CW00589684

POLITICAL PHILOSOPHY NOW

Chief Editor of the Series:
Howard Williams, Aberystwyth University, Wales

Associate Editors:
Wolfgang Kersting, University of Kiel, Germany
Steven B. Smith, Yale University, USA
Peter Nicholson, University of York, England
Renato Cristi, Wilfrid Laurier University, Waterloo, Canada

Political Philosophy Now is a series which deals with authors,
topics and periods in political philosophy from the perspective of
their relevance to current debates. The series presents a spread of
subjects and points of view from various traditions which include
European and New World debates in political philosophy.

Other titles in the series
Kant on Sublimity and Morality
Joshua Rayman

Poverty, Ethics and Justice
H. P. P. [Hennie] Lötter

Politics and Metaphysics in Kant
Edited by Sorin Baiasu, Howard Williams and Sami Pihlström

*Imperfect Cosmopolis: Studies in the History of International
Legal Theory and Cosmopolitan Ideas*
Georg Cavallar

Deleuze and Guattari: Aesthetics and Politics
Robert Porter

POLITICAL PHILOSOPHY NOW

Identity, Politics and the Novel: The Aesthetic Moment

Ian Fraser

UNIVERSITY OF WALES PRESS • CARDIFF • 2013

© Ian Fraser, 2013

All rights reserved. No part of this book may be reproduced in any material form (including photocopying or storing it in any medium by electronic means and whether or not transiently or incidentally to some other use of this publication) without the written permission of the copyright owner except in accordance with the provisions of the Copyright, Designs and Patents Act 1988. Applications for the copyright owner's written permission to reproduce any part of this publication should be addressed to The University of Wales Press, 10 Columbus Walk, Brigantine Place, Cardiff CF10 4UP.

www.uwp.co.uk

British Library Cataloguing-in-Publication Data
A catalogue record for this book is available from the British Library.

ISBN 978-0-7083-2606-0

The right of Ian Fraser to be identified as author of this work has been asserted in accordance with sections 77, 78 and 79 of the Copyright, Designs and Patents Act 1988.

Typeset by Marie Doherty
Printed by CPI Antony Rowe, Chippenham, Wiltshire

Contents

Acknowledgements

This book has taken a long time in coming to fruition, and that it now has is largely due to the advice of my great friend and colleague Lawrence Wilde, who has had to listen to my many interpretations of these novelists and their novels for a number of years while I was working on other projects. He said put pen to paper, so to speak, and I now have, so thanks to him for his encouragement and also for his usual meticulousness in reading the manuscript. Thanks to Howard Williams, the series editor, for showing an interest in this project even in its pre-embryonic stage, and for his continued support for my work from the beginning of my academic career, and Sarah Lewis, head of commissioning for University of Wales Press, for her help and advice during the publication process.

I would also like to thank all the students who have participated in the discussions on my final year Art, Politics and Society module that I have taught previously at Nottingham Trent University and now at Loughborough University, where so many of the ideas presented here have featured. My head of department at Loughborough, Chris Szejnmann, also deserves special thanks for his support towards the end of the project that was crucial in helping me find the time to bring it to completion. Other people who have been supportive or offered advice either directly or indirectly during the project are as follows: Sian Adiseshiah for introducing me to Kristeva's work; Tony Burns; Gary Browning; Keith Fraser; Shevawn Green; Oliver Harrison; Ruth Kinna and Vincent Murphy. Molly has again kept me company throughout the entire project in her perfectly positioned cushion on my desk under the lamp. Sharon Garratt deserves special praise for both putting up with me in general and for allowing me the time to work on the project. In appreciation for always looking after her little brother and for our shared love of novels, the book is dedicated to my sister, Carol Fraser Murphy.

All these chapters were presented as papers as follows and I would like to thank all the participants for their comments: The Utopian Studies Association Annual conferences in Toronto and at the University of Limerick; The Political Studies Association Annual Conferences in London and Belfast; The Workshops in Political Theory Annual Conferences at Manchester Metropolitan University and Manchester University; Loughborough University; Nottingham Trent University; Oxford Brookes University and Durham University for inviting me to present the Henry Tudor Memorial Address.

I am grateful to the following for allowing me to use extracts from the novels considered here: The Wylie Agency for Milan Kundera; Random House for Ian McEwan and Michel Houellebecq; David Higham Associates for J. M. Coetzee. Chapter three is a revised version of 'Class experience in McEwan's Atonement', *Critique: Studies in Contemporary Fiction*. Emphases in quotations in the book are always in the original unless otherwise stated. Terms in square brackets are my amendments and insertions unless otherwise stated.

Introduction

Capitalism is currently undergoing one of its worst crises since the great depression of the 1930s. The response to this crisis by bourgeois elites is to impose an age of austerity encapsulated in the lie that we are all in this together under the banner of a failed neoliberal dogma that caused the crisis in the first place. Given that this 'miserable reality . . . can be changed only through radical political praxis, the concern with aesthetics demands justification' and mine is as follows.[1]

This book offers a political and philosophical examination of the work of four critically acclaimed novelists in order to explore our normative understanding of different forms of identity. The understanding of identity offered here is captured in the idea of the aesthetic self, as discussed in the final chapter of *Dialectics of the Self*, in which I engaged in an immanent critique of the work of Charles Taylor from a Marxist perspective.[2] The aesthetic self emanates from understanding identity dialectically as abstract and concrete, universal and particular, in an alternating movement through which the world is constituted. This understanding of identity implies that the self is a social self, engaging in self-interpretation, language, dialogue and affirming life through our social relations and responsibilities with each other, however contradictory that may be. Out of these contradictions, the aesthetic self refers to the many ways in which those of us who want to challenge the status quo of capitalist social relations do so politically, economically and culturally. In the affirmation of our own identity, we can see possibilities of how it might coalesce in a dialectical manner with the identities of others. When we do so, we can experience epiphanic moments of spiritual and moral uplift that allow us to see the world differently, question its basic assumptions, act in a different manner and so offer us an instance of transcendence. Such is the aesthetic moment that emanates from the aesthetic self.

My focus is on the cultural manifestations of the aesthetic self, by exploring how core concepts in social and political philosophy

can illuminate our understanding of characters and their identities in contemporary fiction. The intention is also to show how
exploring the concepts through the medium of the novel can
enhance our understanding of these concepts and their importance for offering us orientations towards the good. So a dialectical
interplay will take place where the concept informs the novel and
the novel informs the concept. Aesthetic moments can then emerge
that point to transformations in a character's identity on the path
to transcendence.

The four writers considered here either directly employ or
leave their work open to political and philosophical interpretation, which responds to Martha Nussbaum's rhetorical question
in her own studies on literature, namely: 'How should one live?'[3]
Answering this question orientates us towards a vision of the good
life while also impacting on the nature of our identity. This work
takes up that question within the tradition of Marxist aesthetics
that attempts, as Pauline Johnson has argued, to 'determine the
basis of the emancipatory impact of the work of art', which 'acts
to effect a change in the recipient's consciousness'.[4]

Similar books that attempt to explore the links between social,
political and philosophical theory and novels are the aforementioned Martha Nussbaum,[5] studies such as Richard Rorty's
Contingency, Irony and Solidarity,[6] and Judith Butler's emphasis
on using literary texts as vehicles for exploring social theories.[7]
Such an approach has been encapsulated in what has been termed
the 'new aestheticism', where a number of different contemporary thinkers have looked at the way art and literature open up
radically different ways of contemplating identity, politics and culture.[8] What makes my approach distinctive is that it is developed
from within the Marxist aesthetic tradition through the idea of the
aesthetic self, and by offering an immanent critique of the thinkers discussed. Pauline Johnson's book is an overview of the key
thinkers in the Marxist tradition and therefore quite a different
exercise from my own, despite our shared interest in the emancipatory aspect of art through changes in people's consciousness. Terry
Eagleton offers a similar overview of understanding the nature
of art through the notion of the aesthetic as Johnson does, and
covers non-Marxist thinkers in his analysis, as I do. However, he
accomplishes this through a critique of the concept of the aesthetic
as it has been understood throughout modern Western thought,

and not by focusing on contemporary novels, again, as is the case here.[9] My hope, therefore, is that this book will offer an important contribution to the traditions mentioned above, while making an additional and original contribution to the literature that crosses the boundaries between social, political and philosophical theories and aesthetics.

As the focus is on identity, the substance of the investigation relates to the characters in the novels and how and in what ways the concepts employed can either explain or try to comprehend their actions and behaviour. At the start of each chapter there is a brief synopsis of each of the novels, mentioning the key characters that will be considered through the conceptual lens and theoretical framework provided by each of the theorists to be considered. To this end, two novels each from the work of Milan Kundera, Ian McEwan, Michel Houellebecq and J. M. Coetzee are explored by drawing on the following theorists from within the tradition of classical, contemporary, political and social philosophy: Friedrich Nietzsche, G. W. F. Hegel, E. P. Thompson, Julia Kristeva, Henri Lefebvre, Albert Camus, Thomas Aquinas and Theodor Adorno.

The choice of these four novelists should in no way imply that they are the only writers worthy of consideration for the explorations of identity undertaken here. However, they are, in my opinion, among some of the best writers of contemporary fiction because they offer a sophisticated analysis of the human condition that has huge import for the way we view the world. Some of their characters embody aspects of an aesthetic self that produce aesthetic moments of such intensity and poignancy that the possibility for a change in the reader's consciousness, to experience the epiphanic moment of their own transcendence, becomes a real possibility. My contention is that the theorists mentioned above will enhance this process even further through the application of their social, political and philosophical frameworks.

In part I, I consider the work of the critically acclaimed Czech writer Milan Kundera who has often weaved philosophical themes both explicitly and implicitly through his novels. In the *Unbearable Lightness of Being*, set before, during and after the Prague Spring of 1968 and which is the subject of chapter one, the presence of Nietzsche figures prominently. In this chapter, I examine Nietzsche's understanding of art as self-creation, and his notions of the Apollonian and Dionysian, under the weight and lightness of how we live our lives through his doctrine of eternal recurrence. Chapter two offers an examination of Kundera's novella *Identity*, in which he explores the relation of the self to the 'other' through various instances of recognition and misrecognition. To that end, I analyse the core relationship in the novel by adopting an analytical framework from Hegel's theory of recognition, as outlined particularly in his *Phenomenology of Spirit* in the famous section on the master/slave dialectic.

Part II considers the work of English writer Ian McEwan. Chapter three explores what many perceive to be his best work, the widely praised *Atonement*, which was shortlisted for the Booker Prize in 2001 and was made into a very successful film. What is particularly distinctive about the novel is a re-examination of class conflict where the microcosms of English society are played out through characters in a country house shortly before the Second World War, and then in the institutions of the army and the nursing establishment during it. My concern is to highlight the class contradictions present in the novel by utilizing the conceptual framework developed by the English social theorist and historian E. P. Thompson, which focuses on themes such as class experience and class consciousness, class struggle and class hegemony, and fetishism. In chapter four, I examine McEwan's *Saturday*, through the notion of abjection developed by the Bulgarian-French feminist, psychoanalyst, literary critic and philosopher, Julia Kristeva. The notion of abjection implies the rejection of an 'other' through distaste or disgust and by creating protective boundaries to keep this 'other' at a safe distance. The notion of abjection is utilized to explore the extent to which a person should be responsible for due consideration of others less fortunate than themselves, an ethical issue that figures prominently in the novel.

Part III examines two novels by the *enfant terrible* of contemporary French fiction, Michel Houellebecq. In chapter five, I analyse his critically acclaimed but controversial novel *Atomised*, which paints a seemingly bleak picture of society where human identities have become so deeply alienated that, despite many good intentions, the attempt to create a more humane world has failed miserably. To expose and undermine this view of the novel, I employ the alienation theory of the French philosopher Henri Lefebvre to focus on the dialectical relations that emerge in the book. His theory shows us the way that the inhuman forms of alienation

that people experience can allow them to glimpse moments of a
more humane world. Houellebecq's next novel after *Atomised* was
Platform, again a controversial work, given its focus on the sex
industry and undercurrent tones of Islamaphobia. My discussion
of the novel in chapter six is guided by Albert Camus' notion of
the absurd, with the intention of exploring how the novel confronts us with the meaninglessness of existence through which we
try to attain some kind of meaning.

The South African writer J. M. Coetzee, whose work is the subject of part four, was the recipient of the 2003 Nobel Prize for
Literature, and he won the Booker Prize in 1999 for the second
time for his outstanding novel of post-apartheid South Africa,
Disgrace, which I consider in chapter seven. Following Thomas
Aquinas' notion of disgrace, I consider the responsibility involved
in acts of disgrace that take place in the novel, and how atonement
for disgraceful acts can lead towards a path to a more prudential
and virtuous life. In this way, Aquinas' theory attempts to offer
us an understanding of the contradictions of identity that Coetzee
depicts in post-apartheid South Africa. The penultimate chapter considers Coetzee's *Diary of a Bad Year* through the aesthetic
theory of the German philosopher Theodor Adorno and in particular his understanding of commitment in art. The novel explicitly
explores a number of political themes and issues, and on that basis
I draw on Adorno's framework to see whether it fulfils his criteria
of what constitutes committed and autonomous art, or whether it
falls in to didacticism or preaching and thereby descends into bad
art. The conclusion draws the main themes of the book together,
and reiterates the importance of the aesthetic self as a way of
understanding identity in the aesthetic moments that occur in the
selected novels considered.

Part I:
Milan Kundera

1 • *The Unbearable Lightness of Being*: Friedrich Nietzsche and Art as Self-creation

Kundera's *The Unbearable Lightness of Being*[1] is set before, during and after the so-called 'Prague Spring' that lasted from January to April 1968, following the succession of Alexander Dubček to the leadership of the ruling Czechoslovak Communist Party.[2] Dubček was opposed to the coercion and despotism that had prevailed since 1948, and began to argue for the development of participatory democracy, resulting in an explosion of free expression as censorship was lifted for the first time in a communist state. The open nature of this event became known by Dubček's expression as 'socialism with a human face'. As depicted in the book, the Prague Spring was overturned by the armed forces of the Warsaw Pact who invaded Czechoslovakia, arrested all the leaders and forced them to rescind the freedoms that they had given to the Czech people. This momentous event serves as the backdrop for the stories of the main characters: Tomas, Tereza, Sabina and Franz.

Tomas, a brilliant surgeon, is also a womanizer and avoids committed relationships. However, when he goes to a country town to perform an operation, he meets Tereza, a waitress in his hotel, and they talk briefly after she finishes her shift. Tomas leaves for Prague but Tereza follows in pursuit, moves in with him and eventually they marry. He continues seeing other women, which causes Tereza to live a tortured existence. After the invasion, they decide to live in exile in Geneva; Tomas continues his extramarital affairs and Tereza therefore decides to return to Prague to live under Soviet occupation. Tomas at first feels free, but, realizing that he still wants Tereza, he too heads back to Prague. He is then told by the authorities that he cannot continue to be a surgeon unless he signs a retraction of an article that he had written criticizing the Czech regime. He refuses and instead works as a window cleaner. Eventually, he and Tereza decide to escape to the country and work on the land, remaining there until they both meet their deaths in a driving accident.

Sabina, a painter, is one of Tomas' mistresses. She lives an unconstrained life so she also decides to go to Geneva to live in exile after the invasion, rather than remain under authoritarian rule. Once there, she has an affair with a married university professor named Franz. When he leaves his wife to be with Sabina, true to her instincts, she leaves him and spends the rest of her life travelling from one city to the next. Franz finds solace by forming a relationship with one of his students, but always thinks of Sabina. He is eventually killed in a mugging in Bangkok.

My aim here is to try to illuminate our understanding of *Unbearable Lightness* through the work of Friedrich Nietzsche, a thinker who is also of great importance to Kundera. The chapter will focus on Nietzsche's notions of the Apollonian and Dionysian, his emphasis on art as self-creation on the path to becoming a free spirit and the doctrine of eternal recurrence. The intention is to elucidate these themes to help to understand the characters and give a greater insight into the philosophical and aesthetic moments in the book. Let us begin, then, with the notions of the Apollonian and Dionysian in Nietzsche's thought.

Apollonian and Dionysian

In Nietzsche's first book, *The Birth of Tragedy*, he makes an important distinction between the 'duality' of the Apollonian and the Dionysian, named after the Greek gods, Apollo and Dionysus, which he sees as being bound up with the 'continuous evolution of art'.[3] He interprets these 'two very different drives' as co-existing beside each other 'mostly in open conflict, stimulating and provoking one another' to produce 'vigorous offspring' that continues this opposition until they are reconciled in art.

If we focus on the Apollonian side first, in its metaphysical sense, it relates simply to the everyday world as it is, which consciousness attempts to order and comprehend, irrespective of what is or is not beautiful. In its aesthetic sense, the Apollonian consciousness and drive has the beautiful as its object and 'perfection' as its ideal through a process of 'transfiguration'.[4] However, while the Apollonian applies to these objects of aesthetic experience, the 'transfiguration' process also impacts on the psychological identity of the experiencing subject.[5] The Apollonian world this subject finds itself in is, according to Nietzsche, the art world of dream, the 'semblance' of which is the 'precondition of all the arts of image-making'.[6] He maintains that even when the 'dream-reality is most alive', we always understand it is a pretence. Moreover, Nietzsche notes how even everyday reality is also a semblance because it contains beneath it another different reality. He cites this as one reason why Schopenhauer claimed that the ability to philosophize was to have the occasional feeling that all people and things were phantoms or dream-images.

Nietzsche further explains that a person with an artistic temperament approaches the reality of a dream in the same way a philosopher approaches the reality of existence. The artistic person 'attends to it closely and with pleasure, using these images to interpret life, and practising for life with the help of these events', but also confronting 'things which are grave, gloomy, sad, dark, sudden blocks, teasings of chance, anxious expectations, in short the "Divine Comedy" of life'. An emotion of total comprehension attends these experiences and indicates that the dreaming is part of our 'innermost being', the 'deep ground common to all our lives', and gives us 'profound pleasure and joyous necessity'. Consequently, 'every human being is fully an artist when creating the worlds of dream'. The Apollonian realm, then, relates to non-musical arts and is concerned with the 'beautiful representation of phenomenal reality'.[7]

Turning to the Dionysian art world, Nietzsche specifies that it 'is best conveyed by the analogy of *intoxication*'.[8] Again drawing on Schopenhauer, Nietzsche argues that Dionysian 'stirrings' emerge when people suddenly become confused in the way that they understand the world because something has occurred that undermines their capacity to reason. Such a 'horror' also brings about a 'blissful ecstasy' arising from the 'innermost ground' of our being. As these feelings become more intense they 'cause subjectivity to vanish to the point of complete self-forgetting'. They eventually awake 'either under the influence of a narcotic drink' or in the impending 'spring when the whole of nature is pervaded by lust for life', as in the festivals in the German Middle Ages where people wandered from place to place and engaged in song and dance. This 'glowing life of Dionysiac enthusiasts' can be grasped even further,

Nietzsche suggests, if Beethoven's 'Hymn to Joy' was changed into a painting and everyone's imagination was allowed to run free as they 'sink into the dust, shivering in awe'. All the barriers between humans erected due to 'necessity, caprice, or "imprudent fashion"' now 'break asunder' as people are not just united in harmony with each other but are as one. Through song and dance people now belong to a 'higher community' where, forgetting how to talk and walk, they instead are on the verge of 'flying and dancing, up and away into the air above'. They feel as though they are gods moving in 'ecstasy and sublimity', as they once saw the gods move in their dreams. No longer artists, humans have themselves become a 'work of art' as 'all nature's artistic power reveals itself here, amidst shivers of intoxication' in 'blissful satisfaction'. The Dionysian realm, therefore, relates to the evocative power of music, which impacts on the Apollonian capacity for art by making us 'contemplate symbolically Dionysiac universality', and allows the 'symbolic image to emerge with the highest degree of significance'.[9] As Martha Nussbaum indicates, these Apollonian and Dionysian moments are 'passionate, interested, and needy elements of the personality' and constitute what will be Nietzsche's lifelong theme: 'art, indeed, is not for art's sake, but for life's sake'.[10]

Art as self-creation: free spirit

In Nietzsche's second work, *Human, All Too Human*, he adopts the writing style of aphorisms, that is, short observations and reflections, consisting of a long paragraph or just a few sentences. This was a new style of writing and composition for Nietzsche, who was trying to find his own new voice.[11] Interestingly, Kundera himself has commented approvingly on Nietzsche's style by stressing how the mix in length of the aphoristic chapters or paragraphs in his work offers an 'extraordinary sense of rhythm' and has 'no need for filler, for transitions, for weak passages';[12] so the 'tension never slackens' due to the 'thoughts speeding toward us'. Even more importantly, as Alexander Nehamas explains, Nietzsche's style relates to his perspectivism, the contention that there are no facts independent of interpretation, and that there are no neutral standards that can determine which of our interpretations are right or wrong.[13] As Nietzsche exhorts in *Human, All Too Human*: 'you shall learn to grasp the sense of perspective in every value judgement – the displacement, distortion and merely apparent teleology of horizons and whatever else pertains to perspectivism'.[14] For Nietzsche, when we do this we become master over ourselves and our virtues, see clearly the 'problem with the *order of rank*, and how power and right and spaciousness of perspective grow into the heights together'.[15] Indeed, embracing perspectivism is a crucial part of what it means to be a 'free spirit', to whom *Human, All Too Human* is dedicated, even though it does not exist yet.[16] For Nietzsche, the free spirit faces the *'problem of the order of rank'* as its own problem, and in doing so feels the 'force and necessity' of the 'task' that exists within as an 'unconscious pregnancy', even before the task is recognized or even named.[17] As Nietzsche himself says, 'life itself *rewards* us for our tough will to live, for the long war . . . Finally our reward is the *greatest* of life's gifts, perhaps the greatest thing it is able to give of any kind – we are given our *task* back'.[18]

The 'task' then is a process of self-creation where everything is scrutinized about the world and ourselves as we engage in the order of rank. However, Nietzsche's perspectivism does not slip into a relativist position that interprets one view being as good as any other.[19] Instead, he contends that your own viewpoint is the best one for you while recognizing it might not be best for anyone else. Perspectivism must be subject to criticism, but it must also be seen for its affirmative qualities as we make ourselves into free spirits. As Schacht argues, to be Nietzschean free spirits and make something worthwhile of ourselves requires that we do so rigorously and without deception.[20] Accordingly, we must draw on everything that we can learn about the world. So, according to Schacht, Nietzsche thinks that we can employ 'various perspectival techniques that seem to him to be relevant to the understanding of what we have come to be and what we have it in us to become'.

In terms of aestheticism, it provides part of the motivation for perspectivism because Nietzsche looks at the world as an artwork or literary text that can be interpreted in many different ways.[21] Additionally, his aestheticism is also related to his perspectivism through the 'philology of the world', which allows Nietzsche to develop a literary model for many of his views, but also motivates him to create a literary product that cannot be imitated.[22] It is also ambiguous, which is why it undermines both a positive and negative view of art.[23] Hence, for Nietzsche, the real function of art in relation to the self as a free spirit is to make one tolerable to oneself and to others, if that is possible, to beautify life by conceal- ing or reinterpreting one's own character and to make ourselves 'endurable'.[24] Nietzsche notes how on one side this can make us be restrained in our aesthetic practice and stay within conventional forms, but on the other side it also can make us engage in art to '*conceal* or *reinterpret* everything ugly to let the *meaning* of the thing shine through'. Furthermore, the free spirit must 'effect a persistent invitation to the overturning of habitual evaluations and valued habits', and offer a 'schooling in suspicion, even more in contempt, but fortunately also in courage, indeed in audacity'.[25] A free spirit then is engaged in a constant task of remaking the self through the development of its own perspectivism as it questions both itself and the world. The demand that this task puts on us is appositely captured in Nietzsche's notion of eternal recurrence to which we now turn.

Eternal recurrence

In *The Gay Science*, in a paragraph preceded by the title, '*the heav- iest weight*', Nietzsche discusses the doctrine of eternal recurrence as a thought experiment.[26] He asks you, the reader, to imagine what would happen if a demon came into your 'loneliest loneli- ness', to tell you that the life you are living and have lived will have to be lived again and again. All pain and joy would be revisited in the same way and in the sequence with which they happened. Nietzsche then asks: what would you do? Would you collapse to the floor and gnash your teeth and curse this demon? Or would you answer more positively by declaring the demon to be a god and declare the request to be 'divine'? Nietzsche considers that if this thought gained control over you then in the state you are currently in it would 'transform and possibly crush you'. It would be the 'heaviest weight' because the question to be answered is: do you want this over and over again, and how might you change yourself to adapt to that demand so that you '*long for nothing more fer- vently* than for this ultimate eternal confirmation and seal?'

The cyclical nature of the doctrine implies that every deci- sion we make will come back to confront us, so it is rightly seen as 'Nietzsche's most complex and controversial image for the satisfaction that one would ideally take in one's earthly life'.[27] This is why the doctrine lends itself to interpretations that see it as an ethical imperative to live your life as though it would eternally recur, with all the existential impact that imposes on an individual.[28] Advancing on this theme further, Nehamas argues that eternal recurrence is 'not a theory of the world but a view of the self' because it shows how Nietzsche draws on the psychological consequences from the doctrine and applies them to his own life, while also making them the object of his writing.[29] As Nehamas continues, Nietzsche's concern is with the attitude a person must have to respond with joy rather than despair to the thought that their life will reoccur in the same way forever.[30] However, the way Nehamas interprets this challenge is to focus on literary characters rather than real individuals because, he contends, Nietzsche sees 'life as literature', as the subtitle of Nehamas' book infers.[31] For Nehamas, literary characters are bound by the edict of eternal recurrence because they do live their lives over and over again in the same way, as they are part of a pre-ordained story within which what happens to them cannot be changed.[32] For Nehamas, it is 'just this feature of the literary situation that underlies and motivates Nietzsche's view of the ideal person and the perfect life'. To do so, Nehamas maintains, is to engage in a 'paradoxical interplay, between creation and discovery, knowledge and action, literature and life', which is 'at the centre of Nietzsche's conception of the self'.[33] Eternal recurrence therefore places a weighty demand on us as individuals, especially once it is coupled with our need to be free spirits.

Kundera

Kundera himself reflects on the doctrine of eternal recurrence in a discussion of the role of philosophical meditation in his novels. For him, the term philosophy is incongruous because it remains within the realm of abstraction, rather than rooting itself in characters and the situations that they find themselves in.[34] He is then questioned on how he can believe this when the opening sentence of *Unbearable Lightness* refers to Nietzsche's notion of eternal recurrence, which is a philosophical idea, developed in the abstract without characters and situations. Kundera rejects this interpretation and instead says the doctrine is related directly to the

fundamental situation of the character of Tomas because it identifies his dilemma: in a world where there is no eternal return his
existence must be light. Kundera also explains that he apprehends
the self in his novels not just psychologically, but in the 'essence
of its existential problem' and '*existential code*'. So, when he was
writing *Unbearable Lightness* the 'code' of each of the main characters was linked to certain key words. For example, for Tereza
they are 'body, soul, vertigo, weakness, idyll, Paradise', and for
Tomas they are 'lightness, weight', and the 'existential code', which
is not examined in abstraction, 'reveals itself progressively in the
action, in the situations'.[35] Kundera says that he does this by turning the novel into one long 'interrogative meditation' rather than
simply interrogating certain situations.[36] So, 'the novelist is neither
historian nor prophet' but is instead 'an explorer of existence'.[37]

The writer who is the exemplar of this approach for Kundera
is Franz Kafka, because even though he moves away from psychology to analyse a situation, it does not mean that his characters
are psychologically unconvincing. Instead, Kafka takes the 'psychological *problematic* . . . to the secondary level'.[38] Elucidating
further, Kundera contends that it is irrelevant whether a character
in Kafka's work had a good or bad childhood or is involved in a
romantic relationship, as this will have no effect on behaviour or
fate. Unlike Proust or Joyce who would explore these psychological aspects of the character, Kafka reverses the process of inquiry
and so offers another way of understanding a person's identity.
Kundera adds, however, that even if he stands outside the tradition
of the psychological novel, this does not mean that he denies a
character an internal life; instead, his novels explore 'other enig-
mas' and 'other questions', which allows any of his characters to
be 'an experimental self'.[39]

Kundera is, therefore, a type of Nietzschean because he is using
his art as a way to explore existence, ask awkward questions
and pose dilemmas in situations where he examines the 'existential problem' of a character.[40] Indeed, Kundera holds Nietzsche
in high esteem because his first concern is to break up anything
fixed, to attack conventional systems and 'open up rifts for ven-
turing into the unknown'.[41] Consequently, Nietzsche's thought is
'*experimental thought*', so the 'philosopher of the future will be
an *experimenter*' who goes in all different directions that may
even come into conflict with each other.[42] Kundera says that he,

too, follows this edict in his own novels even though the natural impulse is to systematize, but the problem here is that it leads to trying to cover all the implications of your ideas and counter any objections that can be made against them in advance.[43] When this happens, conviction sets in and thought stops dead through the attempt to persuade.[44] Instead, the aim should be to 'inspire' and 'experimental thought' does this by inspiring another thought and so 'set thought moving'.[45] Following Nietzsche, Kundera urges the novelist to 'systematically desystematise his thought', and 'kick at the barricade that he himself has erected around his ideas'. Additionally, Kundera sees Nietzsche's rejection of systematic thought leading to an expansion of thematic considerations to overcome the separation of different philosophical disciplines. The world can then be seen more fully so 'everything human can become the object of a philosopher's thought'. Kundera therefore praises Nietzsche for bringing philosophy closer to the novel, and his doctrine of eternal recurrence is one way of doing this, as we shall now see in relation to *Unbearable Lightness*.[46]

Tomas and Tereza

As mentioned earlier, eternal recurrence[47] appears in the first line of the novel in relation to the predicament of Tomas (3). For Kundera, Tomas' existential problem is that as there is no eternal recurrence his existence is shrouded in lightness. However, the narrator of the novel spends the first few pages pondering over the doctrine by considering it in two ways and not just one as Kundera has done. One way is Kundera's interpretation that sees the doctrine as being absent. The narrator construes this as being negative because it results in meaninglessness, as a life that does not recur is 'like a shadow' and what was contained in it is irrelevant. So the idea of eternal recurrence in this negative understanding implies that 'things appear other than as we know them', because they do not have the 'mitigating circumstances of their transitory nature' (3–4). Making a judgement on any action is impossible because the action is 'transitory' or 'ephemeral' in a world where there is no recurrence, so 'everything is pardoned in advance' and 'everything cynically permitted' (4). Such is the 'moral perversity' of a world where eternal recurrence is absent.

The other way is to interpret the doctrine as being present in the world and acting as an edict, which suggests that 'everything recurs as we once experienced it, and that the recurrence itself recurs ad infinitum' (3). This prospect is referred to as 'terrifying' because the 'weight of unbearable responsibility lies heavy on every move we make' and, invoking Nietzsche, the narrator declares it as the 'heaviest of burdens' (4), which is obviously an implicit reference to paragraph 341 of *The Gay Science* where the doctrine is discussed. The narrator then suggests that if this is the case, we can respond to this burden not by succumbing to it, but by living our lives in 'all their splendid lightness'.

The two oppositions of weight and lightness are then considered in their positive and negative moments. One assumption is that weight should be seen as negative because its heaviness crushes us and pins us to the floor (4–5). However, heaviness can also be positive because the 'heavier the burden, the closer our lives come to the earth, the more real and truthful they become' (5). Similarly, without weight we can become 'lighter than air' and 'only half real' as our movements are 'as free as they are insignificant'. This leads to the ultimatum posed by the narrator: 'what then shall we choose? Weight or lightness?'

The narrator then considers these oppositions in relation to Parmenides, the Greek philosopher of the pre-Socratic school who greatly influenced Plato. For Parmenides, weight and light were binary oppositions, and he designated lightness as positive and weight as negative. The narrator then asks whether Parmenides was correct or not, but leaves the answer open by concluding that the only certainty we can have is that the dichotomy between weight and lightness is shrouded in mystery and ambiguity. The two terms of weight and lightness are crucial then for understanding the problems that the characters in the novel are faced with in their different ways. The question posed to them and to us as readers is whether we choose weight or lightness. If we refer back to Nietzsche, the existential demand put upon us from the doctrine of eternal return means the answer to this question must be that we choose both, depending on the circumstances, as we constitute ourselves as free spirits. This fluidity of the self cannot be bound by one or the other. Interestingly, Nietzsche is particularly critical of the school of Parmenides, the Eleatics, amongst others, for denying the reality of change and so having no real understanding of the 'idea of becoming', which also suggests a more dialectical interaction of the two courses of action.[48]

When Tomas is introduced, the narrator tells us that he or she has been reflecting on him for a long time, but it is only now, through these reflections on weight and lightness, that he can be seen clearly. The dilemma facing Tomas is what to do about Tereza, because against his normal instincts of not getting attached to a woman emotionally (11), he has gradually felt an 'inexplicable love' for her (5–6). He recalls an occasion when he laid down beside her sleeping body and imagined that she was dying (6–7). He suddenly realized then that he would not survive without her, and so would die with her too. Remembering this moment makes Tomas think that this must be 'love declaring itself to him', but he quickly corrects himself (7). He questions whether it was in fact love, as he had only met her once, and wanting to die with her was clearly exaggerated, so he thinks it might be hysteria instead. Tomas is incapable of deciding which and berates himself for it, but he realizes that it is quite normal not to know what you want. The absence of eternal recurrence, the fact that we only have one life, means that it is not possible to make a comparison with our previous existences or to refine these existences in the future. So Tomas' dilemma of whether to stay with Tereza or let her go cannot be tested because there is no basis for comparison. 'Life', then, 'is a sketch for nothing, an outline with no picture', and this leads Tomas to conclude, following the German adage *Einmal ist keinmal*, that 'if we only have one life to live, we might as well not have lived at all' (7–8).[49]

Ironically, the decision is made for him because Tereza arrives at his flat and, having nowhere else to stay, moves in (8–9). Tomas asks himself how he could have made such a quick choice when he has prevaricated for nearly two weeks, but in reality it was resolved for him by the actions of Tereza (9). He even rejects the possibility of sending her away because of her vulnerability, referring to her metaphorically as a 'child put in a pitch-daubed bulrush basket and sent downstream' (10). The narrator then tells us that Tomas did not realize it at this time, but 'metaphors are dangerous' because 'a single metaphor can give birth to love'. However, as part of his own code of 'erotic friendship' he had to exclude all love from his life, as this would make his other mistresses inferior to the one he loved. Nevertheless, Tomas comes to realize that they both look forward to sleeping together so much that they make love not with the sole aim of reciprocal sensual enjoyment, but more in the 'shared sleep' following it (13). This makes him conclude that love can be found not in the need for sexual intercourse, which applies to many women, but in the need for 'shared sleep', which is confined to one woman (14). Indeed, his love for Tereza grows even further when she finds erotic letters from Sabina, and unwittingly reveals so when recounting a dream (15). If it was any other woman, he would have thrown her out but his compassion for her, his 'co-feeling' that made him feel her own emotions, meant that he could not (19–20). There was no way he could aim any animosity towards her and instead his love for her intensified.

Tomas, then, the supposed embodiment of lightness, has faced the *'heaviest weight'* in the form of Tereza. Confronted with the existential problem of whether to choose Tereza or reject her, through circumstance but also through his own actions, he embraced her weight through the very thing that he was denying at the start of the novel: the love that was declaring itself to him. With the demand of Nietzsche's demon before him, Tomas attempted to avoid it, but realized that he could not. His rejection of eternal recurrence was therefore mistaken and his own 'meditative interrogation', in Kundera's words, shows how light and weight cut across him throughout the novel, even though at the outset he is firmly in the light camp. From a Nietzschean perspective, he is certainly a free spirit in that sense, but unlike Sabina, as we shall see shortly, he ultimately has to reconcile his lightness with weight because of the power of love. Love is the mediating factor in that process, an emotion his former self had attempted to bypass. This is not to deny that Tomas is still beset by doubt, as is the case when he returns to Prague after the invasion to be with Tereza and ponders on the way the 'fortuitous love' between them arose from a series of chance happenings (33). But the presence of eternal recurrence in terms of weight, or its absence in terms of lightness, must cut across and confront any character in such a situation.

Even so, by the end of the book, on the night before they go to their deaths, the sense of reconciliation of the interplay between weight and lightness is poignantly present between as well as within them. For example, Tereza asks Tomas if this life they have might not be what he really wanted, to which Tomas replies: 'Haven't you noticed I've been happy here' (304–5)? The general feeling is that he and she are reconciled as one.[50] Pertinently, the book ends in the hotel the night before they will go to their deaths to be crushed under the weight of a truck, but the imagery is saturated in light. As they dance, for instance, Tereza imagines herself flying with Tomas in an aeroplane (lightness), through the storm clouds (weight). Tereza feels happiness and sadness, but while the sadness means that they are 'at the last station', the happiness means that they are together. Indeed, the penultimate sentence of the book affirms the lightness motif that weight and light can coexist, because a butterfly, startled by the overhead light, flies out from the lamp by the bedside and circles the room. The film of the book also captures the reconciliation of weight and lightness when we see Tomas and Tereza for the last time driving to their deaths. After Tomas has told Tereza how happy he is, the windscreen wipers on the window of the truck eventually fade out and the screen becomes bathed in the lightness of white to epitomize the unbearable lightness of being.[51]

As we have seen, eternal recurrence applies particularly to literary characters because they stay forever within a pre-ordained story. All the events happening to Tomas and Tereza will recur again and again because they are 'nailed to eternity as Jesus Christ was nailed to the cross' (4). Interestingly, and to take this further, Kundera himself breaks with the standard chronological order of the novel, which in terms of style also points to the operation of the doctrine of eternal recurrence. For example, parts one and five and parts two and four share the same title: 'Lightness and weight' and 'Soul and body' respectively, and pivotal events, such as Tomas and Tereza's first meeting are revisited and meditatively interrogated (5–6, 46–7). The narrator also recalls events by saying, 'now we return to a moment we already know about' (73) or 'let me return to this dream' (53), so we as readers are drawn into the process of reliving the moments of the characters. Even the reconciliation of Tomas and Tereza that is affirmed in their deaths, which we are informed of a third of the way through the novel (119), returns at the end of the story, not as the actual event, but as something that the reader knows will happen as the final page is turned and the book is closed. The eternal recurrence of their lives becomes an eternal recurrence for us as readers as we go back and forth through their literary existence as they face the existential demand of Nietzsche's demon. As Kundera indicates in relation to

literature in general, the 'novel's *raison d'être* is to keep "the world
of life" under a permanent light and to protect us from "the forgetting of being"'.[52] The doctrine of eternal recurrence is one way
we can achieve that, and the lives of the characters can inform our
own deliberations and actions as we live life as literature between
the weight and lightness of our existence.

Sabina and Franz

Nietzsche's emphasis on art as self-creation on the path to becoming a free spirit is taken to its limits with the painter Sabina who,
we are told, 'consciously cultivated . . . her originality' (83). She
is not bound by conventionality, in fact she is the exact opposite,
constantly engaging in the overturning of habitual evaluations
and habits, in Nietzsche's terms. As part of his perspectivism,
Nietzsche tells his potential free spirits that they need to remember the importance of rank, and affirm themselves as self-creative
beings. Sabina epitomizes this edict because from an early age she
embraced cubism and rejected socialist realism, which unfortunately was dominant when she became a student at the Academy
of Fine Arts (87). However, after leaving, she discovers her own
style of painting as her works become typified by their incongruity,
which she describes as 'beauty by mistake' (97–8). This reflects the
origin of her distinctive style that was present in her first mature
work, which was created from the accidental dripping of red paint
on the canvas. Images collide in her paintings, such as a kerosene
lamp with a steelworks construction site superimposed on it, or a
smashed lamp depicted against a barren landscape (97).

She has these thoughts about her work while she is in New York
with Franz, as the narrator explores how much they misunderstand
each other in the aptly named chapter: 'Words misunderstood'.
Franz sees beauty in the European way as being based on pre-
planning and order in its buildings, whereas in New York it is far
more differentiated and circumstantial, which initially he thinks
adds a poetic dimension to its architecture (97–8). Whereas
such incongruity was appealing for Sabina, and New York is her
favourite city precisely for this reason, for Franz, although it was
interesting, ultimately it horrifies him and makes him long for
Europe. So, while both are operating in the Apollonian realm in

their aesthetic considerations, it is left to Sabina to be the icon-
oclast and go against the grain of order, become ambiguous and
engage in reinterpretation and concealment, in the Nietzschean
sense, in her art. Her own paintings are therefore a reflection of
the strangeness of New York and which spurs her on as a self-
creating free spirit. As we shall see, their misunderstanding of each
other is evinced further through the Apollonian/Dionysian relation
when they have a discussion about music.

For Franz, 'music was the art that comes closest to Dionysian
beauty in the sense of intoxication' (88). For him, while it is possible to get drunk on Beethoven's 'Ninth', Bartók's 'Sonata for Two
Pianos and Percussion' or the Beatles' *White Album*, it is impossible to do so for a novel or a painting. Moreover, he transgresses
any boundaries in music, for example, between classical and pop,
which he finds outdated and insincere. Music's power lies in its
capacity to liberate him from the solitude that often accompanies
the life of an academic by bringing him into society to meet people
(89). He also enjoys dancing and it is a source of sorrow to him
that Sabina does not. He therefore appears to be firmly in the Dionysian realm with music having a powerful impact on his being
in the world. However, this manifests itself in a further misunderstanding between them and another nail in what will be the coffin
of their relationship.

Franz's musings here precede a situation where he and Sabina
are in a restaurant where loud, booming music is playing, much to
her irritation. Franz asks her whether she likes music or not. After
initially responding negatively, Sabina then says yes, but in a different historical period, and has in mind the time of Johann Sebastian
Bach, 'when music was like a rose blooming on a boundless snow-
covered plain of silence' (89). She reflects on how she became
hostile to music and, in a familiar story, concludes that it was the
way it was used under Soviet rule, rather than music itself that was
the problem. Sabina remembers when she was at art school and
how she and her fellow students were made to go to summer camp
and work on a construction site. Joyful music was broadcast while
they laboured from early morning to late at night, masking the
reality of the awfulness of the work, and it was played so loudly
that there was nowhere to escape from it. However, her original
conclusion that this could only happen under Soviet Communism
was disabused when she went abroad to the West and found noise

masquerading as music everywhere. For Sabina, this was a particularly ugly development of humankind both acoustically and
visually. She is not, therefore, rejecting the Dionysian as Franz
supposes, but she is protesting about the way that the Dionysian
moment has been corrupted with the misuse of music. Moreover,
her mention of Bach is a pertinent one, because Nietzsche saw him
as the start of the 'mighty brilliant course' of '*German music*' that
proceeds on to Beethoven, and then from Beethoven to Wagner,
arising from the 'Dionysiac ground of the German spirit'.[53]

Sabina straddles the Apollonian/Dionysian divide and Franz's
failure to understand this is a further example of their misunderstanding of each other, which will eventually force Sabina to end
their relationship. Additionally, even Franz himself is not a true
Dionysian because when he reflects on the incident later in bed
after having made love to Sabina, he realizes that he wanted the
music to be loud and noisy to make words become inaudible (90).
He has spent his whole life as an academic using words in so many
different ways that they are like an illness to him, so he craved
music to be played as loud as possible to overpower and make
redundant the use of words. Franz is therefore undermining the
Apollonian side of human existence and ignoring its dialectical
interplay with the Dionysian. Yet, from a Nietzschean perspective,
it is not a matter of rejecting one for the other, but seeing how the
beauty of music is articulated in other different art forms that the
Apollonian moment encompasses.

The other aspect of Sabina's character distinguishing her as a
Nietzschean free spirit is her aim to root out and expose 'kitsch'
in all its forms (247). For Sabina, kitsch precludes all questions
and has only answers, but only through questions can we attain a
degree of truth. The meaning of her paintings exists in appearance
as a comprehensible lie, which hides below what is an incomprehensible truth that manifests itself through the artwork. This acts
as a kind of rupture to kitsch and endorses Nietzsche's edict that
the meaning of art should shine through the reinterpretation of
something ugly. Ironically, however, Sabina points out that even
those who are opposed to kitsch can become its victims because
they need their own certainties for their own worldview. As an
example, we are told how her work was once exhibited in Germany by a political group who depicted her on the front of the
catalogue covered in barbed wire. Additionally, they had written

a short biography of her in which she is described as someone who had fought injustice and was forced to leave her own country, but was still committed to the cause for liberation from Soviet rule. Outraged, Sabina questioned what they have done, but they responded by asking if modern art is not discriminated against in Communist society, to which Sabina retorts that she is opposed to kitsch rather than Communism (248). Subsequently, she disguises the biography of her life much later when she is in America so that nobody would know that she was Czech, and this stops her life being made into kitsch. Consequently, her attempt to express herself authentically as a person and in her art is an affirmation of her life as a free spirit.

The overturning of habitual evaluations and conventional habits also relates to the way Sabina embraces betrayal rather than fidelity in her relationships and life in general, even though it is generally taught to us from an early age that betrayal is 'the most heinous offence imaginable' (87). For Sabina, betrayal should instead be embraced because it involves 'breaking ranks and going off into the unknown'. She begins this process of challenging valued habits by betraying her own puritan father, an amateur painter, whose mocking of the works of Picasso led her to embrace cubism and leave home for Prague to become a student at the Academy of Fine Arts, as we have seen above. Her father had also forbidden her to go out alone for a year when she was fourteen: he realized that she was in love with a boy of the same age. However, any perceived freedom of expression she thought would be possible once she entered art school was quickly curtailed. She was not allowed to paint like Picasso because of the dominance of socialist realism and the obsession for producing portraits of Communist statesmen. Now, in these pietistic times under another father figure in the form of Russian Communism, her chance for love and her predilection for cubism became limited.

To retaliate, she marries a mediocre actor because of his eccentricity, which her father did not like (87–8). When her mother dies and her father commits suicide, she then seeks to 'betray her own betrayal' and promptly leaves her husband to pursue a life of perpetual betrayals on the path to being a free spirit. (88). Nevertheless, she realizes that one day she would have to resist the urge to constantly run away, but not for the moment (94). For Sabina, her capacity for betrayal is therefore an indication of her free spirit and the lack of weight in a world without eternal return. Even so, it also has its costs and can carry with it the heaviest of burdens in a world where eternal recurrence exists, as we will see with her betrayal of Franz.

Franz eventually leaves his wife to be with Sabina, who promptly, and without warning, vacates her flat and leaves for Paris (111–15). Her free spirit cannot be constrained; instead she is stimulated by the possibility to do what she wants and go wherever she wishes (113). However, on arriving in Paris, she experiences a deep form of inescapable melancholy that she cannot articulate (118). The narrator then introduces the weight and light opposition, and thereby the opposition of a world with or without eternal return, by suggesting that we use the term heaviness when we want to depict a dramatic aspect of our lives. Nietzsche's demon suddenly rears its head because the narrator states that faced with this burden we either take it on and fight with it or collapse and allow it to drag us down. In relation to Sabina, the narrator claims that there was no such burden because Franz had not done anything bad to her and her situation was one of the 'unbearable lightness of being' rather than weight. Again, she ponders on how her betrayals always gave her freedom but wonders what will happen if they cease. Having betrayed everything during her life there seemed little left to betray, and she ruminates on whether the emptiness she feels could be the culmination of all her betrayals (118–19). Leaving Geneva and Franz and coming to Paris has certainly put her in even greater proximity to the unbearable lightness of being, but she is unclear now whether that was or is her aim (119).

Her doubt is exacerbated when she receives the letter informing her of the deaths of Tomas and Tereza and the heaviest of burdens, the weight of eternal return, engulfs her. To see how, we need to go back earlier in her relationship with Franz, where we discover Sabina's love for country cemeteries, especially as the sun goes down and the candles sparkle so much it is as though the dead have come back to life (100). For Franz, however, cemeteries were simply a vile pile of bones and stones, and this is yet another way that they do not understand each other. Unsurprisingly, Sabina tries to overcome the shock she feels about their deaths by visiting Montparnasse Cemetery, but the exhilaration she experienced when visiting cemeteries in her own country is not present here (119). Instead, she is unnerved by the ostentatious designs of the graves and sees the cemetery as a testament to vanity. She notices a burial taking place, joins the group of people attending it, and observes the heavy gravestone waiting to be placed over the grave (120). As a seeker of lightness this horrifies Sabina because it implies that those who are dead cannot come back, but then she rebukes herself because it is obvious that they cannot come back as they are dead. Nonetheless, this makes her think of her father's grave and she is relieved that it was not covered by a stone, because it means that he is able to pardon her for the way she treated him. This was not a concern for Sabina earlier and it is indicative of the weight of responsibility she now feels, the heaviest of burdens, which is something she wants lifted from her shoulders through the imagined forgiveness of her father.

Sabina contemplates the cemetery where Tomas and Tereza are buried (121). She reflects that while her parents died in the same week, Tomas and Tereza died in the same second, and suddenly she realizes that she misses Franz. Recalling his distaste for cemeteries, her latest experience makes her think that he may have been correct. She regrets being so intolerant of him and imagines that if they stayed together longer they might have come to understand each other better, but concludes that the chance is now gone. Her only way out from such weight is the flight into lightness and a nomadic existence, especially away from Paris: if she died there a heavy stone would cover her corpse. It is no surprise, then, much later when she is in California, and this is the last time we hear about her, that she leaves instructions in her will that when she dies she should be cremated and her ashes scattered in the lightness of the wind (265). Sabina's lasting testament is to her desire to be a free spirit even in death.

Conclusion

The Nietzschean notions of the Apollonian and Dionysian, the emphasis on art as self-creation in relation to becoming a free spirit and the dialectical interplay of the presence or absence of the doctrine of eternal recurrence have offered us an important insight into aspects of *Unbearable Lightness* and its main characters. Kundera's own admiration for Nietzsche served as a way to highlight these themes that also addresses us as readers in terms

of the existential choices we face in our everyday lives. Faced with
Tomas' dilemma of being with someone who needs us or staying true to ourselves and our own existential code, what would
we do? Would we allow love to overpower us, and do we have
the capacity and the will to resist such an intense feeling and the
compassion it engenders? Do we mourn with Sabina when she
realizes too late that she and Franz could have had a life together
and their misunderstood words could have become understood?
Is she best pursuing the path of a nomadic free spirit? Would we
have done the same thing? Rightly or wrongly, Nietzsche is telling us to face the world courageously, accept responsibility for
what we do and act in good faith when shouldering the heaviest of
burdens. To his credit, Kundera offers these aesthetic moments in
literature where he maintains quite rightly that 'the novel's spirit is
the spirit of complexity' and its 'eternal truth' is telling the reader
that the world is not as simple as you think.[54] Indeed, John Banville endorses this view by recalling how Franz tells Sabina that a
philosopher had once accused him of having nothing in his work
but 'unverifiable speculation'.[55] For Banville, a similar accusation
can also be applied to Kundera, so *Unbearable Lightness* should
therefore be judged not in terms of its moral, social and political
weight, but solely in terms of art.

However, it is precisely on this issue that E. L. Doctorow has
been particularly critical of what he sees as Kundera's one-sided
approach to politics.[56] Doctorow suggests that all the characters
share the fate of being invented to live under two tyrannies: the
tyranny of Czechoslovakia and the tyranny of Kundera's despair.
For Doctorow, Kundera derides politics and isms in general for
aiming at social perfection and the desire for utopia because they
cause all the troubles of humankind. Yet, this neglects how the history of most revolutions is, according to Doctorow, forged by the
desire to eat and breathe rather than in the perfecting of human
beings. Kundera offers a rejection of politics that Doctorow finds
unconvincing in the real world.

Perhaps this is where a Nietzschean framework, so beloved by
Kundera, must lead us, but we need not stay at the terminus of
this aesthetic moment, or reduce everything to Doctorow's very
important need to eat and breathe, crucial though that is. The
way I have utilized Nietzsche can allow us to see the political
import that manifests itself in taking a step further to say what

might it mean to create a world free from despotic rule. Tomas and Tereza attempt to assert their own identities by escape, first to Geneva, then back to Prague, and finally to the countryside. Their aesthetic moment of transcendence is through the love and compassion that they share between each other and their unison in a simultaneous death. Similarly, Sabina thinks that only by wandering from place to place will she be able to be true to her free spirit and not succumb to kitsch. What, though, if we tried to create a proper political community within which we can attempt to live more authentic lives so that there is no need to escape? What if, in this community, we could engage in a re-evaluation of our own selves and those around us so that the love and compassion between Tomas and Tereza can be expressed in its many different forms? Could it be a place where people overcome their misunderstandings and their words are now understood, a poignant longing that the supposedly free spirit of Sabina desired in the end? We do not know whether such a world might be possible. We muddle on dialectically both understanding and misunderstanding each other, in complex processes of social and political interaction. Perhaps, though, being on this journey to be true to others and ourselves is just as important as the end point of realizing it. This search leads us onto the next chapter, which focuses on Kundera's brilliant and aptly titled novella, *Identity*.

2 • *Identity*: G. W. F. Hegel's Theory of Recognition

Identity tells the story of the relationship between Chantal and her younger lover by four years, Jean-Marc.[1] She is a divorcee whose son died at the age of five and gave her the excuse to escape an unhappy marriage. She works in advertising, and first meets Jean-Marc at a conference in a mountain resort where he is working as a ski instructor; they quickly fall in love. The seeming stability of their relationship begins to unravel when at the outset of the novel Chantal, who is already at a seaside hotel a day before Jean-Marc is set to join her, goes out for a walk. When Jean-Marc arrives and she is not at the hotel, he begins to search for her. In doing so, he mistakes another woman for her and so begins to doubt the distinctiveness of Chantal's identity and concomitantly his love for her. This is exacerbated by Chantal's cryptic comment to him that men do not look at her anymore, which he thinks is indicative of her unacknowledged desires. He tests this by sending her anonymous love letters. The novel then imaginatively develops these antagonisms through the contradictions of identity and the relations of the self to the 'other'.

In *Unbearable Lightness*, the presence of Nietzsche's philosophy was explicit from the outset and throughout the book. With *Identity*, any philosophical presence is nowhere near as explicit but I want to argue that Kundera's focus on the self can be illuminated with reference to Hegel's theory of recognition, as outlined particularly in the *Phenomenology of Spirit*, in the famous section on the so-called master/slave dialectic.[2] The aim is to explore Hegel's philosophical theory for understanding the human need for recognition through the characters of Chantal and Jean-Marc, while also exposing the dangers inherent in misrecognition in relation to the self and the self's relation to the 'other'.

Hegel's theory of recognition

Hegel's theory of recognition is explicated in the *Phenomenology of Spirit* where he analyses the development of human consciousness from its immediate or most primitive stage in an endless process of becoming to attain absolute knowledge. Along this path is the master/slave section where the issue of recognition between two self-consciousnesses plays such an important part. Hegel begins by asserting that self-consciousness can only exist in and for itself when it is acknowledged or recognized by another self-consciousness.[3] So the process of recognition is the tracing of the dialectical relationship between a self-consciousness and another self-consciousness. When a self-consciousness is faced with another self-consciousness it not only loses its self by becoming another being, but also supersedes the 'other' by seeing in the 'other' its own self.[4]

For recognition to be complete and not one-sided, each self-consciousness must engage in a process of mutual recognition.[5] This process begins when two self-consciousnesses move from a state of immediacy to confront each other as one individual to another.[6] While in their immediate state they are aware of their own self, they can only attain proper self-certainty through the dialectical mediation of one self to another. Hegel contends this is only possible 'when each is for the other what the other is for it'.[7] To do this, the two self-consciousnesses first need to stake their own lives by engaging in a life and death struggle where each seeks the death of the other.[8] For Hegel, any individual not participating in this life and death struggle can be recognized as a person but cannot achieve true recognition as an independent self-consciousness. Through the life and death struggle, these self-consciousnesses become truly certain of their own being and so have the capacity to achieve freedom. Ultimately, though, the two self-consciousnesses cannot kill each other because they need each other for recognition.[9] The outcome of this situation results in Hegel's lordship/bondage or master/slave dialectic.

In this dialectic the result of the life and death struggle produces on the one side an independent consciousness, a master, whose nature is to be for itself, and on the other side a slave, who is a dependent consciousness living for another, which is the master.[10] Initially, the master appears to have achieved an ideal position because through his domination he gains recognition from the slave but does not have to recognize the slave in return.[11] Yet, this is only a 'one-sided and unequal' recognition because the slave's consciousness is dependent rather than independent.[12] The master is not 'certain of *being-for-self* as the truth of himself', that is, his self-consciousness needs to attain self-certainty and this can only be supplied through an unconstrained, free consciousness, which the slave, by definition, does not possess.[13] Hence, the master is in the same position as he would be if he had put the other self-consciousness to death.

Conversely, the seemingly negative situation of the slave now takes on a more positive aspect. Its consciousness, which did appear to be dependent, transforms itself into an independent consciousness, not in the relationship between itself and the master, but in its relationship with the external world.[14] The master puts the slave to work but in doing so the slave 'becomes conscious of what he truly is'.[15] By forming and shaping external things or objects, the slave comes to see in these objects evidence of his own independent self-consciousness.[16] The slave attains the self-certainty of his consciousness in his work and allows him to take up once more the 'liberating fight for recognition'.[17] This new fight for recognition requires a 'universal self-consciousness' where being recognized consists not in the domination of another self-consciousness, but in the natural relation of different self-consciousnesses who identify their dignity with the freedom they have in common.[18] This will be a society where the 'strictly particular, personal, individual value of each is recognised as such, in its very particularity, by *all*'.[19]

In George Armstrong Kelly's famous essay on the master/slave dialectic, he identifies three ways to view this relationship 'that are all equally valid and interpenetrable'.[20] One is a social understanding, typified by the work of Alexandre Kojève where master and slave engage in a form of Marxist class struggle.[21] The second relates to the different forms of psychological domination and servitude operating within an individual ego.[22] The third is a fusion of these first two and displays 'the interior consequences wrought by the external confrontation of the Self and the Other, the Other and the Self, which has commenced in the struggle for recognition'. On the social interpretation, Armstrong Kelly argues that at any time in history there are always slaves and masters. Additionally, on the interior psychological interpretation, each human has to struggle with slavery and mastery in relation to his or her own psyche, where the passions and reason may come to conflict and there is an attempt to bring them into harmony. He therefore unites these interpretations by focusing on their interaction where humans have the capacity to either enslave or be enslaved by others.[23]

A passion that can arise out of these interactions and will be pertinent to *Identity* is the notion of love. For Hegel, 'love is a feeling' and 'means in general the consciousness of my unity with another'.[24] Love has two moments, the first is the desire to give up one's independence, and the second is the wish to gain recognition in another person while also allowing the other person to gain recognition in you. Such a denial and affirmation of the self through the 'other' is why Hegel refers to love as 'the most immense contradiction'. However, its resolution lies in reciprocity, a form of mutual recognition, which achieves an 'ethical unity' and thereby implies a higher state of consciousness for those involved in such a process.

People play out these psychological tensions in the real world, and so actively forge the link between psychology and history.[25] This real world is what Hegel refers to as the 'system of ethical life' where recognition and misrecognition govern the relations between people and the social institutions that they have created.[26] In relation to love in the 'system of ethical life', Hegel explains how it manifests itself in marriage and the family and his arguments here have created much controversy, particularly for many feminist commentators. They have suggested that his notion of love is inapplicable to women, as indeed is the master/slave framework itself, because it implies the domination of the male over the female.[27] However, my intention is not to adjudicate on these accusations here, but to try to extricate the positive aspects of Hegel's theory for exploring the relationship between Chantal and Jean-Marc. These characters push the boundaries of recognition and misrecognition through the immense contradiction that love is. The restrictions Hegel might have put on these notions in relation to women do not mean that we need to adhere to them when analysing Chantal's character. Indeed, as we shall see, she is very much the embodiment of reversing the sexism often associated with the master/slave recognition framework. For instance, she is a fiercely independent woman with a high-powered and well-paid job in advertising and, if anything, she resembles the master rather than the slave in her relationship with Jean-Marc.

From mutual recognition to misrecognition

At the outset, Chantal and Jean-Marc appear to be in a state of
mutual recognition but events quickly undermine that stability to
reveal the fault lines bubbling beneath the surface of their relationship. They first meet in a mountain hotel, confronting each other
as two self-consciousnesses in a process of recognition and this is
re-told about halfway through the novel (87–8). As mentioned previously, Jean-Marc is a ski instructor who has been invited to a
cocktail party for the participants of a conference, of whom Chantal is one (87). There are many people present and, even though
they are introduced to each other, it is only in passing and they
exchange only a few words – they do not even catch each other's
names. However, Jean-Marc returns the next day, uninvited, with
the sole intention of seeing her again. When Chantal notices him
she flushes from her cheeks right down to her neckline and this
reveals 'her declaration of love' (87–8). She was red for all to see
because of Jean-Marc, and as she was never to flush again for
years after, the flush carried even greater significance as the 'priceless ruby' of their love (88).

They appear to each other as two self-consciousnesses in a very
abstract manner because they do not know each other's names and
are in a state of immediacy. The self-consciousness embodied in
Jean-Marc comes out of itself and is confronted by another self-
consciousness, Chantal, so he exists in and for himself through
being acknowledged. The flush is the symbol of that recognition
through the mediation of love as an initial feeling. Similarly, Chantal is confronted by the other self-consciousness, Jean-Marc, who,
in seeking her out, allows her self-consciousness to be acknowledged. So starts the process of Hegelian recognition at the outset of
their relationship. At this point their social roles in terms of their
work, she as an advertising executive and he as a ski instructor,
matters not to either of them, but these are power relations in a
life and death struggle of recognition that will come to the fore
when misrecognition rears its ugly head. Indeed, even the flush of
their love will be a key to the unravelling of what is initially their
mutual recognition of each other once we return to their relationship as it begins to be depicted at the start of the book.

When Chantal arrives at the seaside hotel, her emotional equilibrium becomes undermined by two waitresses discussing a TV

programme called *Lost in Sight*, which attempts to trace people
who have disappeared (3–4). One of them makes the comment
that losing someone you love and never knowing what has happened to them could drive you insane (4). Chantal ponders on this
and thinks to herself what an 'unrelenting horror' it would be if
something similar were to happen to Jean-Marc (5). The irony is,
as we find out as the story unfolds, that you do not need someone
to physically disappear to lose sight of them, and this is explored
throughout the novel: the constant changing of the self and identity through recognition and misrecognition.

When she retires to bed after dinner, Chantal is haunted by
images from her past such as her ex-husband, his 'overbearing,
energetic sister' and her former lovers (6). What troubles her most
is the way such dreams can nullify the present, which is her life
with Jean-Marc and the apartment that they share together. She
therefore dislikes dreams precisely because 'they discredit the
present by denying it its privileged status'. Even in her sleep, the
stability of her current life is being disturbed and is in turn destabilizing her consciousness and thereby her current identity.

The next day, she walks along the seaside watching the tourists
and couples with children, and imagines flirting with one of the
fathers or with the single men on the beach (12–14). She thinks
that the idea is amusing and it even puts her in a good mood, but
her conclusion is that she lives in a world where men will never
turn to look at her again. She returns to the hotel to find that Jean-
Marc has arrived and left her a note saying he is going out to look
for her (14–15). Chantal asks the receptionist where he will be,
and the latter tells her that he said she would be on the beach, so
he has gone to look for her there. When Jean-Marc does go down
to the beach we have another instance of misrecognition (16). He
thinks he has seen Chantal looking out to sea and is worried that
she may be hit by an oncoming sand-yacht; he suddenly imagines
that this occurs (16–17). Thinking he is experiencing the moment
of her death, through his tears of anguish he calls out her name,
but he cannot be heard because of the noise of the wind (17). The
death of the 'other' is therefore a realization that without recognition Jean-Marc's self loses its identity. This is exacerbated by the
fact that for him, Chantal is his sole mediation with the world. The
loss of self would be total in his case because he has given himself
over to the 'other' so completely. Indeed, in true Hegelian fashion,

it is through the 'other' that he comes to recognize his own self. However, when Jean-Marc sees that she is fine, he smiles at the comedy of the bereavement he had just played out, but not self-critically, 'because Chantal's death has been with him ever since he began to love her' (17–18). As he runs towards her and she does not respond to his advances, he suddenly realizes that it is not Chantal, and now the woman before him 'became old, ugly, pathetically other' (18).

Both of the characters have begun the move from a position of mutual recognition on the basis of their love for each other to misrecognition. Chantal experiences it through being forced to consider the loss of Jean-Marc, and Jean-Marc experiences it by being forced to consider the loss of Chantal. Even worse for Jean-Marc, however, is that he has experienced this misrecognition by confusing Chantal with an 'other' in reality. Again, what will prove more damaging for both of them is the fragmentation of their identities to such an extent that they will doubt that they ever knew who the 'other' was in the first place. The life and death struggle for self-certainty through the 'other' will take them down this path.

Later we are told that Jean-Marc has often mistaken Chantal for someone else, and he wonders whether this means that she is not much different from other women (20). Such a thought necessarily undermines his love for her because he thinks it is astonishing that he cannot demarcate the love of his life to which no other woman is meant to compare. Consequently, the seed of doubt has now been planted and this will begin to undermine his love for her through the process of misrecognition. This is exacerbated when he finally meets Chantal in the hotel room. While he realizes at last that it is her, he notices that she is not looking like her normal self. Indeed, her face seems aged and her glance somewhat harsh. He thinks that the woman on the beach is her true identity and must logically replace Chantal. Moreover, he believes that he is being punished for his inability to recognize her (21).

The misrecognition deteriorates further when Jean-Marc begins to ask Chantal what the matter is, and she drops the bombshell that she is perturbed because men do not turn to look at her anymore. Jean-Marc is stung by her comment and wants to show her how hurtful she has been despite the love and devotion he has expressed towards her. He thinks about saying 'what about me?', but decides not to and causes her to flush by asking her if her concern is true. For Jean-Marc, the flush is evidence of secret desires, longings, he conjectures, which she cannot resist, and to make matters worse she repeats the mantra: 'men, they don't turn to look at me any more' (21–2). Her confession now destabilizes the mutual recognition that had given their relationship solidity, and this misrecognition unravels itself through the remainder of the book.

In the next chapter, the scene is played from Chantal's perspective and she realizes that saying the phrase was meant to be light-hearted but it came out the wrong way and instead sounded 'bitter and melancholy' (22). She only repeats the phrase to try to rectify matters but it sounds even worse than before (23). She recognizes that Jean-Marc is thinking about his love for her, and she feels saved by it, but she cannot properly believe in it yet and so she pushes him away when he tries to hold her. So she thinks no man will turn his head to look at her, not even Jean-Marc, and she is almost testing him to get a reassurance of his love for her. She is older than him so that could be a reason for her insecurity; this, though, will be at great cost to their relationship.

The narrator then considers whether the previous meeting actually occurred, and suggests that Chantal scarcely recalls the phrase that upset Jean-Marc, concluding that the episode has been forgotten like a host of others (24–5). Significantly, there is no mention of Jean-Marc here and it is only later we find out that he has certainly not forgotten the incident, and it has major ramifications for their relationship and the misrecognition developing between them.

Jean-Marc sees Chantal as his 'sole emotional link to the world' and the way in which he can empathize with the plight of others (81). He notes how people can talk to him about people being imprisoned, persecuted, starved and raped, but the only way he can truly identify with their plight is if he imagines Chantal in their place. She therefore allows him to overcome his apathy and develop his compassion, but only because it is mediated through her. He is then a dependent consciousness symptomatic of the slave, and Chantal appears to be the independent consciousness reminiscent of the master.

He wants to tell her how he feels but thinks she will perceive him as being pathetic, especially as he is plagued by the consequence of what his life would be like if he lost her. The loss is not in the form of something final such as death but as a lack of recognition, where she would turn out to be the woman on the beach, her certainty would become illusory and 'she would mean as little to him as everybody else'. He then tells her this and says that he is worried that he is wrong about her identity (82). As he does so, he sees the pile of brassieres she is hiding the letters in, but instead of them making him see her as a stranger or traitor, he suddenly sees the real Chantal, and tells her to forget what he has said. He realizes that he is partly at fault for sending the letters in the first place and testing her love for him.

We now return to where we began with their first meeting in the ski resort. As we saw then, the flush is a symbol of their love (87). Jean-Marc never sees her flush again, which gives it its extraordinary nature, and why it 'glowed in their faraway past like a priceless ruby' (88). So when she flushes after telling Jean-Marc that it bothers her that men do not turn to look at her anymore, he thinks that she must love or at least desire someone else. Ironically, though, the real reason she is getting hot flushes is because she thinks she might be menopausal (86). As the narrator states: 'It's not good hiding her hot flushes, she's getting old and it shows' (86). Even their symbol of love is misrecognized and takes them further away from mutual recognition.

As the story unfolds, we discover that Jean-Marc has found the letters and she also begins to realize that it is he who has sent them. Unable to communicate with each other, they wrongly analyse each other's motives. Chantal thinks he has done this as a way to get rid of her because she is looking old. He thinks she is hiding the letters because she wants to engage in an illicit affair and the flush causes further torture for Jean-Marc (96–7). He recalls her face flushing when they were walking in the street and asking her why to which she made no response. He becomes 'disturbed that something was happening in her which he knew nothing about' and this makes him jealous because his role as letter writer, as Cyrano, was such a success in seducing her (96). The effects are devastating because Chantal becomes a simulacrum and so does the whole of his own life, because she is the mediation between himself and the world (96–7). However, ultimately his love for her outweighs his jealousy and he decides to write her one final letter (96), but any possibility of reconciliation is undermined by an unexpected arrival from Chantal's past.

The past as 'other'

Jean-Marc is suddenly confronted with the appearance of Chantal's sister-in-law with her three children, and so his consciousness becomes penetrated by a previous life that he had not wanted to know anything about (101). The sister-in-law begins to give an account of Chantal's prior persona and this creates a new identity of Chantal for Jean-Marc, an identity that disrupts his self-certainty of her (102). The sister-in-law reveals that Chantal's ex-husband was smaller than Chantal and she used to mother him and call him her 'little mousie'. She imagines Chantal cradling her brother and she shows Jean-Marc how this might have looked by dancing in front of him, mimicking holding a baby. The children then sneak into Chantal's bedroom and are causing pandemonium but all Jean-Marc can picture is this new identity of Chantal as a cradler of a man she calls her 'little mousie' (104). In addition, her new identity also has the characteristic of being a simulacrum, as not someone Jean-Marc loves but as someone who is guarding letters from a secret worshipper in order to have an illicit adventure. To make matters worse, Chantal has always spoken ill of her sister-in-law's family, but here the sister seems to show real affection for her (105). Another nail in Chantal's coffin is what Jean-Marc sees as her ability to adapt to things she detests and he deduces that she now has two faces.

For example, he used to admire the way she resembled a spy or masked enemy in her job in advertising and so cleverly concealed her contempt for it (105–6). Now, though, she is simply a collaborator going along with the 'detestable power' of advertising and the people in it. In short, he reiterates, she now has two faces (106). However, it is only because of the destabilizing power misrecognition has had on his consciousness that he presents this misleading picture of Chantal. In truth, we are told that she was a poorly paid high schoolteacher before her son was born, and even though she loved her job, she realized that she had to get one with more pay if she was to gain her independence and freedom from her marriage (31). She feels guilty about having to betray her principles but the overriding need was to escape and start afresh. Interestingly, she also cannot imagine this new life without an 'other' and so seeks a man who can offer her a different life from the one she had before; that person was Jean-Marc. Her search was therefore part of the quest for mutual recognition.

When Chantal arrives, the misrecognition reaches the state of a sort of inverse absolute knowledge, as they start to wonder if they really know each other at all. Chantal is as distraught as Jean-Marc as she wonders how on earth they have been tracked down (107). The sister-in-law berates Chantal for not keeping in touch with her even though she agrees that she was right to leave her husband (108). She admonishes Chantal for trying to erase them, and her past, from her life: 'You can't deny you were happy with us', says the sister-in-law, which makes Chantal realize how she had spent so long with that family negating her own self and failing to display her otherness. Chantal cannot believe why she had acquiesced so much during her married life, and even worse she does not know why (108–9). Nevertheless, on reflection, she knows that the answer was her son (109). While he was alive she accepted all the scrutiny, sloppiness, obligatory nudism around the pool, and the lack of privacy. It all filled her with disgust but she resigned herself to it, and if her son had not died she would have lived her life like that until her death. This is why her son's demise gave her freedom and why she feels so guilty about it.

The noise of the children in her bedroom awakens Chantal from her thoughts, and when she goes in she notices that they have entered her wardrobe and scattered her brassieres and underpants, along with the letters, all over the floor. Chantal is furious, and for her, the letters are no longer a sign of a secret that she should be ashamed of; they are now, instead, a symbol of Jean-Marc's deceit and treasonable behaviour (110). For Chantal, Jean-Marc is now with the enemy, he is a spy, just like her sister-in-law. Chantal then declares her right of property ownership of the apartment and her personal possessions (110–11). She says no one has the right to interfere with her things, although it is more to Jean-Marc that she directs this edict, but she disguises this by asking her sister-in-law to leave (111).

Once the sister-in-law and her children have left, Chantal again sees Jean-Marc as being part of the conspiracy of her previous family against her (112). She asserts her power by reminding him that the apartment is hers, and the reason she bought it was to be free and not to be spied upon. Jean-Marc's response is to accept that he is at one with the beggar who camps out on the street, he is on the margin of the world but she is at the centre of it. Using her financial power, she taunts him that this is a fine form of marginality because it costs him nothing. He responds by saying he can leave this marginality at any time whereas she has sold out to conformism with her 'many faces'.

As it happens, Jean-Marc had planned to come clean about his deception of sending the letters but the arrival of the sister-in-law and Chantal's attacks on him now rule that out of the question (113). Through a life and death struggle, the power in their relationship moves decisively towards Chantal as she becomes the independent consciousness associated with the master, and Jean-Marc becomes the dependent consciousness of the slave. In truth, he has always been the slave, but mutual recognition has always stopped them from falling back into the emotional disequilibrium that they are now in. Chantal owns the apartment, earns five times what he does and on that basis she accuses him of settling into a 'plush marginality that cost him nothing'. Consequently, the 'tacit agreement' that they had between themselves not to mention such inequalities was now at an end.

Chantal then reads out the last letter he sent and without a further word disappears into her room. He realizes that her statement that no one has the right to open her wardrobe and go through her personal things is directed at him, and that she knows he is the author of the letters and where they are kept. To his mind, such brazenness only confirms her rejection of him outright (114). When she eventually returns from her room they eat a 'cold meal' and 'for the first time in their life together, they said not a word'. She goes to her room and does not return to the bed that they have always shared with each other. Unable to sleep, he puts his ear to the door of her room and is disturbed to hear her calmly sleeping. He now realizes that he was wrong to have thought she was weaker than him. All along, then, because of the inequality between them of wealth and property she was the independent consciousness, the master, and he the dependent consciousness, the slave. The mutual recognition that kept their relationship in equilibrium was built on shaky foundations and once misrecognition appeared those foundations had to fall. However, as the narrator points out, when they were both in love perhaps Jean-Marc was the stronger, but with the love gone, Chantal is now the strong one, and he has become weak (115). Once master, he is now a slave, but his master status was always tenuous in reality.

Again, ironically, Jean-Marc has misrecognized Chantal's condition because she did not sleep as well as he thought. Instead, she is haunted in her dreams by engaging in orgies with strange men that she finds revolting (115–16). She packs a suitcase early in the morning and is confronted by Jean-Marc (116). She informs him that she is going to London, and when he asks why she tells him that he knows the answer because it was mentioned in the last letter that she had received. This makes him flush, which gives her a triumphant feeling and pleases her immensely. His flush is a further indication that she knows he is the letter writer but, if so, he wonders why she cannot understand the reason he acted as he did (117–18). He concludes that they do not understand each other because 'their ideas have gone in different directions, and it seems to him they will never converge again' (118).

Further instances of misrecognition occur as she goes to London and Jean-Marc follows her, and there appears to be no way that they can ever get back to a position of mutual recognition, however temporary. Nevertheless, Kundera introduces a controversial plot device to bring the two of them back to equilibrium that has annoyed some readers:[28] we discover it has all been a dream (152). The penultimate chapter has Jean-Marc holding Chantal in his arms and crying out to her, 'wake up! It's not real!' (152). The narrator then ponders on where fantasy and reality meet but leaves it up to the reader to decide (152–3). The final outcome for the two of them is that Chantal wants to keep watching Jean-Marc to make sure nothing can take his place (153). She says she will leave the lamp on all night and every night to make sure that happens.

Conclusion: from misrecognition to mutual recognition

A reading of Hegel's theory of recognition can also fit into the perspective of Kundera's use of dream, due to the notion of a self-consciousness attempting to adjudicate between the master of reason and the slave of the passions within one psyche. Throughout the book Chantal is plagued in her dreams by former lovers trying to seduce her, by ugly men she finds revolting, engaging in orgies with her and women kissing her on the lips. Her dreams are nightmares but the supposed real aspect of her life is also a nightmare, because the mutual recognition she has with Jean-Marc increases her anxiety and loss of identity of both herself and him.

In a useful discussion on this issue, François Ricard argues that in Kundera's novels dreams are not prophetic or psychoanalytic but offer a 'purely aesthetic treatment' that 'is attached to the dream's content, not as to the cause or the effect or sign of something else, but for its own sake and its own enigmatic beauty'.[29] The dreams are on a par with the real stories and themes running throughout Kundera's novels in an ontological equality.[30] So, as Ricard indicates in relation to the authorial intervention mentioned before, *Identity* does not have a border, as fantasy and reality interpenetrate each other.[31] Ricard sees Kundera as an heir to Kafka in this respect and quotes Kundera from his *Art of the Novel* for support, where he describes Kafka's work as epitomizing the way in which dream and reality cannot be distinguished from each other. [32] For Chantal and Jean-Marc, the fantasy world and reality merge and both are nightmarish, as what they thought were solid identities begin to fragment and diffuse into some 'other'. It is, as Ricard says, a nightmare that both characters, and us as readers along with them, are plunged into.[33] The internal and external fight haunts both characters between their rational and passionate sides. From our Hegelian framework, a master/slave fight to achieve recognition both within themselves and in relation to the 'other' is taking place. The thought of Chantal being the subject of orgies she does not want to participate in, for example, is just as real as her concerns that men do not turn to look at her anymore; not even Jean-Marc. For him, the thought of Chantal's betrayal is as real as the imaginings he has that she does still love him.

The dialectics of identity therefore implies that we can never truly know an 'other' forever, so mutual recognition must always be contingent. For Hegel, and it seems for Kundera, the process of recognition and misrecognition never ends. Dialectically, absolute knowing is not a rigidified absolute but a contingent one, liable to change. It is absolute only on the understanding that it can be contingent. The desire of Chantal at the end of the book is to watch Jean-Marc forever without blinking so that he cannot change but this is a forlorn task. What we should be doing instead is trying to understand the fluidity of the self, and recognizing that we are not one self but multiple selves in our dialectical interactions. We therefore experience a perpetual process of recognition-misrecognition-mutual recognition-misrecognition-recognition. Mutual recognition in all its forms is our ethical aim

in our relations with others, but seeing it as always being contingent means that we keep ourselves on guard to stop us becoming
either master or slave. Chantal and Jean-Marc's relationship shows
us the dangers in assuming mutual recognition as being static and
permanent rather than realizing its potential mutability. This is
why we need to keep the lamp on, not to make sure the 'other'
cannot change, but to illuminate our complex relations between
others and ourselves in a world of shared understanding.

However, this brings us to the problem of the political in Kundera's work that we touched on in the previous chapter. As we have
seen, Hegel's theory of recognition is played out psychologically
and inter-subjectively between a self and the 'other'. The way Kundera depicts this process through Chantal and Jean-Marc is with a
deeply psychological narrative that at times seems wrenched from
any social context. When that social context does intervene, for
example, with the power Chantal has from her wealth and the status of her work, doing an advertising job for the money rather than
the teaching that is more true to her authentic self, misrecognition
seems inevitable. The lack of recognition and inequality Jean-Marc
has in relation to her is not a stable foundation for their relationship, and taking this further and politicizing it, neither is it a sound
basis on which to construct and organize a society. In a different world, one not simply based on the power of money, Chantal
would do what is most authentic to her self-certainty in the social
world and that would be teaching. Then, Jean-Marc might not see
her as a sell-out or traitor and this could be a more firm foundation
for mutual recognition between each other. Similarly, Jean-Marc's
attempt to assert his own identity in the world vicariously through
Chantal is a negation of his own self. He is not staking his life
and experiencing the evils and trouble of the world through his
own self-consciousness in relation to other self-consciousnesses.
The path to mutual recognition means that we cannot as individuals remain in the bedroom with the lamp on, watching each other
and hoping that we do not change. In fact, Chantal should realize
that she must change her identity and find a way to go back to her
vocation as a teacher. Then she can be a more authentic being both
for herself and to gain mutual recognition from Jean-Marc. Similarly, by Jean-Marc engaging with the world and approaching its
problems directly, his identity will change for the better and he will
gain mutual recognition from Chantal. Even more importantly,

beyond the interplay of recognition between the two of them, follows the recognition gained in the ethical life of the community from their work and actions. This political dimension of Hegel's theory therefore allows us to deepen the experience of recognition in positing how different the world could be, not only for Chantal and Jean-Marc, but also for ourselves.

Part II:
Ian McEwan

3 • *Atonement*: E. P. Thompson and Class Experience

Writing in 2005, four years after the publication of *Atonement*,[1] Ian McEwan praised the recently deceased American writer Saul Bellow for his pluralism in being able to write about all different strata of society. In contrast, McEwan argued, 'in Britain we no longer seem able to write across the crass, and subtle distortions of class – or rather, we can't do it gracefully, without seeming to strain or caricature'.[2] Consequently, then, it would appear that this is what McEwan was attempting to do in *Atonement*. Additionally, and in connection with this emphasis on class, in an interview of the same year, Robert McCrum quotes McEwan as saying that 'children who receive the education their parents did not' are set 'on a path of cultural dislocation'.[3] Indeed, what is particularly distinctive about the novel is a re-examination of class conflict where the microcosms of English society are played out through characters in a country house shortly before the Second World War, and then in the institutions of the army and the nursing establishment during it. The story centres around three main characters: Robbie, the son from a lower social class whose mother is the cleaning lady for the upper-class Taliss family, and the sisters of that family, Cecilia and her younger precocious sibling Briony, an aspiring writer. Briony causes the downfall of Robbie and Cecilia's possible relationship by falsely claiming that he was responsible for a crime, the rape of Briony and Cecilia's cousin Lola, which was actually perpetrated by Paul Marshall, the capitalist confectioner friend of their brother, Leon. Robbie is wrongly sent to prison and is eventually released after three years to fight in the Second World War with the action focusing on the retreat to Dunkirk.

Additionally, Robbie Turner is the embodiment of this situation of class and cultural dislocation. His 'father' was a Romany gardener and his mother the general help for the Tallises. Robbie, however, through his contact with the Tallis family as a child, becomes absorbed into the bourgeois mores of upper-middle-class life, and with the patronage of the father, Jack Tallis, he goes to grammar school and then to Cambridge. One of McEwan's particular concerns is the exploration of the effects that this cultural dislocation has on Robbie. In contrast, Cecilia is deeply imbued with the identities relating to an upper-middle-class background, but what happens to Robbie, and the class prejudice of her family that allows him to be sacrificed in this way, begins to fragment her class identity and make her more class-conscious of those below her in the class system. In one sense, this is also a class and cultural dislocation for Cecilia.

My concern is to highlight these class and cultural contradictions present in the book by utilizing the conceptual framework developed by E. P. Thompson, while also drawing on Marx where necessary to inform Thompson's categories.[4] The chapter will explore *Atonement* through the notions of class experience and class consciousness, class struggle and class hegemony, and fetishism. Focusing on these notions of class identity will reveal the power relations they engender, particularly in relation to Robbie and Cecilia, but also Paul Marshall as the personification of capital. Thompson's analysis will be shown to be particularly fruitful in exposing these class contradictions especially as Cecilia's character is also repeatedly used to break through the fetishism operating within the Tallis household, where the workers and their labours are not so much taken for granted, but not thought about at all as long as their tasks are completed to the required level of satisfaction. This focus on class is relatively neglected in the literature on *Atonement*[5] despite its crucial importance to the novel, and it has certainly not been approached through a Thompsonian framework. However, before outlining Thompson's theory we first need to briefly mention the way the novel has been constructed because that will have implications for how we understand the motives and actions of the characters. To do so means dealing with the irony of one of the main protagonists, Briony.

The irony of Briony

Starting with the ending, we now realize that Briony has deceived us. In the final epilogue of the book, we are introduced to the now-ageing and terminally ill Briony in 1999, and discover all that has gone before was various drafts of a novel that was part of her atone-ment. The novel within the novel has been in ironic form and Briony's name is of course a play on this word and we now know that we have been told a story by an 'unreliable witness' (336). The title of the novel is also pointing us towards irony, because we can split the word of atonement as a-tone-ment, that is, a tone was meant. So the clues are there for us to see that we are being presented with something that is not quite as it seems. The novel must be re-read with this in mind.

Briony tells us that she wrote the first draft of the novel in January 1940, the second draft in June 1940 but then does not tell us when the third one was written (369). The latest draft, the one we have just read, was written in March 1999. At the end of this version, Robbie and Cecilia are united and Briony meets them to tell them that she will retract her story and hopefully begin to achieve her atonement. She relates that from the second version onwards she set out to describe the crime perpetrated by Marshall, Lola and herself. She also states that it is only in the last version that a happy ending occurs, as all the other drafts were pitiless (370). The 'true' ending has Robbie die at Dunkirk on 1 June 1940 and Cecilia die in September of the same year by the bomb that destroyed Balham Underground. Briony cannot think what would be served by having a sad ending like that now.[6] So, she never went to see them and the final part of the book is totally fictitious. She did attempt to go and visit Cecilia after Robbie was recently reported dead, but was too much of a coward and turned back once she got to the church on Clapham Common (370–1). All that is left for Briony now is her descent into dementia.

The characters cannot speak for themselves as they are all speaking through Briony's interpretation of them because, as she says herself, as a novelist 'with her absolute power of deciding outcomes, she is also God' (371). Were they just like Briony depicts them or is she presenting them in a way that she wants us to see them? What is true and what is embellishment by Briony needs to be carefully scrutinized when we form judgements about the characters. With that established we now need to outline Thompson's understanding of class.

Thompson on class

Thompson's basic understanding of class is as both a relationship and an historical phenomenon that brings together a number of apparently unrelated events in our everyday experience and in our consciousness.[7] Class is not a structure or a category but something that has happened and happens in human relationships. Class is dynamic and based on agency just as much as it is based on conditioning. Thompson argues that this dynamic understanding of class becomes lost if we stop class dead and anatomize its structure to give a pure specimen of class the way certain sociologists do. For Thompson, this is as unrealistic as trying to give a pure specimen of love or deference, because the relationship must be embodied in people as they live their lives. Consequently, we can no more talk about love without lovers nor deference without squires and labourers. Class happens, then, when people come together through either inherited or shared common experiences, and articulate and feel the identity of their interests against other people, whose interests are different from and usually opposed to theirs.[8]

Thompson argues that if we stop class at a given historical point then we simply get a multitude of individuals with a multitude of experiences.[9] Instead, we need to observe people over an 'adequate period of social change', and then patterns in their ideas, relationships and institutions can be discerned. For Thompson, then, class is defined by people as they 'live their own history, and, in the end, this is its only definition'. In that sense, class can only be understood as a cultural and social formation that arises from processes over a 'considerable historical period', which in his study *The Making of the English Working Class* is between 1780 and 1832.[10]

When Thompson looks back on this period with his understanding of class as agency, he notes how he is going against a number of orthodoxies that either depict working people as passive victims of laissez-faire (the Fabians), mere statistics as a labour force or migrants (empirical economic historians) or ignored in place of identifying those individuals that were pioneers for the forthcoming welfare state. While Thompson recognizes some truth in these approaches he rejects the first two because the agency of working people becomes obscured, and he rejects the final one for engaging in retrospective history rather than history as it actually occurred.[11] On the third view, only those who succeeded are remembered and so the 'blind alleys, the lost causes, and the losers themselves are forgotten'. Thompson's concern is to rescue the losers such as the 'poor stockinger, the Luddite cropper, the "obsolete" hand-loom weaver and the "utopian" artisan' from 'the enormous condescension of posterity'. He argues that doing so makes us realize that however outlandish their actions or ideas, 'their aspirations were valid in terms of their own experience'.

Thompson also suggests that the productive relations that people are born into, or enter involuntarily, mainly, but not totally, determine the class experience.[12] Out of this emerges the notion of class consciousness, which is the way such experiences are handled culturally through 'traditions, value-systems, ideas and institutional forms'. Whereas the class experience can be seen as being determined in some way, class consciousness is not because it arises in different times and places in different forms.

The dangers in not following Thompson's edicts here are evident in his criticisms of alternative understandings of class. For example, Thompson criticizes sociologists such as Ralf Dahrendorf, who not only formulates a theory of class without any reference whatsoever to a concrete class situation, but also defines class through the social roles people are in within a particular social organization.[13] As Thompson indicates, this begs the question of how these people came to be in these social roles and how these social organizations with their property rights and authority structures also came into existence. These are, of course, historical questions, which need to be explained by seeing the experiences of people and their institutions develop over a period of time.

Additionally, Thompson argues that there is a tendency in Marxism in particular to assume that class is a thing, where the working class itself is meant to have a 'real existence, which can be defined almost mathematically', by reading how many people stand in a certain relation to the means of production.[14] The danger of such an approach is that it results in imposing on the class a class consciousness that it is meant to have, but rarely does, if it was fully aware of its own position and its proper interests. It then falls to the elitism of a party, sect or theorist to disclose class consciousness, not as it is, but as it ought to be. Writing some fifteen years after this discussion in the *Making*, Thompson later equates this approach explicitly with Leninist vanguardism for engaging in the politics of substitution where the vanguard know better than the class itself what its consciousness is meant to be.[15] The failure of the class to have the required consciousness the vanguard prescribes is dismissed, in this erroneous understanding of class, as false consciousness, which Thompson of course rejects.

Similarly, Thompson criticizes those who derive class from a theoretical model of a structural totality as in the case of Louis Althusser,[16] because it means that we will wrongly suppose that class is 'instantaneously present' and 'derivative, like a geometric projection, from productive relations', without realizing that it is dependent on class struggle.[17] Failure to realize this results in 'endless stupidities of quantitative measurement of classes, or of sophisticated Newtonian Marxism in which classes and class fractions perform their planetary or molecular evolutions'. The error arises from wrongly supposing that classes exist 'independent of historical relationship and struggle, and that they struggle *because* they exist, rather than coming into existence out of that struggle'. For Thompson, class struggle is the more universal concept and it comes before both class and class consciousness in the historical process. People find themselves in a society that is structured in certain ways, such as through productive relations. Depending on their position they either experience exploitation or try to keep control over those they exploit, they identify opposing interests and begin to struggle around these issues, and in doing so discover themselves as classes and so develop a class consciousness. Class and class consciousness then emerge from class struggle.

Thompson's point that class is not a thing relates to the important notions of fetishism or reification, even though he does not use these terms. Fetishism or reification refers to the process whereby social relations between people take on the form of a relation between things in capitalist commodity production as Marx pointed out.[18] Commodities viewed fetishistically as things hide the fact that human toil has been expended in their creation along with the exploitation and alienation that has accompanied it. Breaking through fetishism exposes these social relations and as Lukács, whom Thompson also appears to be implicitly drawing on here, emphasized, fetishism or reification permeates everything in capital.[19] Viewing class and in particular the working class as a thing ignores the social basis on which they are constructed.

Thompson also emphasizes the notion of class hegemony in his reconsideration and re-affirmation of his notion of class.[20] He argues that when he analyses the class struggle taking place in the eighteenth century the form it takes is one of the gentry and the crowd that operates through a 'paternalism-difference equilibrium', where to some extent these two factions are 'prisoners of each other'. Against those theorists who see only consensus here, Thompson contends that there is instead a 'polarization of antagonistic interests' that become manifest in a 'dialectic of culture'. His point is that in the eighteenth century resistance may be less articulate, but it is up to us to give the articulation through our analysis of these resistances. Doing so means penetrating the 'theatre of class hegemony and control' and recognizing that acts of liberality and charity can be interpreted as acts of class appeasement where giving from above is an act of getting from below. For Thompson, these gentry-pleb relations are not so much an uncompromising raged battle, but rather a more nuanced form of jousting where both sides recognize 'what was possible and also the limits of the possible beyond which power did not dare to go'.[21] As such, plebeian culture is bounded by gentry hegemony, but the plebs are constantly on the lookout for moments where they can assert their own advantage.[22] For Thompson, the notion of hegemony is essential to understand how these social relations were structured.[23] Moreover, such hegemony must be maintained by the rulers through the 'constant exercise of skill, of theatre and of concession', but it is never all encompassing because it 'imposes blinkers, which inhibit vision in certain directions while leaving it clear in others'.[24] Although Thompson does not mention it explicitly here, this again is a rejection of the notion of false consciousness and is instead an understanding that this 'self-activating culture' that is derived from people's 'own experience and resources' can offer resistance to forms of domination and as such allow an 'ever-present threat to official descriptions of reality'.[25]

Thompson's contribution in this area was certainly not without controversy at the time[26] but I want to show its continuing relevance by briefly considering more recent re-evaluations, which actively identify and discuss the notion of class experience and how Thompson figures within these discourses. One important development has been in relation to feminist theorists,[27] who have, as Andrew Sayer points out, looked at class as a cultural phenomenon by seeing class as gendered and gender as classed.[28] Moreover, these writers maintain that gender and class are not separate phenomena and can only be grasped jointly rather than abstracted from and then rejoined. Sayer argues against this procedure because, while he recognizes that these two aspects of experience are lived together, he contends that they are responses to different sources of inequality and domination. By abstracting class from gender, then, we can better understand class experience, while also not forgetting that issues of gender are important as well. Consequently, for Sayer, it is the moral dimension to class specifically that he is interested in, and it is the work of Thompson that he endorses in this area for showing how moral norms are crucial, not only in relation to consent and compliance, but also to resistance to domination and injustice.[29]

However, aside from the gender issue what is important in the generic approach of these feminist theorists is the emphasis that they put on understanding class in relation to culture and identity, and how they address the 'complexities of class' as 'something which is *done*'.[30] Class is an active process, and as we have seen, this was captured in Thompson's framework through his emphasis on 'making' class through the agency of constituting subjects. In this regard, I want to briefly discuss the work of Beverley Skeggs, to show how she gives continued credence to aspects of Thompson's framework.

In her work on class that links the latter to the self and culture, Skeggs recognizes the importance of Thompson's work in this area because of his focus on class experience, and for giving preference for those who made history rather than having history simply imposed upon them.[31] For Skeggs, Thompson gave a tremendous amount of explanatory power back to those who were 'living class' to challenge structuralist accounts, and in doing so provided a new methodological legacy that has been used across a number of fields of enquiry,[32] and which, of course, I am going to employ to analyse *Atonement*. Nevertheless, despite her closeness to, and endorsement of, Thompson's position, Skeggs attempts to make a distinction between her notion of 'living class' and class consciousness, which as we have seen is a crucial concept for class agency. For Skeggs, 'living class' is part of how class is made, whereas theories of class consciousness 'assume that the working class person will develop an awareness of their positioning and therefore come to operate through class interests'.[33] But in Thompson's case at least no such assumption is present, because it would be as determining as the structuralism that he is opposed to. As we have seen, for Thompson, developing a class consciousness may or may not arise. It all depends on how people handle their class experience and, of course, is linked to the overcoming of class hegemony, which again may or may not be penetrated. That he hopes this will happen is without doubt, but it is not an assumption that it will. Skeggs is, therefore, closer to Thompson than she realizes and indeed her work can be understood as an extension of his own, given her further emphasis on class struggle and her desire to defend the working class from the condescension of those who consider themselves their betters.[34]

Thompson's categories can be fruitfully utilized to expose the nature of class experience in the various ways mentioned above, to enlighten our understanding of the class-based aspects of *Atonement* by isolating class from gender, as Sayer himself says we should. With the main notions explained, we now need to apply them to *Atonement*, beginning with class experience and class consciousness.

Class experience and class consciousness

Thompson emphasizes that to understand class properly we need to see how people came to be in their social roles in their social organization. Looming large over this is the microcosmic arena of the Tallis estate where the first and crucial part of the book is played out. The Tallis family can be designated as being part of the upper-middle class, but the background of the family is shady, and seems to show that there has been a deliberate and sustained cultivation of an upper-middle-class lifestyle to hide their more mundane and lower-class origins. For example, in the dining room there is a picture in the style of Gainsborough showing an aristocratic family – parents, two teenage girls and an infant, 'all thin-lipped and pale as ghouls', in front of a Tuscan landscape (126). Briony as narrator informs us that no one knew who they were, and the assumption was that Jack's father, Harry Tallis, thought it would give a form of solidity to the household. Emily Tallis reiterates this point and notes again how the intention of her father-in-law was to 'create an ambience of solidity and family tradition' (145). This solidity was required because we discover that Harry Tallis grew up over an ironmonger's shop and made the family fortune by patenting padlocks, bolts, latches and hasps, and so imposed on the house his taste for all things solid, secure and functional (19).

When Cecilia attempts to develop a family tree, she discovers
that on her father's side and until her great-grandfather opened a
humble hardware shop, the ancestors disappear into farm labour-
ing, with 'suspicious and confusing name changes amongst the
men, and common-law marriages unrecorded in the parish registers' (21). Moreover, she also finds that 'grandfather Harry Tallis
was the son of a farm labourer, who, for some reason, had changed
his name from Cartwright and whose birth and marriage were not
recorded' (109). The irony is, then, that the claims of the family to
being upper-middle class rest on a shady past, which a change of
surname from Cartwright to Tallis would certainly indicate. The
Cartwright family as the forefathers of the Tallis family had obviously moved from a low-class to a high-class position. It follows
that, given their background, they should not be snobbish or look
down on Robbie, but Emily, in particular, does this, even though
she has married into the Tallises' money, albeit seemingly coming
from a wealthy background herself.

Robbie's class experience is one of assimilation into a higher class
through the simple fact that he moved freely between the bungalow
he lived in and the main house through his friendship with Cecilia
and Leon, and his patronage by Jack Tallis (86). Both began when
Grace, Robbie's mother, was employed as a cleaner after Robbie's
father leaves when he is six. Leon and Cecilia adore Grace and this
was the saving of her and also the making of Robbie (87). So Robbie is going to be set on the path of a class and, in McEwan's own
term, cultural dislocation with of course disastrous consequences.

With such an upbringing behind him, Robbie never experienced
any social unease even when people who did not like him at Cambridge tried to embarrass him about his background (86). Far from
hiding it, Robbie told them that his father had walked out on him
and that his mother was a cleaner who supplemented her income
as an occasional clairvoyant. Moreover, when he also realized that
he was more intelligent than many other people at university, such
assimilation was complete and he had no need to display any form
of arrogance in the process. So in the Thompsonian sense, if we
contemplate Robbie and those around him over time, we can discern that Robbie's unusual class experience, given the rigid class
structure of the time, results in him being more class-conscious,
and to a large extent proud of his lower-class background, than
those around him. As we shall see shortly, Robbie is also important

as a catalyst for the raising of Cecilia's class consciousness, which makes her begin to question her own upper-middle-class background and share and empathize with the common experiences of working-class people.

Briony, the narrator, tells us that another basis for his openness was that he had 'his politics to protect him, and his scientifically based theories of class, and his own rather forced self-certainty. I am what I am' (79). What these scientifically based theories of class that he had are not explained. However, Briony as narrator describes through Cecilia how the latter watches him through the window as he rolls a cigarette, which she describes as a 'hangover from his Communist Party time', and which is dismissed as 'another abandoned fad, along with his ambitions in anthropology, and the planned hike from Calais to Istanbul' (22). Cecilia, again via Briony, also slightly mocks Robbie by asking him to roll her one of his 'Bolshevik cigarettes' as they walk together in the garden (25).

This depiction of Robbie as being a bit of a dilettante from Cecilia's point of view, via Briony, of course, is also displayed via the landscape gardening he undertakes on his return from Cambridge, and his 'last craze' with medicine now taking over as his new one, indicating both his pretentiousness and his presumptuousness since it was Cecilia's 'father who would have to pay for it' (19). If we follow Thompson, who attempted to save those at the bottom of society from the condescension of posterity, then we also need to save Robbie from the condescension of Briony here.

Robbie defends his class background and does not seek a class compromise with his upper-class peers at Cambridge, but by the time he returns to the Tallis estate on the fateful day in 1935 it appears that he is becoming assimilated into upper-middle-class society and thereby forgetting his roots. In relation to his posh accent, for example, it is unclear whether he changed it or whether it developed naturally with his interaction with the Tallises. In the Dunkirk episode when Corporal Nettle asks him: 'What's a private soldier like you doing talking like a toff?' (193), Robbie does not bother to respond, but did his new-found social mobility change him in the end? Did Robbie Turner become a turncoat and suffer the ultimate price for doing so? The class experience of being a relative part of an upper-middle-class family and his assimilation into Cambridge life might have changed him in the end, and seen his interests now merge with the interests of the upper-middle classes. However, what is also of ironic import in this episode is that Robbie has suffered so much class prejudice over the incident but is now mocked as someone who has enjoyed class privilege.

Nevertheless, it is revealing that when he is on the way to the fateful dinner, he considers that he is now only free for the first time (91). His headmaster had chosen Cambridge for him. His teacher had chosen the subject, English literature. Landscape gardening, the occupation of his 'father' was just a passing bohemian fancy. Now he was set on the path of medicine, something that he was choosing to do, and literature was an excellent preparation for such a vocation with all its instances of human suffering. However, literature was not the most vital of pursuits for an enquiring mind. The same case could be made for psychoanalysis, communism or medicine, but for Robbie making his own decision is the most important thing, and that now allowed him to find an outlet for his 'practical nature' and 'frustrated scientific aspirations'. He will take lodgings in a strange town and begin, so his story is only starting once he has left the Tallis family even though he is still dependent on Jack Tallis to fund his medical endeavours.

Again, Thompson's theme of agency is important here because, despite the freedom Robbie has received by transcending his class origin in terms of his education and upbringing, we are led to believe that this was accomplished under structural constraints. Moreover, his choice of occupation is to give something back to society by being a doctor whose humanism emanates from his examination of the moral dilemmas that take place in the literature that he has studied while at Cambridge (92). He has also taught children when he was in France before going to university, and seems a far more considerate character than he is given credit for by Briony as narrator. Moreover, the fact that he does possess a number of creative skills – learned in literature, teaching, landscape gardening and his ambition to then become a doctor – puts one in mind of Marx's famous dictum that humans under communism will be able to develop their talents to the full and as such, 'hunt in the morning, fish in the afternoon, rear cattle in the evening, criticise after dinner . . . without ever becoming hunter, fisherman, shepherd or critique'.[35]

However, there are moments where he does appear insensitive to the class relations of the house, given that his mother is the cleaner there, as we shall see when we consider Cecilia and the presence of fetishism. But, again, we need to consider whether this is due to Briony's depiction of Robbie, rather than what Robbie was really like. McEwan, writing as Briony, gives us a number of occasions where she is letting her jealousy for Robbie, given his preference for Cecilia over her, slip out as we have just seen in her account of his beliefs and actions above. More potently, she constantly makes reference to him as Malvolio, a character in Shakespeare's *Twelfth Night*, as in the passage when she describes Robbie's possessions in his room in the cottage. She mentions a photograph of him playing Malvolio who is mocked and treated as a figure of fun as the other characters pretend to him that Olivia is in love with him (82). 'How apt', she says and so sees Robbie as a lovelorn fool. Malvolio behaves so outrageously in *Twelfth Night* that he is imprisoned as a madman, but when the truth is revealed that he has been tricked and he is released he declares revenge on everyone. A fate that does of course, in a similar way, await Robbie, who, like Malvolio, comes from a lower-class origin.[36]

Thompson's rejection of the structural Marxism of Althusser is also pertinent here in terms of experience as emotion and empathy. As Thompson illustrated, an understanding of class through this theoretical model of structural totality leads to comprehending class like a geometric projection by statically reading it from the productive relations that are being examined. The experiential aspect is omitted in such a one-sided and static account of the nature of the class experience. For Thompson, the class experience is related to emotion and feeling, and it is worth reflecting on the fact that one of McEwan's stated aims in *Atonement* was that he wanted to 'play seriously, with something rooted in the emotional rather than the intellectual'.[37] Indeed, at the heart of McEwan's own moral philosophy is this emotion through empathy and compassion for others, which he says is 'at the core of our humanity'.[38] He makes this claim as one of his criticisms of the 9/11 bombers who, he maintains, could only commit such an atrocity because they lack the capacity to imagine, feel or empathize with the suffering caused to the 'other', something that Briony herself lacks also. When we link this with the way Thompson thinks that people come together in struggle to share their experiences and fight a common enemy, he is drawing on something deep within human beings, which rejects the egoism generated in class-based systems, and so forges class alliances.

This lack of empathy is also countered in an important scene where Robbie, as he approaches Dunkirk, is veering in and out of conscious awareness due to his wound (246). We have to presume that these again will be embellishments by Briony in her correspondence with Nettle, but functionality in our relations with each other is contrasted with feeling and emotion. When Robbie and Nettle find a cellar to sleep in, which presages the downward spiral to Robbie's death, Robbie is too plagued by his exhaustion and thoughts to sleep (261). He feels the letters from Cecilia in his pocket and replays the mantra that she always says to him, and which ironically she used to say to Briony as a child when she had nightmares, '*I'll wait for you. Come back*', but although the words are not meaningless, they were not having as great an effect on him now. The waiting of one person for another was now simply like an 'arithmetical sum, and just as empty of emotion'. The hope that he had previously almost dissipates given the situation that he and the other soldiers are in and the horrors of war that they had been part of and witnessed. Robbie ponders on the fact that Briony may change her evidence so those who were guilty would now be innocent, but what is guilt now? Everyone is guilty and no one was, given the mayhem of war. Robbie concludes to keep quiet about it down in the cellar and in doing so invokes Briony's name as an accomplice in sleeping it all off as he falls into delirium (261–2). Briony as narrator is doing two things here. One is to try to evade her own culpability for what she has done by shrouding it under the greater catastrophe and horror of war. The other is to reduce emotion and feeling to a mere mathematical proposition that, as in Structural Marxism, can be read statically.

However, Robbie then contemplates staying in France and rescuing those caught up in the war, the way he had rescued the twins that had gone missing on that fateful night, which he now recollects (262). He remembers Cecilia running across the gravel to him as he was being led into the police car. He then imagines all that has happened going in reverse and even envisages being forgiven by a Flemish woman who they met on the way back for not being able to save her and her son (262–3). He is awoken from his reverie by Nettle who informs him that he has been shouting in his sleep and thereby annoying the other soldiers (263). Nettle cares for Robbie and it is a nice counterpoint to Robbie's irritation with his coarseness earlier on. Nettle has become a true friend and comrade on the journey, and now he wipes Robbie's forehead, makes him drink some water and tries to counter his suggestion to stay with the news that the boats have arrived and they will be away in the morning (263–4).

Robbie retreats into his reverie and muses on the contrast between the 'unruly, free spirits' of the poets who were revered at Cambridge, only because they did not know the need to survive as a body of men, all pulling together in support of one another (264). Cecilia comes back into his thoughts and the fact that she is waiting means his hope returns. 'Arithmetic be damned', Robbie says, in response to his previous thoughts. Her love, their love, is not just a mathematical equation with no emotion: it is the reason why he has survived. So emotion triumphs over cold calculations that do not take account of the experiential aspect of our existence and our relation with others. Whether Briony as narrator now believes this is debatable. We know that her sources for this part of the novel are the love letters between Robbie and Cecilia housed in the Imperial War Museum and her correspondence with Corporal Nettle. Either way, empathy and emotion do win out, even though Robbie will not survive and the ending of this section of the book sounds his death knell. Responding to Nettle's advice for Robbie to keep quiet, Robbie declares, 'I promise, you won't hear another word', and that is not because he will be asleep but because he will be dead (265).

If we now turn our attention to Cecilia, we can see that she is a prisoner of her upper-middle-class milieu and the low expectations her family, particularly her mother, have of the role of women in society from her background: get married to someone wealthy and have children. We see a growing class experience into class con-sciousness in Cecilia mediated through her love for Robbie and the realization of, through the way that he is eventually treated, the expendability of people from lower-class backgrounds to those above them. As we have seen Thompson point out in relation to the notion of class as a relationship, we cannot have love with-out the lovers, and Robbie and Cecilia are personifications of this class relationship. Robbie's fate and original background is a crucial catalyst in identifying shared interests against a common enemy – the Tallis family along with Paul Marshall – which uses its class power to maintain its position in society, and subordinate the lower classes.

Cecilia tells Robbie that she has cut herself off from her family and will never speak to her parents, brother or sister again because of what they have done to him (205). So Cecilia has turned her back on her upper-middle-class background and identifies her interests with Robbie against the interests of her family, admittedly all through the mediation of love, but it does involve a fracturing of her previous consciousness that accepted the established hierarchical order of class society. Robbie, however, appears to have forgotten his class background in the dizzying lights of upward social mobility, but he is brought down to earth with the brutal nature of the upper-middle classes when they need a convenient scapegoat.

All this causes Cecilia to begin her class solidarity with Robbie. After the rape has occurred, Cecilia joins her family, Marshall and the policemen in the drawing room as they await Robbie's return. She stands alone in the centre of the room, staring at each of them and cannot believe that she is associated with such people, or be able to tell them that she and Robbie are in love (179). When she leaves the room with a cry of anger, they are all relieved and even relaxed now that she has gone. Cecilia also makes the point that her different class position, her siding with Robbie against them, has resulted in her seeing the 'snobbery that lay behind their stupidity' (209). For Cecilia, such snobbery was evident in a number of factors, such as Emily never forgiving Robbie for getting a first and her father losing himself in his work so as not to confront Robbie's plight. Additionally, her previously beloved Leon went along with everyone else like a 'grinning, spineless idiot'. Consequently, Cecilia does not speak to her parents, brother or sister again once Robbie is sent to prison (208).

The break from her family and her class background is extended when she becomes a nurse. Cecilia says that she is happy with her new life and her new friends because she 'can breathe now', which could mean that she can express herself, free from the class restraints of her family (209). Moreover, the fact that she is living in lodgings described as 'net curtained and seedy', but now feels more free to express herself despite these less than salubrious surroundings is testament to her rejection of her class background (330–1). Consequently, there could only be one choice for her when she was confronted with Robbie or her family.

Her solidarity with Robbie in her heightened state of class consciousness through the mediation of love becomes further evident, when, despite what has befallen him, Robbie becomes troubled because Cecilia had not spoken to her parents, brother or sister since November 1935 when he was sent to prison (208). This causes him even more concern given how much she loved her family, the house and the park (209). Cecilia does not write to them and they do not know her address. It is only through Robbie's mother, Grace, who has sold the bungalow and moved to another town, that she receives letters from them. Although she lets them know that she is fine, she stresses that she does not want to be contacted by them. Even when Leon comes to the hospital and to the nurses' hostel, she avoids him and then walks past him, wrenching her arm free when he grasps it (208–9).

Robbie knows he could never go back, but he is concerned that she is destroying a part of herself for his sake. When he tells Cecilia his worries she writes back to him and her class awareness becomes even more apparent because she still cannot believe how they all turned against him, even her father, and believed the evidence of, as she says, a 'silly, hysterical little girl' (209). Moreover, she says that they encouraged Briony because they gave her no room to turn back. Again, this might be special pleading from Briony the narrator here, especially when she has Cecilia say, 'she was a young thirteen', albeit while at the same time saying she never wants to speak to her again.

However, Robbie and Cecilia could be seen as being susceptible to class misperceptions themselves, because they both assume that young Danny Hardman is guilty of the rape. Indeed, Cecilia persistently says that it is he they should be questioning, which causes Briony to note how it was understandable but poor form that Cecilia should be covering for 'her friend' by casting suspicion on an innocent boy (181). The apology from them to 'Able Seaman Hardman' when they are told by Briony that it was actually Marshall comes in the fictional final chapter, so Briony does it on their behalf (347). Again, though, we should be cautious about Briony's role here as narrator. How do we know that she is not lying about Cecilia and Robbie in their accusation against Danny (346)? Think of how, when Briony breaks the news to them that it was in fact Marshall who was guilty, Briony the narrator of this definitely fictitious scene states: 'Given all that had happened, and all its terrible consequences, it was frivolous, she knew, but Briony took calm pleasure in delivering her clinching news' that she had just come from the wedding of Marshall and Lola. 'Calm pleasure'? Why? Because she wants to show that they made a mistake just like she did and again it is her way to escape culpability for what she has done. The fact that this scene is completely fictitious should make us even more suspicious of Briony's account.

Cecilia is guilty of class misconceptions herself in another instance when she tells Robbie about the story of the father of two twins that were born in the hospital. One of them dies, and when the father, who is a bricklayer's mate, comes to see the surviving baby and his wife, Cecilia and the other nurses assume, because of his occupation, that he would be some 'cheeky little chap with a fag stuck on his lower lip' (213). Cecilia tells Robbie that he was in fact a 'very handsome fellow, six feet tall with blond hair', causing her nursing friend Jenny to describe him as being like a Greek god. He had a clubbed foot like Byron and was so sweet and gentle and patient in comforting his wife that they were 'all touched by it'. Maybe, though, this is the breaking down of class barriers in the stereotyped attitudes of the upper-middle classes to the working class. You would think that Robbie would have disabused her of such misconceptions, but again the hand of Briony might be at work.

Overall, then, we can see how the class experience develops into class consciousness for Cecilia on the microcosmic level. Just as with Robbie we do not know how she might have turned out given the onset of the Second World War and her and Robbie's untimely deaths. However, she renounces any privileges from her family and finishes her days as a nurse in drab lodgings until disaster strikes in the infamous flood in Balham tube station. I will further expose the class-conscious nature of Cecilia in relation to the discussion on fetishism. For now, we need to turn to a class experience from the other side of the divide and that is with the capitalist Paul Marshall.

Marshall, along with Lola, is complicit with Briony in letting the innocent Robbie be accused of the rape and sent to jail. Again, we need to remember that it is through Briony as narrator that we get to understand Paul Marshall, and he is generally a person without any redemptive qualities, a bit like Briony herself. The class experience for Marshall is particularly related to his place in the productive relations as an exploiter of labour in his chocolate factory (49). His chocolate Amo bar was a 'vision' on which he had been 'enslaved' for nine months as he moved between his board-room and the factory, barely visiting the large house he had bought on Clapham Common. After initial difficulties around distribution and an advertising campaign that had upset some bishops, Marshall luxuriates in the increased sales, and counters the problems with the unions on production quotas, overtime rates and new factory locations, by charming and coaxing them 'like children'. The new challenge in front of him was the possibility of the war taking place, which he sees as an excellent business opportunity to increase further the sales of his Amo bar to the extent that it could become part of the standard-issue ration pack (49–50). His alacrity for such a development leads some to call him a warmonger, but Marshall says that this will not deter him from his 'purpose' and his 'vision'. That this vision is simply to make as much money as possible regardless of the cost to others is, of course, nowhere near the forefront of his considerations.

Again, though, it is also pertinent that some of his failings are illustrated through Cecilia as her class consciousness begins to develop. Consider how Emily admires Paul Marshall and bemoans how Cecilia, with her modern forms of snobbery developed while at Cambridge, would consider such a man with a degree in chemistry 'incomplete as a human being' (152). What was the point of her going to Cambridge to read Austen, Dickens, Conrad and so on when they were all in the library downstairs? Why did she believe that made her superior to anyone else? Emily then marvels, unconvincingly, at Marshall as a chemist finding a way to produce chocolate, but then revealingly notes how he can undercut his competitors and so increase his profit margin, which she admits is 'vulgarly put', but would offer 'untroubled years' for her daughter, a bit like Emily herself. Cecilia, though, sees through Marshall, and at one point as she contemplates what it would be like to be married to someone like him whom she sees as 'so nearly handsome, so hugely rich, so unfathomably stupid', she recognizes that he would give her 'bone-headed boys with a passion for guns and football and aeroplanes' (50). Robbie, the more sensitive soul, would be a better husband and father as Cecilia begins to realize.

Jack Tallis is not as impressed with Marshall as Emily, as is evinced by his comment in their phone conversation. Emily says how Marshall, like Jack, wants rearmament but in his case it is so that he can sell more of his chocolate to the government (153).

Jack's response is to dismiss Marshall's ambition by stating: 'I
see. Ploughshares into tinfoil'. That is, Marshall is using valuable
resources to make something useless.[39] Additionally, Marshall
exerts a ghostly presence in the war itself when we are told that
one of the chocolate Amo bars is shared amongst Robbie and his
fellow soldiers on the retreat back to Dunkirk. The bitter irony
is that the man who profited at Robbie's expense is still profit-
ing even further by supplying his commodities for the war (239).
Similarly, Marshall's profiteering also materializes when Briony is
treating the injured soldiers who have returned from the retreat,
and we learn that some of them had 'sodden crumbs of Amo bars'
in their pockets (304). That we can link this object back through
its social relations to its production under conditions of exploitation by a particularly nasty capitalist and a pretty poor specimen
of a human being in Marshall, the real rapist, leads us onto the
presence of fetishism in the novel.

Fetishism

The workers are almost an unseen presence within the Tallis household, but their semi-subterranean existence does come to the fore at
times to expose and thereby undermine the fetishism that surrounds
them. As we have seen, Thompson rejects seeing the working class
as a thing and this corresponds with a rejection of perceiving social
relations and commodities as things also. Cecilia is often the vehicle
through which the fetishized relations are given a social understanding as in the case when she enters the kitchen where the evening
meal is being prepared and she notes the following:

> The labour in the kitchen had been long and hard all day in the heat,
> and the residue was everywhere: the flagstone floor was slick with the
> spilt grease of roasted meat and trodden-in peel; sodden tea towels, trib-
> utes to heroic forgotten labours, drooped above the range like decaying
> regimental banners in church. (104)

The striking imagery here of the preparation of the evening meal is
like a battle under a situation of duress – the searing summer heat
– but also, and more importantly, under the hierarchical power
of the Tallis family over their workers. The labour is 'forgotten'

by the Tallises because they are in thrall to fetishism and have no interest in any suffering that may have occurred in the making of their dinner. Again, it is the raising of the class consciousness of Cecilia that exposes how the workers and their labours are treated as things.

Cecilia's role as a vehicle of de-fetishization also emerges when she is about to go onto the patio, and as she steps out she smells the aromatic plants that are growing in between the cracks of the paving stones (106). It makes her recall that it was a previous temporary gardener, whom no one could now picture or even name, who had suggested doing this, and as nobody at the time understood what he had in mind, she concludes that was probably why he was sacked. This again indicates a heightening of Cecilia's class consciousness here, which in this instance is through the mediation of labour that has used nature to be creative but is concealed through fetishism. The aromatic smell does not arouse such thoughts in the other characters, and indeed, we are told that as they stand around the plants are 'crushed underfoot'.

Similarly, it is through Cecilia that the labour of Grace, Robbie's mother, which remains fetishistically hidden in the objects of the house that she cleans, becomes apparent. When Cecilia takes a vase of flowers to put in Aunt Venus' room, she places them on a chest of drawers, and then we are told that she does not leave immediately. She observes how the sheets on the bed 'would be starchily pure' and notes how the seat of a 'Chippendale sofa had been so carefully straightened' that sitting on it would be a 'desecration' (45–6). Additionally, she smells the wax that has been used to polish the furniture and concludes through the fetish of the objects that 'Mrs Turner must have passed through that morning' (46). There is almost a spiritual dimension to the labour performed here through the use of the word 'desecration'. As we saw in the example of the preparation of dinner in the kitchen, the tea towels themselves are described as symbolizing regimental flags in a church. So not only is the treatment of objects and humans as things undermined, but the impression is one of a spirit-like quality that has been attained in the recognition of the 'heroic' labour expended.

Indeed, Cecilia's recognition of Grace's work is in contrast to the incident when Robbie tells his mother that he has been invited to dinner, and she says that must have been why she was polishing the silver all day (89). All Robbie can say in reply is that when he sees his face in the cutlery he will think of her, but the implication is that he has not thought about the social relation hidden in the fetishized objects of the cutlery.

One final example of the presence of fetishism and the invitation to break through its shrouding of social relations is in relation to the Meissen vase that belonged to Uncle Clem, Jack Tallis' brother and only sibling (22–3). The vase itself is quickly de-fetishized in the story because we are told that Uncle Clem received it from the inhabitants of the French town of Verdun during the First World War, which he had evacuated and saved the lives of some fifty women, children and old people, before it was shelled (22). He had to leave it in a farmhouse while he fought in the war and later retrieved it by wading across a river one night before rejoining his unit. The story is told in one of his last letters that he wrote home before he died, a week before the Armistice. While the labour expended on the object is not being exposed here, the human social relation behind it is through Uncle Clem's actions. It is an interesting counterpoint to the inability of the Tallises to see through fetishism when it is all around them, yet they can do so in this instance because it involves someone close to the family unit. Overall, the respect for the vase was down to the heroic exploits of Uncle Clem, and Cecilia considers that putting flowers in it, wild flowers in particular, is an appropriate tribute to him. This is why Jack Tallis wants the vase to be used, despite its value: in honour of his brother's memory. Moreover, this also brings forth the contradiction that Marx himself describes in terms of the opposition between use value and exchange value. The fact that capital is a system that emphasizes the rule of exchange value over use value leads directly to fetishism, and here through the ultimate sacrifice of his brother this fetishism is undermined. For Cecilia, we are informed that she had no view on the matter, although she did at times wonder how much it would fetch at Sotheby's, which might suggest that she is edging towards fetishism. However, in the incident where the vase breaks in a minor struggle between herself and Robbie the following is what she thinks the vase stands for:

> Her dead uncle, her father's dear brother, the wasteful war, the treacher-
> ous crossing of the river, the preciousness beyond money, the heroism

and goodness, all the years backed up behind the history of the vase reaching back to the genius of Horoldt, and beyond him to the mastery of the arcanists who had re-invented porcelain. (29)

The attack on fetishism through the consciousness of Cecilia could not be clearer because she refers not only to the heroic actions of her uncle, but its use value beyond monetary worth and the labour that had created the vase in the first place.

Class struggle and class hegemony

Thompson's emphasis on class struggle and class hegemony also illuminates instances of insubordination from the servants, which become manifest in a number of ways. As we have seen, for Thompson, class struggle occurs when people find themselves in social and productive relations where they experience domination or exploitation that causes them to share their interests with each other and so resist. Within this process is the theatre of class hegemony, with the opposing forces attempting to subvert the rules of the game. Moreover, Thompson's aim is also to rescue from the condescension of posterity those whose stories have not been told or have been ignored in mainstream historical narrative, and bringing to the surface the subterranean existence of the workers in the Tallis household is one way we can do that in *Atonement*.

An interesting illustration of these notions occurs when Cecilia displays a class alliance with the workers against her mother, and avoids confrontation through class compromise in the realm of hegemonic control. As we saw earlier, the workers have been asked to make a roast dinner on a very hot day and at the last minute Emily Tallis decides that the roast should be turned into a salad instead due to the sweltering heat (105). Betty's annoyance and insubordination are encapsulated by ironically asking Emily if she wants the roast potatoes in a salad. When Emily replies in the affirmative, Betty then ironically lists other salads that could be conjured out of the roast dinner, such as a Brussels sprouts salad, horseradish salad and so on. When Emily suggests Betty is making a fuss over nothing, Betty appeals to Cecilia by stating that the roast was what they were asked to make, and they have been making it under hot and barely tolerable conditions. Cecilia intervenes to make the peace and not have her mother humiliated by the insubordination of the workers, which she says is a familiar dilemma, and so shows that this is a recurring battle between the workers and Emily as representative of a subordinating class in the household. Cecilia achieves the re-establishment of an equilibrium between these opposing forces by lying to her mother that Leon would be upset by not having one of Betty's roasts, given that he has already boasted about its quality to Marshall. She then assuages her mother by suggesting having a salad on the side as well. Emily, who is in thrall to fetishism, thinks nothing of the labour that has been expended by the workers, but Cecilia in her new state of heightened class consciousness does, and this also reveals the nature of hegemonic control being fought over by the workers and her mother. As Thompson indicates, the act of giving from above is also the act of getting from below and this is certainly the case in the class compromise that is present here.

Class struggle as insubordination and the challenging of hegemony also occurs in another incident. After Robbie has been sent to prison and Briony is now a nurse, Emily tells Briony in a letter that 'wretched Betty dropped Uncle Clem's vase' carrying it down to the cellars, and it 'shattered on the steps' (279). Emily suspects that this may have been deliberate because Betty claimed that 'the pieces had simply come away in her hand', but this was 'hardly to be believed'. One suggestion here is that Betty was innocent because unknown to anyone else the vase had been mended by Cecilia after the incident with Robbie and was therefore likely to break again.[40] While this is certainly possible, it is also the case that Betty had also lost a ration book and they had to do without sugar for two weeks. Reading between the lines here it could be that Betty has appropriated the ration book again as a subversive act against the supposed domination of the Tallis family and in solidarity with Grace's predicament in seeing her son wrongly sent to prison.

Conclusion

The preoccupation with class and cultural dislocation that appeared to interest McEwan when writing *Atonement* has been explored here through a Thompsonian framework utilizing the categories of class, class experience, class consciousness, class hegemony, class struggle and fetishism. The emphasis on class experience and class consciousness was particularly prevalent in exposing the cultural dislocation of Robbie and his movement from a lower-class to an upper-middle-class milieu, and back to a working-class one through his conviction of a crime he did not commit. More efficaciously, Cecilia's own class dislocation that was mediated through what happened to Robbie, along with her love for him, led to the development of an increasing class consciousness in relation to those around her, albeit while still retaining some aspects of class prejudice, although given her class background this is hardly surprising. Indeed, what should be commended is the way Cecilia was crucial in undermining the fetishism that pervades the Tallis household and the way she acted in class alliance with the workers, and Robbie, within the realm of class hegemony. Just as Thompson strove to save those who have been left in history to the condescension of posterity, so through Thompson's framework imposed on *Atonement*, we have saved those who would otherwise be ignored or simply dismissed without a class-based reading of the novel. Through the struggles of the sacrificed Robbie, to the even more potent raising of consciousness in Cecilia, the workers with their forgotten and heroic labours in their subterranean existence are brought back to life through the penetration of the fetishism that abounds in the Tallis household. That such a Thompsonian reading of *Atonement* allows us to explore the different manifestations of class experience that are present is testament both to the power of his approach and to McEwan's capacity to write about class so cogently.

4 • *Saturday*: Julia Kristeva on Abjection

The narrative of McEwan's *Saturday* is related in the third person as the feelings and thoughts of Henry Perowne, a wealthy neurosurgeon living in London, seemingly oblivious to outside realities.[1] He is awoken from his comfortable existence as his privacy is invaded by a member of a lower social class in the form of Baxter, an 'other' who has not before entered his consciousness and does so by a freak turn of events. On his way to a squash game on 15 February 2003, the day of the march against the Iraq war, Perowne's car is crashed into by a BMW containing Baxter and his two criminal associates. There is an altercation and Baxter punches Perowne in the chest. Perowne only escapes a full beating because he realizes that Baxter is suffering from Huntington's disease, lets him know the fact and offers him help. Perowne manages to escape the situation but Baxter comes back later, towards the end of the book, with one of his men, to exact his revenge in a microcosmic form of terrorism. He forces his way into Perowne's house while his family are celebrating the publication of his daughter Daisy's first book of poems. He holds a knife to the throat of Perowne's wife, and tells Daisy to strip with the supposed intention of raping her. Eventually, Baxter is overpowered, thrown down the stairs and knocked unconscious. By a twist of fate he is taken to hospital and, given the intricacy of the operation due to him having Huntington's disease, Perowne is called out on his night off to prolong Baxter's life a little longer, even though his descent into death is inevitable due to his incurable condition.

The work of Julia Kristeva, and in particular her notion of abjection in confrontation with an abject 'other', is utilized to illuminate our understanding of this novel. For Kristeva, the negative moment of abjection emerges from the dialectical interplay between what she refers to as the semiotic/imaginary and the symbolic.[2] Abjection acts as a threat or rupture to the symbolic realm of order and is linked to the issue of identity through understanding the subject problematically, because it is often in a process of rejecting what is 'other' to itself. What will be argued here is that in *Saturday*, McEwan's main protagonist, Henry Perowne, exemplifies this dialectical problem of abjection. This chapter therefore explores the impact of Kristeva's notion of abjection on Perowne's identity in its dialectical interaction between himself, a generalized abject 'other' and a particular form of this abject 'other' in the character of Baxter. The aim is to show how Perowne's abjection becomes humanized in the process of considering the abject 'other'. I begin first by briefly outlining the main aspects of Kristeva's notion of abjection, relating it to Perowne's general abjection to the 'other' and then mapping the core aspects of abjection onto the Perowne/Baxter confrontation.

Abjection

To understand how abjection arises, Kristeva makes a distinction between the imaginary/semiotic realm and the symbolic in the process of signification in relation to theories of meaning, language and the subject.[3] The semiotic refers to the drives and articulations of a subject in a 'preverbal functional state that governs the connections between the body (in the process of constituting itself as a body proper), objects and the protagonists of family structure'.[4] In contrast, the symbolic realm depends on language as a sign system whether it is vocalized or gestural and so dependent on the rules of grammar and syntax.[5] The symbolic realm is where signifying involves people speaking as unambiguously as possible, as in the case of scientists or philosophical logicians,[6] whereas those forms of expression found, for example, in music, dance and poetry typify the semiotic. The semiotic can be associated with the expressions that emanate from the unconscious and the symbolic with the conscious expression, whether written, spoken or gestured with sign language, of a stable sign system.[7] For Kristeva, then, a subject that is immersed in this movement in and between the semiotic and the symbolic is always a 'subject in process',[8] which is shaped by context, history, culture, relationships and language.[9] Moreover, given the role of the unconscious, subjects have identities that emerge in this process often in ways that they were not fully aware of.[10] So, Kristeva 'undermines any notion of a unified subject' and instead exposes its always tenuous identity.[11]

The subject constitutes itself within this interplay between the semiotic and the symbolic, and while there is a positive moment in the forging of an identity in this process, there is also a negative aspect present that Kristeva captures with her notion of abjection. For Kristeva, abjection involves how a person or a subject engages in 'violent' and 'dark revolts of being' against something 'other', which is seen as a threat coming from outside or inside and is 'ejected beyond the scope of the possible, the tolerable, the thinkable'.[12] Although the 'other' is there in close proximity to this subject, it cannot be assimilated by it. The 'other' 'beseeches, worries, and fascinates desire' in this subject, 'which, nevertheless, does not let itself be seduced'. The subject internalizes its apprehensive desire and through its nausea rejects this 'other'. The subject that engages in abjection of the 'other' has a sense of certainty it is proud of and cherishes because it 'protects it from the shameful'. Even though there is a form of resistance from this subject, it is at the same time 'drawn toward an elsewhere as tempting as it is condemned'. This 'other' is therefore part of the subject, 'within', and part of some 'other' person, 'without'. Kristeva develops the 'within' side of abjection through an understanding of the psyche where she explains how the ego that merges with its master, the superego, drives the abject away to the outside.[13] However, the abject does not follow the rules of the game set down by the master, the superego, and constantly challenges it. As Kristeva indicates, 'to each ego its object, to each superego its abject'. She sees this subject being destabilized as it moves back and forth in a 'vortex of summons and repulsion' where the abject and abjection are its 'safeguards' or 'primers' of its culture.[14] So that which 'disturbs identity, system, order' and has no respect for 'borders, positions, rules' is what causes abjection.[15] Consequently, for Kristeva, abjection operates in the 'in-between, the ambiguous, the composite' and is 'immoral, sinister, scheming, and shady: a terror that dissembles, a hatred that smiles, a passion that uses the body for barter instead of inflaming it, a debtor who sells you up, a friend who stabs you'.[16] The abject both 'beseeches and pulverises' the subject and is part of its 'very *being*'.[17] As Kelly Oliver explains, given the all-pervasive nature of abjection within individuals, all societies must be premised on the abject in terms of creating boundaries and rejecting what is antisocial, because they are designated into 'classes, castes, professional and family roles, etc'.[18] Abjection is an ongoing aspect of human existence that is confronted either consciously or unconsciously on a daily basis, hence Kristeva's reference to the power of its horror.

To illustrate this process of abjection further, Kristeva offers the example of 'loathing an item of food, a piece of filth, waste, or dung', which the subject responds to with 'spasms and vomiting' to protect itself by moving to one side and turning away from these objects on a path of separation.[19] She contends that food loathing is both the most basic and most archaic form of abjection because of the responses occurring in a subject, in this case a baby, when presented with, for example, curdled milk whose surface skin appears harmless but induces a 'gagging sensation' and 'spasms in the stomach' when either seen or touched with the lips.[20] The subject experiences nausea and in the midst of dizziness, balks at the milk and separates itself from the mother and father who offer it.[21] The subject then wants none of the milk in any way and so expels it, but as the food is not an 'other', the subject expels itself, spits itself out and so abjects itself in the moment it is also trying to establish itself. Kristeva sees this double action of rejection and affirmation as appearing to be insignificant, but it actually turns the subject 'inside out, guts sprawling', so the parents see that the subject is in the 'process of becoming an other at the expense of [its] own death'. The baby protests through sobs, convulsions and vomit as 'it reacts, it abreacts. It abjects'. Abjection has, therefore, an instinctual quality that is manifest at the earliest stages of human existence, and which we carry with us for the rest of our lives.

Kristeva refers to the subject by whom the abject exists as the '*deject*' that separates, situates and strays, rather than 'getting his bearings, desiring, belonging or refusing'.[22] The deject is 'dichotomous', 'Manichaean', engages in dividing, excluding, and although he is somewhat aware of his abjections, he does not really want to know them. He even includes himself among his abjections and so 'casting within himself the scalpel that carries out his separations'. The deject privileges place over being by asking where he is rather than who he is, but his space is always 'divisible, foldable, and catastrophic', which is why he is a 'deviser of territories, languages, works'. The deject persistently demarcates his universe in response to the abject that constantly questions his solidity, and so makes him start this process anew. As a '*stray*', the deject is a 'tire-less builder' who is on a journey through the night and whose end is always receding. Although the deject senses the danger and loss the abject possesses for him, he cannot help taking the risk as he continually tries to differentiate himself from this 'other', and 'the more he strays the more he is saved' as he gains his 'jouissance' (enjoyment) by straying into excluded territory.

Abjection of the subject is also based on the 'recognition of the *want* on which any being, meaning, language, or desire is founded'.[23] Kristeva notes how psychoanalysts at her time of writing, 1980, were just taking into account only the 'object of want' as a 'fetishized product'. Yet, her emphasis is on understanding the experience of want as logically prior to being and object in a 'working of imagination' whose 'foundations are being laid here'. As such, abjection and 'abjection of self, is its only signified. Its signifier, then, is none but literature', according to Kristeva.[24] She interprets all literature as being a 'version of the apocalypse' that is 'rooted . . . on the fragile border (borderline cases) where identities (subject/object, etc) do not exist or only barely so – double, fuzzy, heterogeneous, animal, metamorphosed, altered, abject'.[25] Literature is the 'privileged signifier' of abjection and the medium that can involve the 'unveiling of the abject'.[26] It 'represents the ultimate coding of our crises, of our most intimate and most serious apocalypses'. As Anna Smith elucidates, for Kristeva, literature is a way to 'record human distress' and its 'potentially renewing effects . . . make it a transformative register of contemporary life'.[27] Similarly, as Nöelle McAfee notes, for Kristeva, 'literature offers a way to help work through what afflicts us'.[28]

Kristeva's understanding of abjection posits a subject in a perpetual process of movement between the semiotic and the symbolic, as it confronts an abject 'other', both within the mind and without. The subject is a mixture of drives, impulses, unconscious and conscious moments in the forging of an identity that is continually being reconstituted. In the form of the deject, the subject is dividing the world from himself and privileging his own existence over others. Kristeva identifies literature as the medium for exploring this abjection of the subject and the possibility of overcoming such abjection. Let us now go inside the mind of Henry Perowne as he is confronted by the within and without of the abject 'other' both generally and in the particular form of Baxter.

Perowne and the abject 'other'

Henry Perowne, a wealthy neurosurgeon, has the perfect life and family. He lives in a sumptuous house in central London, which he describes as a 'palace' (270) over which he is 'king' (269), and from where he surveys the outside world that consists, from his view, of a pedestrianized square with circular gardens (4–5). The 'daily traffic' passing through the square consists of office crowds at lunchtime, Indian boys from the local hostel, lovers, 'crepuscular drug dealers' and a mentally ill old lady who shouts 'go away!' for hours and sounds like a 'marsh bird or zoo creature' (5). At the end of the novel after the traumatic encounter, he reflects further on this scene and tries to remember the square at its best, which he says is 'weekday lunchtimes, in warm weather', when the office workers appear and have their lunch and the garden gates are open (272). He then makes a comparison between these people who work and are 'confident, cheerful, unoppressed', to the 'various broken figures that haunt the benches'. He suggests that employment is the key to this division between these two groups rather than just class, because 'drunks and junkies come from all kinds of backgrounds, as do the office people'. Hard work is the answer for Perowne, but given the unreliability of this 'enfeebled army haunting the public places of every town . . . no amount of social justice will cure or disperse' them. He concludes that it is simply a matter of 'bad luck' that people are in this predicament, and Baxter, ridden with Huntington's disease, will be emblematic of that fact. The examples of the abject 'other' for Perowne, therefore, are some of the most vulnerable people in society and he is a deject attempting at the beginning of the novel to draw boundaries between himself and them. Not content with demarcating the abject 'others', Perowne also has a very optimistic view of those who could be on his side of the divide. For example, he sees the office workers as being 'unoppressed', which they may be on a lunch break when they are free from work, but not necessarily when they get back into the office with the day-to-day routine of tasks and managerial hierarchy to contend with. Quite rightly, Lynn Wells refers to Perowne's musings here as a 'comic vision' because it implies that 'anyone can make it if they try', and it can also be added that this is the eternal message of the capitalist society Perowne feels so at home in.[29]

On his way to get his car, and now acting as a deject by straying into the real world of the abject 'other', Perowne encounters
a street cleaner who is about the same age as him (73). Perowne
notes how the worker is 'oddly intent on making a good job' and
deduces that such activity is 'futile' as the marchers further back
are dropping all their rubbish on the floor, and due to the general
'daily blizzard of litter' sweeping across the city (74). As their eyes
meet, Perowne in a 'vertiginous moment . . . feels himself bound to
the other man, as though on a seesaw with him, pinned to an axis
that could tip them into each other's life'. Perowne then ponders
on how, in a previous age where a supernatural force had allotted
people to their stations in life, it must have been 'restful' if you
were prosperous, even though you could not see how such a belief
justified your prosperity. He refers to this as a form of 'anosognosia', a term from psychiatry indicating a lack of awareness for
one's own condition, and then contemplates on what we do see
now that we understand this. His judgement, given the 'ruinous
experiments' of the twentieth century around matters of 'justice
and redistributed wealth', is that there are 'no more big ideas'.
Improvement in the world, he maintains, is only possible, 'if at
all, by tiny baby steps'. Perowne then makes a general claim that
'people take an existential view' on such matters and deduces it is
just bad luck if someone has to sweep the streets for a living: 'the
streets need to be clean. Let the unlucky enlist'.

Lynn Wells interprets this exchange as one of the occasional
experiences Perowne has throughout the novel where 'he feels a
deep connection with such people, and appreciates the basic inter-
changeability of human life'.[30] However, that is clearly not what
is happening here. Although he is saying that he feels 'bound to
the other man', the image of the seesaw tells us that this is a game
of, in one sense, class struggle. If Perowne is up, the street cleaner
is down, someone has to clean the streets and someone has to be
a wealthy neurosurgeon. If the street cleaner is up, then Perowne
goes down, but the exchange here is of a different variety, because
it is not the occupational status that would be an issue, rather it
is the 'justice and redistributed wealth' aspect that would come to
the fore. Having thought this through, and described all attempts
at redressing the imbalance of the seesaw as 'ruinous', Perowne's
conclusion is to leave the street cleaner to his fate. In one sense,
although he does recognize the need for piecemeal reform with his

reference to 'baby steps', he appears to be endorsing the position that he was describing in previous hierarchical ages: people should know their place and stay there so life will be 'restful'. Perowne succumbs to anosognosia himself because he does not realize how this fatalist position, which he states as if it is an axiomatic fact, serves his own prosperity and draws the boundary between himself and the abject 'other'. He personifies the deject privileging place over being by asking where he is, and luxuriates in his high social position, compared to who he is. The encounter with the street cleaner as the abject 'other' does disturb his solidity, but Perowne quickly re-asserts it. The abject therefore challenges his super-ego and destabilizes his consciousness, but he erects a boundary that tells him it is perfectly fine to cordon himself off from this abject 'other'. However, this incident and discussion of the abject 'other' is particularly crucial here, because it presages just a little later the pivotal event that will tip the seesaw balance of a life of the abject 'other' into the life of Perowne, the confrontation with Baxter and his men. This is where 'justice and redistribution' will be demanded, and a rupturing of the 'restful' life Perowne has will occur. It will now be Perowne's turn to be 'unlucky', as he is enlisted into a confrontation with a hostile abject 'other', and the boundaries that he has created to protect himself become blurred as he falls into the abjection that he is meant to despise.

Perowne and Baxter

Perowne's first encounter with Baxter is just before the car accident. Perowne, while waiting to turn his car into the street on the way to his squash game, sees him from a distance with his two tall associates as they appear out of a lap-dancing club (79). Baxter is described as being 'thickset and short and wearing a black suit' whereas his companions, we later discover, are dressed in 'trainers, tracksuits and hooded tops – the currency of the street, so general as to be no style at all' – although it is an attire that his own son Theo adopts when he does not want to make decisions about how he looks (84–5). After the accident, Baxter, accompanied by his two men, approaches Perowne and offers him a cigarette (87). Perowne declines while observing how, in a moment of abject repulsion, Baxter is 'one of those smokers whose pores exude a perfume, an oily essence of his habit'. He is also not helped by his physical demeanour as he is a 'fidgety, small-faced young man with thick eyebrows and dark brown hair razored close to the skull', with a bulbous mouth and a 'general simian air' (87–8). Even the suit distinguishing him as being the leader of his two street-dressed associates seems ill-fitted (88). As McEwan himself has commented, 'when Perowne is looking at Baxter' he 'feels a kind of visceral distaste',[31] and from our Kristevan perspective we can see how it is a clear confrontation with the abject 'other' that originates from our earliest instinctual responses to something that we do not like.

However, through the altercation with Perowne, a different aspect of Baxter's character emerges. As Perowne detects that Baxter has Huntington's disease, he reasons that telling him is his only chance to avoid a beating. So, in an act of 'shameless blackmail' and thereby a fall into his own abjection, Perowne says to Baxter: 'Your father had it. Now you've got it too' (94–5). Through his own abjection, Perowne now sees how, in confrontation with this abject 'other', the power in the situation moves towards him, and this becomes more manifest as Baxter sends his men back to the car to allow him to talk to Perowne alone about his illness (95). As a deject, Perowne has tried to demarcate himself from this abject 'other', but as a stray he takes the risk of moving into this sphere of abjection and in doing so saves himself and achieves his jouissance (enjoyment). Yet, this is only a temporary state because through this conversation the depiction of Baxter as an ape-like numbskull begins to be challenged and this will affect Perowne profoundly.

To understand his medical condition correctly, Perowne asks Baxter about his background and we discover that he grew up in Folkestone, is now living in his father's old flat in Kentish Town, and that he 'didn't get on with school' (96). Perowne then asks him outright if anyone has mentioned Huntington's disease to him and his silence confirms it. Perowne's power increases as he assumes, not simply his normal role of doctor in the world of the medical, but in this terminal case, the 'shaman', a priest with magical powers, in the realm of the 'magical' who it is 'unwise to abuse' (95). When Perowne lists the responses that have been made to try to combat the illness, Baxter knows them all, causing Perowne to admit: 'You're well up on this then', to which Baxter ironically rejoinders: 'Oh, thank you, doctor' (97). Perowne's initial assumptions about this abject 'other' are being questioned and undermined. From a Kristevan perspective the realm of the symbolic, the world of science and logic, is not a realm that Baxter is excluded from, as one would expect when confronted with the knowledgeable neurosurgeon that is Perowne. Baxter is just as informed as Perowne on the science of Huntington's disease and that allows them both to communicate with each other on this symbolic level. Perowne's confrontation with this abject 'other' and his own fall into abjection is blurring the boundaries that his deject self has created and tried to privilege.

This is evinced even further when, due to Baxter's condition, a mood swing seems about to engulf him as the 'muscles in his cheek are independently alive' and Perowne observes the following:

> In this transitional phase of perplexity or sorrow, the vaguely ape-like features are softened, even attractive. He's an intelligent man, and gives the impression that, illness apart, he's missed his chances, made some big mistakes and ended up in the wrong company. Probably dropped out of school long ago and regrets it. No parents around. And now, what worse situation than this could he find himself in? There's no way out for him. No one can help. (97–8)

This is quite a touching moment where the abject 'other', someone Perowne initially viewed with instinctive visceral distaste, takes on a different form, which allows a moment of reciprocity and movement across the boundary between them. Of course, Perowne, the embodiment of someone demarcating his own realm and borders from the abject, then undermines this view slightly by remarking that he is 'incapable of pity', because clinical experience had done that to him a long time ago (98). However, as we shall see later, this moment of conscious awareness of the abject 'other' of Baxter who confronts Perowne's superego will have an important bearing to play on the change in his character, once the attack occurs towards the end of the novel.

Despite this, Lynn Wells suggests that Baxter is 'characterised as merely sub-human', but this ignores the poignant passage quoted above.[32] Additionally, it also seems to Wells that, unlike the descriptions of other 'minor' characters, she mentions the 'much-loved Cockney lady who helps clean the theatres' (9) and the 'Filipino nurse' (105), for example, 'Baxter's race is unspecified'.[33]

But, being a Cockney does not tell us the race of the woman either; she could be black for all we know, so it is a little difficult to see what the portent of Wells' claim is here. Nevertheless, Wells pursues this line of reasoning in an interview with McEwan, who also seems slightly perplexed at her interpretation of Baxter. She refers to Baxter being a 'blank' compared to the examples of the Cockney and the Filipino above, and mentions that after she had given a conference paper on *Saturday* some people approached her and said that Baxter was black or Baxter was white and a skinhead.[34] Although Wells does not refer to it, there is one explicit example where Perowne does refer to Baxter as a blank, which is after he has completed the operation on him (257). Perowne writes up his notes as follows: 'known as Baxter' in the name space, and in the date of birth section he states, '"est. age plus minus 25". All the other personal details he has to leave blank' (257). This, though, does not mean that Baxter himself is a blank because the type of perfunctory details on such a form would hardly delineate a more concretized person anyway. However, even the little we know of Baxter gives us more of an identity for him than being a blank and this is aided by McEwan's own discussion of him.

McEwan's own response to Wells is to say that he never intended Baxter to be black and he reiterates the biographical background delineated above.[35] He also makes the point that given the novel is written through the character of Perowne, it has to be his perception of Baxter, and not McEwan's, but McEwan then adds: 'I didn't spell it out, but in social terms, Baxter is clear enough'.[36] Despite this explanation, Wells pursues the theme and maintains that whereas other characters, even the most 'peripheral', are described in 'very specific cultural terms . . . when Perowne looks at Baxter, none of that comes through'.[37] This leads McEwan to state quite bluntly that when 'Perowne is looking at Baxter . . . he doesn't see anything except culture', and posits Leonard Bast from E. M. Forster's *Howards End* as a 'distant kind of literary ancestor for Baxter', because he is intelligent and has read the literature on his condition. He is also 'very lonely with this, and the kind of company he keeps can offer no kind of solace'.[38] At this point, Wells changes the subject, but it is clear that she has not grasped the full complexity of Baxter's character. Moreover, to suggest that his character is a blank compared to even the most peripheral characters can easily be refuted by the references to the novel made above. Indeed, instead of McEwan marginalizing Baxter, as Wells suggests, it is Wells who is doing so by not paying due attention to what we do learn about him even through the limited perspective of Perowne.

Wells also enlists the support of Elizabeth Wallace, who sees Baxter as 'one-dimensional' and weak, suggesting that if he 'stands in for a larger and more persistent menace – the militant poor, the citizens of the developing world, or even an Arab extremist – then McEwan's fantasy becomes especially facile'.[39] How this can be the case when Baxter has the life of Perowne's wife in his hands, and could have perpetrated the rape of his daughter is a little unclear. However, McEwan himself offered a useful explanation on this issue in an interview in 2006. He was asked about the topic of terrorism in the novel and why he had introduced it, not on the basis of Muslim terror, but out of a 'homegrown', 'very, local, very immediate' variety through a 'deranged group of young men', one of whom, the leader, Baxter, is suffering from a neurodegenerative disease.[40] McEwan responds by stating that the concern in both types of terror is still the same because in both cases it raises the question: 'what does a rational person or a society that regards itself as rational do in the face of irrational behaviour?' He also contends that there is 'something very contaminating about aggressive and irrational behaviour', which raises the further question of 'how do you defeat a vile opponent without becoming a little bit vile yourself', or is it always inevitable? So it is the general principle of rational versus irrational behaviour that McEwan is preoccupied with, in all its different forms. Or from our Kristevan perspective it is whether confrontation with an abject 'other' forces us into abjection ourselves. Baxter is just one way to express this behaviour, as is the reaction of Perowne.

From a Kristevan perspective, Perowne's own abjection lies in his boundary making in relation to the abject 'other' in the general form of the undesirables of the world, and in the particular form, initially at least, of Baxter. What Kristeva tells us though, as McEwan confirms, is that we become complicit in this abjection ourselves, both in the mind and in our actions. McEwan's own answer when we are faced with such a situation is to 'invoke a common humanity' that can be 'shared by all'.[41] The question is whether this common humanity begins to permeate and undermine the abjection Perowne feels to the 'other' at the end of the novel.

Does the ending mean that the comfortable life for the wealthy middle classes, of which Perowne and his family are emblematic, largely cocooned from the realities of the everyday world, go on as normal or not? Has the boundary between Perowne and the abject 'other' been reconstructed and reasserted both within his mind and without, or is Perowne's identity and knowledge of himself and the world changed for the better?

Lynn Wells sides with the former interpretation by declaring that 'one gets no sense of a need for urgent cultural change from the novel's ending', and this 'papers over the implications of the disparity between the doctor and the street-thug'.[42] Additionally, Wells notes that there is 'no direct indictment of Henry Perowne's vision of things, and if McEwan's famous irony is at play here, its subtlety has obviously been lost on readers and critics alike'. This echoes the hostile review by John Banville, who considers the book, like Perowne himself, to be beset by self-satisfaction and arrogance, acting as a source of comfort for Western readers against the challenge posed by external threats to their culture.[43] In relation to Banville in particular, however, as Dominic Head notes, such a reading is only possible if Perowne exemplifies Western culture, but his philistine attack on 'literary culture' suggests not and thereby undermines such arrogance.[44] Head also makes the persuasive point that Perowne, as a medical scientist, would make possible the transcending of cultural differences through his discoveries, and this gives the novel its 'mood of consolation'.

There are ways to undermine these negative judgements even further once we see the effect that confronting the abject 'other' of Baxter will have on Perowne. For example, when he is called to perform the operation on Baxter, Perowne's wife questions why he should help someone who has assaulted him and invaded their home in such a violent manner (238). Perowne's response is to say: 'I have to see this through. I'm responsible' (239). Yet the responsibility that he feels is not simply because he has thrown Baxter down the stairs to protect himself, but also because he fell into abjection by using Baxter's illness to undermine him and allow himself to escape. As Perowne himself states: 'If I'd handled this better this morning, perhaps none of this would have happened' (240). It is Perowne's own actions that have led to this situation of Baxter being on the operating table with a blood clot on his brain. So Perowne now realizes what it means to become an abject 'other' himself, and as the narrator explains, 'despite the various shifts in his attitude to Baxter, some clarity, even some resolve, is beginning to form. He thinks he knows what it is he wants to do' (233). He resolves not just to perform the operation on Baxter, but also to do right by him. For Perowne, this means convincing his family that they should drop any charges and influencing his medical colleagues to confirm that Baxter will be unfit to stand trial anyway (278). This outcome is not simply due to Perowne feeling guilty because he has succumbed to his own abjection, it also arises by operating on and caring for Baxter, which fragments the boundary that he has created between himself and this abstract 'other', a boundary that seemed so strong at the start of the novel.

For instance, at the end of the operation, Perowne asks for Barber's 'Adagio for Strings' to be played as they close up the cut in Baxter's skull (256). Perowne knows that this piece has been 'played to death on the radio', but he likes it being put on at the end of an operation because its 'languorous, meditative music' indicates that his long labour is finally coming to an end. As he listens to the music, the bandage is secured and all the gowns and trappings covering Baxter are removed. Perowne sees this as the 'stage at which the patient's identity is restored' and becomes an 'entire person' again, as though the 'unwrapping of the patient' is a 'return to life'. He muses that if he had not seen it so many times before 'he could almost mistake it for tenderness'. He then goes to the end of the operating table and cradles Baxter's head in his hands, while ruminating that the 'meditative, falling line of the orchestral strings seems to be addressed to Baxter alone'. Again, the poignancy here lies in the way the clinical nature of what needs to be done, the cradling of the patient's head to protect it while all the things covering Baxter are removed, is being contrasted with what those actions represent in human terms: 'tenderness'. There is also an understanding through the sadness of the music that Baxter is only being brought back to life for a short time because his disease will eventually kill him.

As Perowne reflects a little later when he goes to see Baxter in the intensive care unit, the only thing left for him is the 'reprieve' of 'sleep and death' (262). Perowne's abjection, his rejection of Baxter as an abject 'other', has therefore been further undermined and so changed his consciousness for the better. Indeed, even the philistinism Perowne purports to have, and which Head draws attention to, is slightly undermined here. Perowne is certainly adamant that books, cinema and even music cannot compete with the elation and importance of his own medical work (258), but he still feels the need to play music at the end of an operation. Moreover, he also recognizes the power of the music for challenging the boundaries that he has created between himself and Baxter as the abstract 'other' in the movement between the symbolic, the science of neurosurgery, and the semiotic, the potency of Barber's piece. This is despite the fact, as Perowne recognized above, that the work has been played repeatedly on the radio, but for him at least, it has not lost any of its resonance. Interestingly, although without attempting to suggest that this was in McEwan's mind when using this music, it did serve as the soundtrack for the hugely successful film *The Elephant Man* where a similar case of abjection occurs.[45] The film was based on the tortured life of Joseph Merrick, called John in the film, who had a severe disease that caused major deformities to his body. Merrick was certainly emblematic of an abject 'other' in the way he was treated by society, and even by Dr Frederick Treves, who initially was more interested in the disease for his own medical advancement rather than the health of the man. However, Treves overcomes his own abjection and attempts to make Merrick's life as comfortable as possible for his remaining few years before his inevitable death. The playing of the 'Adagio' is particularly moving in the final death scene when Merrick removes the pillow he needs to keep him upright so he can breathe when he sleeps, and so lies down to die.

The transformative effect on making Perowne transcend his hostility to the abject 'other' gains further support in the intensive care unit when he sits down next to the sleeping Baxter's bed (262). Perowne notices from his watch that it is now 3.30 a.m. and he really should be going home, because he might fall asleep in the chair. However, he convinces himself to stay now that he is here, 'almost by accident', and deduces that he will not fall asleep as he is 'alive to too many contradictory impulses'. Perowne's supposed self-certainty in his deject view of the world is being destabilized through his confrontation with Baxter as the abject 'other'. Baxter is someone who has threatened and transgressed the inner sanctum of Perowne's life, and should not even register in the conscience or superego of his mind if Wells and Banville are correct. Yet, he clearly has done, and again, in a very poignant passage as he sits

beside Baxter, Perowne puts his hand round Baxter's wrist and
takes his pulse, even though it is not necessary as it is already cal-
culated on the monitor (262–3). Perowne does it 'because he wants
to' and sees it as a 'matter of primal contact' that is 'reassuring
to the patient'. Nonetheless, although the process is meant to be
completed over a count of fifteen seconds, Perowne suddenly realizes that he has been doing it for longer. He concludes 'in effect,
he's holding Baxter's hand while he attempts to sift and order his
thoughts and decide precisely what should be done'. So now the
physical boundary between himself and the abstract 'other' has
been breached, and the tender image of Perowne holding Baxter's
hand suggests again that he is not the person he used to be, especially as he will decide to help Baxter as much as he can, even
against the wishes of Perowne's own family. Indeed, although he is
conscious after the day's events that he is now 'timid, vulnerable',
'weak', 'ignorant' and 'all he feels now is fear', it is doing right by
Baxter that is his 'one small fixed point of conviction' (277–8).
The deject has had his superego confronted with the abject but it
is no longer possible to shut this 'other' out. Consequently, Perowne is a far more complex and flawed character than he at first
appears. Peter Childs has interpreted this change by observing how
Perowne has become 'a still contented but now anxious man'.[46]
However, while the 'anxious' epithet is undeniable, I am not sure
'contented' is the right way to describe the other side of Perowne's
character. Being contented implies being satisfied with what one
has and desiring nothing more, which is certainly not the case with
Perowne. Secure might be a more apposite word given that he and
his family are safe from danger, but Perowne knows, in his new
state of consciousness, that this is only for the present time.

A change in Perowne's identity is also evident in the incident
when Baxter and his sidekick force their way into the house.
Indeed, Kristeva's emphasis on the power of literature as a place
for exploring the abject and offering the possibility of transcending it also has particular relevance here in terms of what happens
to Baxter. While holding Perowne's wife at knife-point, he forces
Daisy to strip with the apparent intention that he and his accomplice will rape her (217–18). They then see that she is pregnant and
this deters them, so Baxter instead forces her to read out one of her
poems (219). Unbeknown to Baxter, she recites 'Dover Beach' by
Matthew Arnold, and the power of the poetry has a profound and

'elated' effect on Baxter, making him declare the poem 'beautiful'. He is even more amazed that she wrote it, which of course she has not. (222). Baxter then says quite poignantly that it reminds him of where he grew up, and in this new mood he tells Daisy to get dressed, much to the annoyance of his associate Nigel (222–3). The poem makes Baxter think differently about the world, and Perowne observes how it had 'cast a spell' on Baxter, made him fall for the 'magic', and made him want to live (278). Even more tellingly, Perowne concludes that 'Baxter heard what Henry never has, and probably never will, despite all Daisy's attempts to educate him' on the power of literature (278). Perowne reflects that no one can forgive Baxter's use of the knife, but the effect on him of the poem, its capacity to produce in him a 'yearning' that Perowne himself 'could barely begin to define', deserves some sort of recognition (278–9).

Ironically, Baxter is a testament to the power of literature as a humanizing force that can allow us to break out, however momentary, from our own abjection. Moreover, Perowne's resistance to this power indicates the limitations on his capability for understanding the nature of his own abjection when confronted with the abject 'other' through this medium. If Perowne was to follow Daisy's advice and read more literature, perhaps his sensitivities would be heightened, and it may not have to take a knife at the throat of his wife and the general terrorizing of his family to make him confront his abjection and thereby humanize it in relation to the abject 'other'.

As Peter Childs also perceptively points out, Perowne is a 'living fiction to the extent that he considers himself apart from the violence of the streets, which he spies from his bedroom window, or the horrors of the world, about which he reads in the papers'.[47] The confrontation with Baxter as the abject 'other' has crashed through that pretend world and shown him the harsh realities of the real one. In Perowne's favour, however, as I showed earlier, he did recognize that music can have a transformative effect on our emotions and responses to the abject 'other', even if he cannot see how that can occur for him through literature and poetry. Previously, it was Samuel Barber's 'Adagio for Strings' that had this effect on him and again, although I am not trying to read McEwan's mind in choosing this poem, it is also ironic that Barber set 'Dover Beach' to music.[48] As McEwan himself maintains, 'perhaps more than any other art form, music consistently delivers satisfaction and formal protection that are only ever found in the best poetry'.[49] We can only speculate whether Perowne would be drawn to poetry via the medium of the music if it were by a composer whose work he admires, but it does offer up a possible way in which his philistinism might be reduced even further.

Kristeva's point about literature offering us an unveiling of the abject and thereby a possibility of transcending it, however momentary, is what gives literature such power. It is not just Perowne who is humanized by confrontation with the abject 'other', but anyone who reads the novel should be also, as long as you are open and receptive enough to reflect on your own abject status. The comfortable middle classes, so emblematic of Perowne, would therefore do well to heed the abjection within and without that his contradictory character expresses. Despite what critics such as Wells and Banville say, that is what I think McEwan is exploring in this novel, which Kristeva's notion of abjection helps us to unearth even further.

Part III:
Michel Houellebecq

5 • *Atomised*: Henri Lefebvre and Alienation

In the critically acclaimed but controversial novel *Atomised*, Michel Houellebecq paints a seemingly bleak picture of a deeply alienated humanity that, despite many good intentions, has failed to create a humane world.[1] The story centres on two half-brothers, Michel, a molecular biologist, and Bruno, a teacher. Both are dysfunctional in their own ways due to their upbringing – they were abandoned by their mother at an early age – and the instrumentalism prevalent in capitalist consumer society that engulfs them as adults. Michel is introverted and apparently unemotional, whereas Bruno is obsessed with eroticism and seems to have found his ideal partner in Christiane who shares his sexual adventurousness. However, she is paralysed in a sex act and commits suicide and Bruno descends into madness and is committed to a mental institution. Annabelle, Michel's childhood sweetheart, is the victim of Michel's unrequited love until she comes back into his life when they are older and they try to forge a relationship with each other. Tragedy strikes as she develops cancer when pregnant with Michel's child, and she, too, attempts to kill herself knowing that she will die of the disease anyway. Shaken by her death, Michel resolves to return to his scientific work and develops the possibility of human cloning, which he bequeaths to humanity after his apparent death off the coast of Ireland.

So, the supposed answer to the failures of humanity that emerges from the novel is the creation of a posthuman society. We discover at the end of the book that it has been written in the future by a posthuman clone, and that the human race is almost extinct. On this basis, a number of critics have interpreted the novel's message as negative and nihilist.[2] However, I argue that there is a glimmer of hope for a humanist world that occurs in the book, particularly through the character of Annabelle and her relationship with Michel. The way to unearth this subliminal interpretation of the novel lies in the notion of alienation itself. Alienation must be understood dialectically, but the commentators on this novel instead view it one-sidedly, as complete negation, without any moment of disalienation and the possibility of supersession or transcendence. In contrast, I follow Henri Lefebvre's dictum that the 'drama of alienation is dialectical', because it is through the inhuman forms of alienation that people build the human world and offer the possibility of a different one.[3]

By focusing on the dialectical relations between the apparently totally alienated characters of Annabelle and Michel through a Lefebvrean lens, the one-sided interpretation of the book as completely negative begins to be undermined as does the posthuman ending. Michel is almost posthuman himself in his inability to feel, and fails to requite Annabelle's love for him during their childhood and early teens. Yet, when she comes back into his life years later, and in particular after her death, he realizes that it was because of her that he managed to form an image of love, and this, the posthuman narrator tells us, was 'his guiding thought in the last months of his theoretical work' (363). The posthuman ending of the book is therefore a warning about what will happen should we forget our belief in love. It is through love, then, despite the difficulties and damage it can cause, that a humanist society can avoid the purported all-encompassing process of atomization and alienation, and the end of humanity itself. Annabelle is a symbol of this humanist hope. To show this more positive reading of *Atomised*, I begin by outlining the main aspects of Lefebvre's dialectical understanding of alienation and then apply it to the novel through the character of Michel and his dialectical interactions with Annabelle.

Lefebvre on alienation

For Lefebvre, common understandings of alienation that see humans alienated from themselves and turned into things are vague and do not capture the multidimensionality of the concept.[4] To correct this, Lefebvre argues that the concept of alienation must be made particular, relative, historical and comprehended socially, and then there can be no absolute alienation or absolute disalienation.[5] Instead, alienation and disalienation relate to each other dialectically in a movement of 'alienation-disalienation-new

alienation' as these moments cut across people in their daily lives
and relations with each other. Hence, alienation and disalienation
dynamically exist in real situations that can be discerned through
analysis.[6] Moreover, even when people achieve moments of disalienation there is always the possibility of alienation returning
because of this 'perpetual dialectical movement' of being alienated
and not being alienated. For Lefebvre, this means that we should
recognize that even greater alienation is possible through disalienated activities. As examples, he cites the disalienation of joining a
group that will combat the alienation of solitude, but does not rule
out the possibility of new forms of alienation arising from being a
part of a collective entity.[7] Similarly, engaging in leisure activities
can be disalienating because they allow people to escape from the
drudgery of work, but if these become mere 'entertainments and
distractions' then they, too, contain moments of alienation.

Lefebvre suggests that the worst form of alienation occurs when
it is 'unrecognized' or 'non-conscious', but this should not conceal
that even being conscious of alienation is a form of disalienation
itself, because it can still result in even deeper alienation through
failure, frustration or privation. This can lead to the most extreme
form of alienation which is reification, the reduction of activity
and consciousness to things by which they are ruled. However,
Lefebvre maintains that although reification is the end point of
alienation, it does not exhaust the concept because alienation takes
many forms and is 'infinitely complex'.[8] To penetrate this complexity and identify moments of alienation and disalienation, of that
which alienates and that which disalienates, means understanding these categories in a dialectical movement and as a 'process of
becoming'.[9] Given the diversity of situations within which these
moments arise, Lefebvre admits that it can be difficult to offer the
objective criterion that would allow us to expose and classify them
in more specific terms. Instead, he suggests that it is best to catalogue a typology of alienation to allow alienated and alienating
situations to be discerned.[10]

Lefebvre also contends that another important aspect of alienation is to distinguish between the '*other*' and '*otherness*' so that the
dialectical relationship between these two moments becomes more
apparent.[11] He argues that alienation is the outcome of a relation
with 'otherness' that makes us 'other', because it rips us away from
ourselves and turns an activity into a thing. Ironically, this process

is creative because it allows a self-consciousness to understand itself through what it is not, and without this negative moment it becomes stifled. 'Otherness', then, is crucial to human perception even though it acts as a source of uncertainty and anguish.[12] So Lefebvre suggests that we should use the 'other' as an accessible accomplice and friend, and although we initially feel uneasy in its presence, we overcome this uneasiness because we see it as a fellow human being. There is, therefore, a dialectical movement between the 'other' and 'otherness' that is defined as 'knowing, gaining power over otherness and vanquishing it' and so bringing it close to one's self.

The danger in coming into contact with the 'other' is a moment of disalienation that can turn into more forms of alienation, because the movement from 'other' to 'otherness' reveals something unknown or distant from what is near. Again, Lefebvre recognizes that as the things we are familiar with move away from us, this can make us uneasy and experience an alienation that is also partly a disalienation, because it is a challenge to our consciousness.[13] What we must not allow is for the 'otherness' to dominate the 'other' as we will be completely alienated from ourselves.[14] Instead, we need to affirm the 'movement, the passing, the supersession' and avoid the shuddering halt that is the 'greatest alienation of all'.

Lefebvre also sees the dialectics of alienation operating in relation to the notion of love.[15] He wonders how love can arouse such emotion when it is expressed between two people and so aligns them with one another. What is it, he muses, that allows people in love to communicate this feeling and through it overcome their many differences and misunderstandings?[16] His answer is that something remains in these exchanges, a '*moment*', an 'illusion and a reality', which 'vanishes', but also 'makes itself known' as 'lived time appears once more through all the veils and distances'.[17] Despite this almost intangible quality, Lefebvre designates that love can take two forms: 'passionate love', which he sees as alienating, and 'elective love', which he sees as disalienating.[18] He contends that elective love is far more prevalent and normal than passionate love and it is typified by not fetishizing either the lovers, or their physical and spiritual relationship. Elective love also imposes obligations on a couple while disalienating the alienation that arises through loneliness.

Lefebvre's dialectical understanding of alienation therefore produces the key terms of alienation/disalienation, other/otherness and passionate love/elective love, which through a process of becoming offers the possibility of supersession. When we now examine *Atomised* through a Lefebvrean lens that centres on understanding alienation dialectically, we will see that the one-sided interpretation of the novel as depicting total alienation and an all-encompassing nihilism becomes undermined.

The alienated Michel

At the beginning of the novel, Michel is the epitome of an alienated self. The alienation he experienced even when he was a young boy now appears to have completely engulfed him, and so seems to justify the completely negative interpretation of his character. After his leaving party, for example, he takes the deserted motorway back into Paris and he 'felt like a character in a science-fiction film he had seen at university: the last man on earth after every other living thing had been wiped out. A post-apocalyptic wasteland' (13). We are told that human emotions are not his concern and he knew little of them anyway (139). However, we are also informed that 'like most people he loathed what the sociologists and commentators liked to call the "atomised society"' and he thought it was important to stay in touch with one's family, even if it meant a certain amount of routine (185–6). So, immediately here, there are indications that his alienation is not complete and moments of disalienation are present. From Lefebvre's perspective, we need to be alert to the process of alienation-disalienation-new alienation and becoming that, as we have seen, cuts across people's lives and their social relations with each other. These moments need to be analysed and identified in relation to Michel who will veer dialectally between them. It is no surprise that, after these disalienating thoughts, he then drifts back into an alienated moment by pessimistically concluding that while relationships with family can endure compared to other relationships, 'finally, they too gutter out' (186).

The complex where Michel lives in Palaiseau appears paradisiacal as it has an approval rating of 63 per cent of the tenants and epitomizes what is meant by the quality of life due to the human

scale of the buildings, luxurious lawns and convenient super-
markets where he can buy his frozen ready-made meals for one
(12–13, 194). When his local Monoprix supermarket has an Ital-
ian fortnight, Michel ruminates that 'this life so well organised,
on such a human scale; happiness could be found in this; had he
wanted for more, he wouldn't know where to find it' (143). In
reality, the place's soulless nature is revealed by the limited human
contact Michel has, which extends only to the mechanical nod of
a cashier as he buys his food (139) and in an accidental encounter
with a neighbour (13). In need of company, which again suggests
a moment of disalienation, Michel acquires a canary, which falls
onto the balcony of a fellow female tenant five floors below. This
incident allows Michel and the female tenant to acknowledge each
other as neighbours when taking the rubbish out, something that
would have been unthinkable before given their self-contained life-
styles within their separate apartments (14). Even so, his alienated
isolation simply resumes and takes its course.

Lefebvre offers a number of examples where he considers the
manifestations of alienation to be present in society, and one
chimes nicely here with Michel's character and predicament.
Lefebvre considers how certain American sociologists have discovered what he refers to as the 'other-directed man, one of the
other-directed people'.[19] This man, exceptional only in his banal-
ity, detects the opinions of others, mostly important people, and
conforms to them.[20] He is the product of the 'manipulation of
individuals and consciousness by modern technology', in a world
dominated by 'bank accounts and credit, the growth of suburbs
and new housing estates, the rising cost of setting up home (mort-
gage, furniture), and more generally, "consumer society"'.[21] He is
the 'alienated man in an alienating society', and to a great extent
so is Michel.

However, following Lefebvre's framework we must focus on
alienation through disalienation in a process of becoming, and
there are a number of moments of this in Michel's character.
For example, while Michel is languishing in this alienated state,
a moment of disalienation is present because 'he himself wanted
nothing more than to love someone, he asked for nothing' (140).
He realizes that he seems incapable of loving someone but that
does not mean that he lacks the desire to. As we shall see, it is
Annabelle that will make him understand what love is in the

elective sense and weaken his alienation. But before considering her, there is another important female who causes moments of disalienation in Michel's life and that is his grandmother.

In a very moving episode, Michel has to go to the hospital to visit his grandmother who has had a stroke and is close to death (105–6). On arriving, he is initially stoical as befits his unfeeling frame of mind, but his aunt is there and she attempts to dissuade him from seeing his ailing grandmother in her current state. He ignores her advice and resolves that: 'What had to be endured, he would endure' (105). His grandmother has been allocated a room of her own, and when he enters, the image before him looks nothing like her. She has tubes cascading from her body, her hair is undone, and she is 'simply a creature of flesh and blood . . . given up into the hands of the medical profession' (106). Despite the shock of what he has seen, he has the fortitude to hold her hand as he has always done. His hope is that she recognizes his touch and knows that it is him. There is a clear aspect of compassion that the supposedly unfeeling and alienated Michel shows here when confronted with the disalienating force of the reality of his grandmother's suffering. His grandmother also has a crucial humanizing effect on him especially when we read the brief account of her harsh life recounting how she has worked on the farm from the age of seven, and then in a factory following the death of her husband (106). After she retired at sixty, she agreed to look after Michel, and she gave him everything she could, from feeding and clothing him to loving him unconditionally. The posthuman narrator then notes that there are those who devote their lives to others as his grandmother has, and it is no surprise that those who do so are 'invariably women' (106–7).

That the seemingly unfeeling and supposedly totally alienated Michel realizes this himself points to a further moment of his disalienation. Moreover, as a homily on the human condition in relation to women the passage is striking in its solicitude. Additionally, the feelings Michel has towards his grandmother lead him to conclude that it was undeniable that women had better qualities than men because they displayed more love, compassion and worked harder. For Michel, men had proved themselves superfluous in comparison.

Nancy Huston, who regards Houellebecq as 'one of the most ardent living advocates of nihilism',[22] responds to this overt disalienating and humanist moment in the novel by stating that Michel's grandmother is probably only 'worthy of heartfelt praise' because she is 'beyond sexuality and desire'.[23] Huston even dismisses the clear affirmation of the female spirit within the book in relation to the grandmother, and Annabelle in particular.[24] For example, Huston notes Michel's comment above but expresses surprise at such sentiments given Houellebecq's hostility to women's liberation. Consequently, she explains how women generally in his work, even when they are loveable, still meet with 'some horrendous fate'.[25] Annabelle, and Bruno's girlfriend Christiane, both commit suicide, of course. The latter due to her paralysed state and the former due to cancer. It is only in relation to grandmothers that a more positive viewpoint emerges, according to Huston. However, because of the undialectical and one-sided reading of the novel that she puts forward, Huston cannot see the disalienation that is present or, as in the case here, when she does, she unnecessarily and mistakenly restricts its presence. So keen to attack Houellebecq the man, Huston misses the nuanced humanism of the novel.

Another incident that suggests Michel is not absolutely alienated, and is related to both his grandmother and Annabelle, occurs after he has been in despair when contemplating theoretical understandings of human consciousness (267). What he concludes, given the unsatisfactory way other scientists have dealt with this problem, is that a 'new paradigm' was required (268). This is meant to be the invention of a posthuman clone, but then he has an 'unusually happy dream', which after a few fruitless days offers him an almost epiphanic and disalienating moment (269). The dream is about him being 'beside a young girl as she gambolled through the forest, surrounded by flowers and butterflies'. The image, he later registers, is from a 30-year-old memory of a TV show called *Prince Sapphire*, which he used to watch at his grandmother's every Sunday afternoon and 'found an echo in his own heart'. Again, overtly, his grandmother is arousing heartfelt emotion in the supposedly unemotional Michel, along with an unnamed girl that appears to be Annabelle, because when they were young, they would also wander through the countryside together (58). So his grandmother and now, more crucially, Annabelle are important catalysts for moving Michel from moments of alienation to disalienation in a process of becoming.

The humanism that the dream stimulates in the apparently alienated Michel is displayed further when, as he awakes, he feels happy, full of life, and when he goes out for a walk, realizes that he 'was alone but not lonely' (269). He wants to learn how to belong and thinks that talking to his female neighbour who works for a lifestyle magazine would help him. He surmises that 'it must depend on common psychological traits which even he possessed' (269–70). Even so, he still thinks his neighbour could teach him more and goes to ring her doorbell but, receiving no answer, he returns to his apartment, engages in some self-reflection, and considers whether he might be depressed (270). The dialectic of alienation and disalienation is working its way through him and so producing his anguished and uneasy state.

Having come across a cruise brochure in the junk mail, he contemplates the possibility of taking a trip, but leaving that to one side, he decides to affirm life in a sensible and happy manner (271–2). Yet, what interrupts his reverie here again is an intervention relating to his deceased grandmother. He receives a letter from the council telling him that her resting place is to be moved to allow the building of a car park, and summoned back home to oversee the removal of her remains.

On his return, he notices how much the village has changed and feels the mixed emotions that arise when revisiting the place of one's birth (275). However, almost immediately, Annabelle is brought to the forefront of his consciousness as he sees the seat where they used to sit after school. The posthuman narrator offers an ominous description of fish swimming against the current in the dark waters, and the sunshine only briefly breaking through the clouds as a symbol of the darkness that will shroud them with her death. Yet, the glimpse of sunshine is also symbolically pointing to something more positive, which as we shall see, is the humanizing and disalienating effect that she will have on Michel.

When he goes to the graveyard to oversee the removal of his grandmother's remains, the posthuman narrator informs us that death is not easy to comprehend and it takes courage to confront it (275). By the time the grave has been unearthed, rather than seeing the coffin which has largely decomposed, Michel catches sight of the emaciated skeletal bones with the 'skull caked with earth' and 'clumps of white hair falling over empty sockets', and he is forced to look away. Now he understands what death is, and what life is.

Ironically, such a stark image of death forces him to re-humanize the corpse so that he suddenly imagines his grandmother 'darning in front of the television, walking towards the kitchen' (276). So the alienation of death is being disalienated in his consciousness by conjuring back to life the memory of his grandmother. As he eventually walks away in a disoriented state, he enters a bar, orders a drink, suddenly notices that he is trembling, and eventually falls into a gentle doze. The grandmother and Annabelle therefore undermine Michel's alienation and re-affirm moments of disalienating humanism. Unsurprisingly, it is after this incident that he has his second meeting with Annabelle, which brings into play Lefebvre's notions of the 'other' and love.

The other and love

As we have seen, Lefebvre's dialectical understanding of the 'other' allows for the possibility of alienation and disalienation. Similarly, love can take on alienating forms as in passionate love or in the disalienating form of elective love. My contention is that Michel eventually realizes the power of elective love through the 'other' of Annabelle, and this challenges those commentators who see no hope in their relationship.

Jack Abecassis, for example, has the merit of grasping the dialectical nature of the novel, but his focus is on Michel and Bruno.[26] Abecassis notes how Michel is cerebral, non-sensual and incapable of love, whereas Bruno is the sensual one, but ill-equipped sexually to completely fulfil his desires because he has a small penis, finds it difficult to maintain erections and ejaculates prematurely. Abecassis suggests that the result for Michel is withdrawal from the libidinal economy, whereas Bruno embraces it only to become its victim.[27] Abecassis proposes that what is distinctive about the novel is 'the deflation of the *regime of desire*', a movement which he detects as a new tendency in French fiction.[28] As he indicates, *Atomised* is 'about the erasure of humanity as we know it and the creation of immortal and asexual clones'. He sees this allegorical story being played out in the lives of Michel and Bruno who are 'exemplars of late twentieth century nihilism and despair'. Consequently, Abecassis contends that there is a 'broken dialectic' between them resulting in a Kierkegaardian 'Either/Or' where no

mediation is possible.[29] On one side is repression and nihilism in
the form of Michel, whereas on the other is self-destruction and
despair in the form of Bruno, resulting in the ending of humanity.[30]
For Abecassis, Michel allegorically represents the end of desire as
his life is composed of 'that almost completely neutral zero value
through which one must pass from the negative to the positive':
the new posthuman society.[31] However, while Abecassis offers a
perceptive understanding of the dialectical relationship between
Michel and Bruno, he does not detect that there is an unbroken
dialectic between Michel and Annabelle, which is eventually mediated through love and so undermines Abecassis' understanding of
Michel as an embodiment of nihilism.

Jerry Varsava also tries to justify the pessimistic interpretation
of the novel by accusing Houellebecq of advocating views 'that are
clearly indebted to dated Marxist orthodoxies', despite declaring
that he is an ex-Marxist.[32] One antediluvian view of Marx that
Varsava sees Houellebecq subscribing to is the determinist, teleo-
logical interpretation of historical development known as the base/
superstructure model.[33] This allows Houellebecq, and by implication Marx, to see 'human history as a woeful existential tale whose
tragically sad ending is the inevitable consequence of mechanistic
historical laws' and a denial of free will.[34] Marx's answer to this
state of affairs, and Houellebecq's for that matter, is, according
to Varsava, the edict of the eleventh thesis on Feuerbach, that the
'point is not to interpret the world in varied and interesting ways
but to "change it"'.[35] But the question must be asked: how can
we change the world if, as Varsava suggests, we are determined in
such a way that free will is denied? If Houellebecq is at one with
Marx here, then we do have the capacity to change the world and
the presumed determinism of the novel is undermined.

The spontaneity of the eleventh thesis on Feuerbach does not
sit easily with the depiction of Marx emphasizing the inexorable
outcome of the laws of history as suggested in his base/super-
structure model, which Varsava sees Houellebecq as adopting and
endorsing.[36] For Varsava, Houellebecq is contending that the economic base of advanced capitalism determines the social mores of
interpersonal relationships and gender politics. However, despite
identifying the spontaneous moment in Marx, Varsava instead
suggests that the characters in *Atomised*, just as with Marx's bour-
geoisie, are conditioned by 'socio-historical circumstances over

which they have no meaningful influence, and these circumstances lead inexorably to personal tragedy and social dissolution'. For Varsava, then, the novel is completely without hope and his evidence for this is what happens to the main characters: 'one failed marriage, one failed father-son relationship, one psycho-emotional crippling, and four suicides'.[37] He also accuses Houellebecq of using Annabelle as a further emblem of the 'futility of love in a liberal, narcissistic age', because she cannot get Michel to love her later in life.[38] The link between Annabelle and Michel and the effect that she has on him through a process of alienation and disalienation is therefore missed. Far from being simply determined by the world, Michel is going to change it, and it is not just in terms of offering a posthuman society, which Varsava oddly refers to as a 'fascistic Technostate where the citizenry need not work to any considerable degree, and sex is readily available'.[39] While it could be argued that a society based on a reduction in labour time and open sexuality might not be fascist, the main point is that Varsava ignores the other possibility of a different humanist society that Michel proposes, which we will interpret through Lefebvre's notion of elective love. It is another commentator, Michael Karwowski, who comes closest to realizing that the love between Michel and Annabelle might challenge these negative interpretations, but ultimately he also falls back into the nihilist thesis.

Karwowski approaches the novel by classifying Houellebecq as part of the existential tradition, because his characters look for meaning through their suffering.[40] Karwowski argues that although it appears that Michel and Bruno seem to give up on life, in the case of Michel he is at least offered the possibility of an emotional relationship with Annabelle.[41] Michel can respond only to her, and this allows Houellebecq to posit this possible true love of Michel against the free love that has developed in society. For Karwowski, then, the 'nub' of Houellebecq's work is this contrast between true love and free love, which itself is a metaphor for 'humanity's search for personal fulfilment and contentment, in a word, for human significance'. Nevertheless, Karwowski suggests that Houellebecq is not promoting any agenda despite his emphasis on the importance of love, and sees Houellebecq as being like any great artist, acting 'as the vanguard of humanity's search for meaning'.[42] Karwowski then falls back into the sort of nihilist stance that other critics attribute to Houellebecq's work.

Karwowski argues that Houellebecq's 'existentialist angst' shows the 'experience of the futility of human life as lived in terms of self-fulfilment'.[43] For Karwowski, 'love is not possible through the elevation of the self' because 'our experience of sexual permissiveness has taught us that much'.[44] It is through 'selflessness' and the abandoning of the self or ego that human fulfilment can occur, and this is what, according to Karwowski, Houellebecq's experience of life tells him: 'we must lose our life to find it'. Consequently, Karwowski argues that this alternative is summed up in a dream in the novel where Michel has two choices: being and non-being and without a moment's hesitation he chooses the latter.[45] For Karwowski, the negative interpretation stands, but if we follow Michel through this moment of alienation into disalienation this negative interpretation begins to break down. Indeed, Karwowski's focus on the two types of love here is perceptive but he chooses not to take this further. If he had, then he would see that it is through Annabelle and her effect on Michel that the Lefebvrean elective love, what Karwowski calls 'true love', gives us a more subtle interpretation of the novel that points towards a disalienating humanism.

Annabelle and Michel

The rekindling of the relationship between Michel and Annabelle will reveal a more positive understanding of Michel's predicament and the elective love that is engendered between them. The starting point is when they meet again in their home town. When Michel looks at her, he thinks that she is as beautiful as ever and he cannot believe that she is aged about forty, reflecting that she looks about twenty-seven or twenty-eight (276). She is in town due to her father dying of cancer, a fate that will befall her, and reveals to Michel that she also lives in Paris like him (277). Michel says nothing and still appears to be in a state of shock after seeing his grandmother's remains. Annabelle informs him that she is now a librarian, and had heard what Michel was doing through Bruno, whom she had bumped into at an airport three years ago. She then confesses to Michel that she has thought about him many times and was angry with him for not replying to letters that she had sent him over twenty-three years ago. As she walks Michel to the station she says to him: 'We're at the same point now . . . the same distance from death'. Finally, Michel does utter some words to ask her if she will see him again to which she agrees, and invites him to dinner the following Saturday. This is the beginning of their dialectical interaction with each other on the path to Michel's realization of elective love and his disalienation and supersession.

Beginning with Annabelle, it appears that she is the embodiment of a totally alienated self because she has not had a happy life due to her obsession with love, and because men treated her simply as another piece of meat (278–9). Annabelle's search was for a disalienating elective love, only to receive the alienating passionate love in return. She has decided to give up on her quest and now has an empty existence, reading in the evening, making tea, seeing her parents and looking after her nephew and nieces (279–80). Reliant on sleeping pills and tranquilizers to assuage nightly fears at times, she concludes that death cannot come quick enough (280). Michel says nothing, but is not in the least surprised by this because women are 'looking for a tender relationship that they never find, for a passion they no longer feel; so they begin the long, difficult years' (280).

However, it is through their newly formed relationship that moments of disalienation emerge, albeit dialectically in and against moments of alienation. For example, they decide to get into bed together and Michel is amused by the idea of Annabelle suggesting that they have sexual intercourse, but as she is not on the pill nor has a condom, she offers to take him orally which he accepts (280). The experience is pleasant for Michel although it is not intense, but there was some poignancy in the act because 'it symbolised their second meeting, their interrupted destinies'. The humanist emotion that Annabelle sparks in a dialectically disalienating Michel is encapsulated in his caressing her before she goes to sleep, and in his appreciation of the sensuality that her body arouses in him, as he too descends into his slumber (280–1).

The next morning, the posthuman narrator briefly contrasts their lives and while hers had been one of hedonistic sexual freedom for which she had suffered, Michel's indifference to it all meant that he had been on its periphery and hardly touched by it (282–3). His life was worshipping at his local supermarket and researching molecular biology (283). Even so, Annabelle wants them to try to have a relationship, even though it is so late in their lives. In a poignant moment she confesses to Michel that she still has her train pass from the last year they were at school together, and it reduces her to tears every time she looks at it. Caught up in the anguish of it all, she declares: 'I can't understand how things can have gone so wrong. I just can't accept it'. At the moment, Michel cannot respond to this expression of elective love, albeit gone wrong, and the posthuman narrator informs us that as they begin to see each other, it was still the case that 'in the midst of the suicide of the West, it was clear they had no chance'. But again, moments of disalienation through elective love do break through at times.

For example, Annabelle goes back on the contraceptive pill and they start having sex, but for Michel, just touching her body and being asleep next to her is even more pleasurable (284). He then dreams about being brutally attacked by a gang using razors, which leaves him practically blind and his hand almost cut off. He comforts himself that 'in spite of the blood and the pain, still he knew that Annabelle would stay by him, she would shield him with her love forever' (284–5). Again, this is an astonishing statement given his alienation is meant to be all-consuming. He is the man who is about to develop the possibility for the end of humanity, but through the power of elective love he is affirming the human. Nevertheless, Michel's disalienation is dialectically entwined with further alienation, because although he felt deep compassion for the love that Annabelle could give, but which had been wasted, it was also the case that 'a glacial reticence had taken over his body; he simply could not love' (285). As we shall see, though, he will realize that he can love in the elective sense but only when she is dead.

The alienation pervading their relationship is also evident when their agreement to have a baby together results in Annabelle becoming pregnant but then developing cancer of the uterus. She has to have an abortion, her third, and also a hysterectomy to stop the cancer from spreading. Amidst this awful situation, they go for walks and sit on the bench as they did as children (333–4), which again points to moments of an awakening of elective love. But we are also informed that the rules in the real world were different and inhuman (334). Consequently, they are told that the cancer is still present and will spread, and treatment would have only a 50 per cent chance of success (335). Annabelle holds Michel in her arms for a long time; she hears him grind his teeth and finds his face 'wet with tears' (336). Knowing what her fate will be, Annabelle attempts to commit suicide and falls into a coma. The note she leaves that Michel finds says: 'I have decided to die, surrounded by those I love' (337). It is now that her effect on Michel through the disalienating power of elective love and contact with the 'other' will begin to penetrate his consciousness.

When Michel goes into the hospital room to see her, as the sunlight illuminates a lock of her hair, he notes that although 'a little paler than usual, her face, eyes closed, seemed completely at peace. All worries seemed to have disappeared, to Michel she had never seemed so happy' (339). Even though it is too late, he kisses her head and lips and strokes her hair (340). Michel reflects that it was not completely their fault given the struggle, rivalry, vanity and violence that epitomizes the world. Even so, neither of them had done anything to change it and make it a better place. When he remembers that he did at least try to have a child with Annabelle, this fills him with joy and he consoles himself that although her death is inevitable 'at least for some weeks she had felt loved'. So Annabelle had at last experienced the disalienating effect of elective love with her supposedly unfeeling 'other' in the form of the alienated Michel.

That the elective love is having a profound impact on Michel is further evinced when this passage is then followed by some verses from a book on Buddhism that he has been carrying around with him for some weeks, and which exhorts everyone to be and remain happy and live in friendship. One verse that is quoted here states that if a man 'practices universal love / At his Death, he will have no thoughts of hatred' (341). Michel will disappear with such a thought in his mind and this is a testament to the disalienating elective love that he will come to experience fully. However, at the same time in this instance, there is a movement back to an alienated state in his consciousness as follows.

Knowing Annabelle is close to death, Michel asks a man at the information desk at the hospital for a piece of paper, and receives a sheaf of headed notepaper from him (342). The posthuman narrator tells us that 'later, it was this letterhead which would help Hubczejak, the researcher who defends, popularises and eventually brings into being Michel's posthuman clone, to identify the text among all the papers at the Clifden house' in Ireland. Michel

then writes a short poem about Annabelle on this paper and he
says to himself that there is no way that she will leave life with
'bad grace' as some do by clinging on to it. This poem is an indication of Michel's research that will signal the possibility of the
end of humanity. The death of Annabelle prefigures the death of
all, and the possibility of a posthuman future. Michel states, '*Our
bodies will become cold, barely present / In the grass, my Annabelle, / Which will be the death too / Of every individual*' (343).
The posthuman narrator states that Michel had never known love
and neither had Annabelle either, but this is clearly contradicted by
what is said above.

When Annabelle dies two days later, we are told that she is to
be interred in the same place as Michel's grandmother, and he feels
again utter desolation (344). Annabelle leaves instructions that she
wants to be cremated (345). At the funeral, 'at the moment when
the flames leapt from the huge burners, Michel turned his head
away'. The ostensibly unfeeling Michel cannot bear to look. Similar emotions erupt within him when, again following her wishes,
they scatter her ashes in the garden of her parents' house among
the roses. Michel thinks back to their childhood together when she
would come to the station and take him in her arms (346). 'He
looked at the earth, the sun, the roses; the suppleness of the grass.
It was incomprehensible' (346). Michel suddenly breaks into tears
and resolves to return to his work. Annabelle is the catalyst for
this decision, but as we shall see, his task is not simply to develop
the possibility of a posthuman society; another alternative occurs
to him, which is the possibility of a society based on elective love.

Supersession

Lefebvre's emphasis on the dialectical nature of alienation raises
the possibility of supersession, and I now want to show how the
latter takes place at the end of the novel in the character of Michel,
through the mediation of elective love with Annabelle.

Michel takes the aeroplane to Clifden where he will finish his
research, and 'he had the feeling that his whole life had been leading up to this moment' (347). When he reaches the research centre
where he will spend what is left of his life, he realizes that 'he could
not dispel the feeling of sadness, of cold inside' (348): the sadness

I interpret as the loss of Annabelle. Indeed, up until that point, in his last days when he is finalizing his cloning theory, 'many times, warm, peaceful images of Annabelle flitted across his memory, and images too of his grandmother' (353). We are also told that Michel's 'great leap' was 'the fact that he was able, through somewhat risky interpretations of the postulates of quantum mechanics, to restore the possibility of love' (363). Indeed, just before this statement, we have Michel's last recorded words, which are not to call for a posthuman society but rather to emphasize the importance of elective love. As Michel poignantly puts it: 'the lover hears his lover's voice over mountains and oceans; over mountains and oceans a mother hears the cry of her child. Love binds and it binds forever' (362).

The image of Annabelle indicated the possibility of love for Michel and 'was probably his guiding thought in the last months of his theoretical work, about which we know so little' (363). Yet, what we do know about these final weeks when this 'guiding thought' of the possibility of love was so prominent is that he had now 'made his peace'. His 'anxious, faltering expression' was now 'stilled' as he embarked on 'long, dreamy walks along Sky Road with only the sky itself as witness'. Could it not be that he is hearing his lover's voice, the voice of Annabelle, as the 'ocean glittered, refracting a shifting light onto the rocky islands beyond the headland' (363)? Even the cloud that he sees is described as 'strangely physical' and perhaps symbolic of the presence of Annabelle.

The supreme irony is that at the very moment Michel is signalling the possibility of a cloning process to end humanity, he is disalienated and humanized by Annabelle. Annabelle is Michel's only real link with being human and she has made him human through the power of elective love. With that being fulfilled, and Annabelle dead, his work is accomplished and his own life ends. What he bequeaths to the human race is the possibility of becoming a posthuman society, or realizing the importance of compassion and love for one another. It is then a further irony that Hubczejak is the one who suggests that Michel's 'great leap' was to 'restore the possibility of love' (362–3). Despite this, Hubczejak develops only the 'most radical' of Michel's theories, which is the posthuman one, and ignores the theory based on the possibility of love. The posthuman narrator then explains that Hubczejak's 'unrelentingly positivist' reading of Michel's work led the former to 'underestimate the extent of metaphysical change which would necessarily accompany such a biological revolution' to a post-human society (376). Hubczejak misconstrued the underlying philosophy of the research, but this did not in any way delay the project being implemented because most people now accepted that a 'fundamental shift was indispensable if society was to survive' and 'credibly restore a sense of community, of permanence and of the sacred'. Science and a technical solution to humanity's problems was the path taken by Hubczejak and those he influences, but it is not the only path. As the posthuman narrator says at the end of the novel, the human race 'never quite abandoned a belief in love' and this is why the book has been written as a 'last tribute to humanity' (379). Annabelle is Michel's only real link with being human and she humanized him through the disalienating power of elective love.

Lefebvre's understanding of the dialectical nature of alienation through the categories of alienation/disalienation, other/otherness and passionate love/elective love on the road to supersession, therefore, shows how the negative and nihilist interpretations of *Atomised* come to be undermined. The novel is undoubtedly a pessimistic portrayal of modern alienation, but by realizing, in Lefebvre's terms, that the drama of alienation must always be dia-lectical in a process of becoming, the humanist moment and the possibility of hope shines through.

6 • *Platform*: Albert Camus and the Absurd

Houellebecq's next novel after *Atomised* was *Platform*, again a controversial work with its focus on the sex industry and under-current tones of Islamaphobia.[1] The story is told in first- and third-person narrative by Michel, a civil servant who works in the Ministry of Culture in Paris, and lives a relatively lonely life, with his main desires being fulfilled by engaging in sex tourism while on holiday, drinking and watching banal television programmes. His life changes when his father is murdered and Michel eventually receives his wealthy inheritance. In the aftermath of the death, he goes on a vacation to Thailand and falls in love with Valérie, an employee of the tourist firm that is organizing the trip. She also shares his sexual adventurousness. After an idea from Michel, Valérie and her boss decide to set up holidays devoted exclusively to sex tourism but their plans are thwarted when Islamic terrorists attack one of the resorts, setting off a bomb in a bar and shooting holidaymakers, Valérie included. She dies instantly, causing Michel to descend into madness and what will be his own demise.

In this chapter, I analyse the novel utilizing Albert Camus' notion of the absurd.[2] The presence of Camus as an influence on Houellebecq appears in the first sentence of *Platform* where the first-person narrator Michel states: 'Father died last year', which draws parallels with the first line of Camus' *The Outsider*,[3] where the first-person narrator similarly states: 'Mother died today'.[4] Additionally, the surname of Michel in *Platform* is Renault, which is similar to Camus' character who is called Meursault. Further resemblances occur with Michel saying that he would happily, and without compunction, shoot the North African man who had killed his father and Meursault shooting the Arab on the beach in Algiers, also without any remorse. Meursault has been described as the 'absurd hero *par excellence*' because of his lack of 'social non-conformity' and his rejection of conventional mores.[5] As we shall see, Michel's identity is also the embodiment of the absurd man who adopts a similar stance to Meursault and attempts to make sense of the world, whilst realizing its incomprehensibility. Consequently, the notion of the absurd is explored as Michel's outsider status becomes challenged in his relationship with Valérie and forces him to ask the fundamental question on the meaning of life. To this end, Camus' notion of the absurd is first explained and then used to explore Michel's identity. The chapter ends by considering the issue of Islam that caused controversy both in relation to the novel and to Houellebecq himself.

The absurd

In *The Myth of Sisyphus*, Camus states that his notion of the absurd is a 'starting point' rather than a 'conclusion' so his discussion will be 'provisional', descriptive of an 'intellectual malady' and contain no metaphysical belief.[6] Accordingly, prejudging his position is not possible due to these assumptions that also act as both the 'limits' and 'only bias' of the book, which he has to make clear due to 'certain personal experiences'.

Camus begins by relating the notion of the absurd to suicide because deciding if life is worth living or not is the fundamental question of philosophy due to the 'actions it entails'.[7] Answering this question can result in people either committing suicide or, alternatively, dying or getting killed for 'ideas or illusions that give them a reason for living'.[8] His concern is to deal with the issue of suicide within individual thought rather than as a social phenomenon, which is the way it has been approached previously.[9] He explains how the act is 'prepared within the silence of the heart, as is a great work of art', and amounts to a form of 'confessing' that death is preferable to life.[10] This feeling occurs because a person suddenly sees the world stripped of its illusions and makes him or her 'an alien, a stranger', separate from life like an actor without a stage or setting.[11] Absurdity is the basis of this feeling as we are forced to consider the 'exact degree to which suicide is a solution to the absurd' and which is the subject of Camus' essay.[12] So, being true to oneself, believing in the 'absurdity of existence', is what will dictate your actions in the world.

Camus considers that you can answer either yes or no to the question of suicide, but there are also those, the majority of people, who choose to prevaricate because of the immense power life has over us.[13] We get into 'the habit of living before acquiring the habit of thinking', which can lead us into the 'act of eluding', as we hope for a life that will 'transcend', 'refine' and give meaning to this life, while also betraying it.[14] Confusion is the outcome, especially as some people think that the refusal to give life meaning implies life is not worth living. For Camus, there is no necessary link between these two judgements and instead what we need to consider is whether the absurd dictates death. To answer this raises the only problem that Camus is concerned with: 'is there a logic to the point of death?', and he concludes that it is only by 'absurd reasoning' that he will find an answer.[15]

Where, though, do we look for the absurd? For Camus, it exists in the everyday world and on 'any street corner', albeit often in an 'elusive' manner.[16] To find it is difficult because we can never truly know a person but we can observe their deeds and actions.[17] Camus gives the example of seeing an actor perform on numerous occasions, and although one might not know the actor personally, through viewing a number of parts played, some knowledge of him or her is possible.[18] This reveals that people define themselves in make-believe as well as in their genuine desires. The acts that people carry out and the attitudes of mind that they have partially reveal a 'lower key of feelings', even though they are 'inaccessible in the heart'. Camus asserts that it is evident that he is 'defining a method' here, not of knowledge, but of analysis, which 'acknowledges the feeling that all true knowledge is impossible'. For Camus, just as great deeds and thought have their origin in a ridiculous and mundane beginning, so too does the absurd.[19]

The banal nature of our existence is aptly summed up by Camus as: 'Rising, tram, four hours in the office or factory, meal, tram, four hours of work, meal, sleep, and Monday, Tuesday, Wednesday, Thursday, Friday and Saturday'. The weariness of this life raises the question of why we continue with it, and brings in a moment of 'amazement' resulting in either 'suicide or recovery'. Weariness may be sickening, but that is good because 'everything begins with consciousness and nothing is worth anything except through it'.[20] So when we perceive the world even in all its beauty there is at the heart of it 'something inhuman', a 'strangeness', a 'denseness', which can 'negate us' – this is 'the absurd'.[21] However, these 'absurd discoveries' of the everyday should be treated not simply as facts, but in terms of their consequences in making

us ask the fundamental question on the meaning of life.[22] We use
our intelligence and adopt a rational and scientific understanding
of the world to do this, but for Camus, although we can 'seize
phenomena and enumerate them', we cannot comprehend them or
the world of which they are part.[23] A rational and scientific understanding of the world may be sure, but it can teach us nothing
in its certainty in a world that is 'not reasonable'.[24] Indeed, the
absurd itself arises from this confrontation between the irrational
and the 'wild longing for clarity whose call echoes in the human
heart'.[25] It originates in the collision between human need and the
unreasonableness of the world on which the 'whole consequence
of life' depends.[26] Consequently, the three main characters in the
'drama' of our existence are: 'The irrational, the human nostalgia,
and the absurd', which he also refers to as the 'odd trinity'.[27]

Camus then wants to explore the meaning of the absurd and its
consequences.[28] He claims that the absurd can only be grasped, not
simply in the person or in the world, but in their unity together.[29]
He sees this consequence again as a 'rule of method' that illuminates the 'odd trinity' and gives us a 'data of experience' that 'is
both infinitely simple and infinitely complicated'.[30] The trinity cannot be divided because to 'destroy one of its terms is to destroy
the whole' so there can be no absurd outside the human mind, or
outside the world, and like everything else its terminus is death. So
the very thing that might crush us, that we do not want to face,
must be retained, Camus maintains, so that we engage in a 'confrontation and an unceasing struggle'.[31] There is a 'total absence of
hope', but not despair, and a 'continual rejection', but not renun-
ciation, and a 'conscious dissatisfaction', but not an 'immature
unrest'. When confronting the absurd our aim is 'not to be cured,
but to live with one's ailments' because we must seek out what is
'true' and not 'what is desirable'.[32]

For Camus, 'absurd reasoning' can illuminate how the mind
works when it begins with the premise that although there is no
meaning in the world, ultimately meaning can be discovered within
it, while at the same time being infused with the anxiety that such
a realization entails.[33] The absurd is 'lucid reason noting its limits'
and reasoning itself must be 'faithful to the evidence that aroused
it'.[34] The evidence is the absurd because it represents the 'divorce
between the mind that desires and the world that disappoints', the
'nostalgia for unity, this fragmented universe and the contradiction

that binds them together'. Evasion is not an option, and neither is trying to engage in 'suppressing the absurd by denying one of the terms of its equation'. You have to ask yourself whether you can live with the absurd or 'die of it' so as not to descend into 'deceit' and a 'retreat before what the mind itself has brought to light'. Then you will be 'able to remain on that dizzying crest – that is integrity and the rest is subterfuge'. Camus realizes just how difficult this journey is and, again referring to method, suggests that it is a matter of 'persisting' and thereby avoiding the temptation, perhaps through the solace of religion, to abandon the absurd.[35] By 'persisting' it is possible to feel an 'irreparable innocence' and to demand of oneself to 'live *solely*' with what you know, 'that nothing is', which allows you to explore the possibility 'to live *without appeal*'.

Camus then returns to the issue of suicide and decides that the problem now needs to be reversed, so that the previous task of finding out whether life had to have meaning in order to live is now subject to the realization that if life has no meaning then it will be lived better. Consciousness brings the absurd to light within individual experience and so produces a 'conscious revolt', which is a perpetual confrontation between a person and their insignificance, and offers a constant challenge to the world.[36] The first consequence of this revolt is 'defiance', and the second consequence is to experience the 'reasonable freedom' of death and the absurd to feel the 'pure flame of life'.[37] Faced with a universe within 'which nothing is possible but everything is given, and beyond which all is collapse and nothingness', we need to decide to accept and draw strength from it, refuse to hope and embrace a 'life without consolation'.

Camus contends that to live in such a universe and believe in the absurd means exchanging the quantity of experiences for the quality because the 'whole equilibrium' of life 'depends on the perpetual opposition between my conscious revolt and the darkness in which it struggles'.[38] Freedom itself has no meaning except in relation to its limited fate, so 'what counts is not the best living but the most living' where 'value judgements are discarded here in favour of factual judgements'.[39] Even if living in this way was deemed to be dishonourable, Camus maintains that we are bound by 'true propriety' to live in a dishonourable manner.[40]

Camus explores the notion of 'most living' a little further and asserts that it begins when most people have imposed upon them the same number of experiences even though they retain their own 'spontaneous contribution, the "given" element' in them. He states that he cannot judge that and can only comment on the 'immediate evidence', where he sees a 'common code of ethics' that 'lies not so much in the ideal importance of its basic principles as in the norm of an experience that it is possible to measure'. Admitting to stretching a point somewhat, Camus makes the comparison between the Greeks who had their 'code of leisure' while 'we have the code of our eight-hour day'. However, it is through the mere quantity of experiences that the 'adventurer of the everyday' wins his or her 'own code of ethics' and so 'break all records'.[41] This breaking of records means facing the world as much as we can, confronting it with 'contradictions' and by 'playing on words'.[42] The absurd tells us that 'all experiences are unimportant and it urges towards the greatest quantity of experiences', but the latter does not depend on the 'circumstances of our life', it 'depends solely on us'. If we compare ourselves to another person who has lived the same number of years, the world will always give us a similar amount of experiences, but our role is to make ourselves conscious of them. So 'being aware of one's life, one's revolt, one's freedom, and to the maximum, is living, and to the maximum' as 'lucidity dominates' and the 'scale of values becomes useless' as we pursue our lives.[43] 'Passion' is therefore the third consequence of the absurd.[44]

For Camus, then, the absurd gives us the three consequences of 'revolt', 'freedom' and 'passion' and by the 'mere activity of consciousness we transform into a rule of life what was an invitation to death'. In doing so, we must reject the possibility of committing suicide. Consequently, the starting point of an 'anguished awareness of the inhuman' means that the 'absurd returns at the end of its itinerary to the very heart of the passionate flames of human revolt'. We now need to consider how Camus' notion of the absurd can illuminate our understanding of Michel.

Michel: the absurd man

When we first meet the forty-something Michel, both he and his life are mundane. He is, from Camus' perspective, the 'everyday' person, a creature of habit, doing his eight-hour day as a civil servant, a 'cushy little number' as his father disparagingly told him (8), and then spending the evening eating ready-made food, such as 'instant mash with cheese' (18), and watching trash on television until he falls asleep (6, 8–9). When he attends his father's funeral he reflects that he made an 'excellent general impression' as he is 'always clean shaven' and he normally wears a 'grey suit and sober ties', albeit while not looking 'particularly cheerful' (5).

His work in the public sector is, ironically, given his uncultured existence, planning finance for exhibitions in the Ministry of Culture (12). He tells us that he has been there for about fifteen years, his starting salary was adequate and then he aged and was a bystander as various changes in policy were implemented (25). He sees himself as 'courteous, well-mannered, well-liked by colleagues and superiors' (25–6), and in general a 'harmless human being and moderately amusing' (85–6), although he does have an 'anxious bureaucratic face' (39) and can be 'egocentric' and 'neurotic' (32). He also thinks critically about the world, which brings him into contact with the absurd. Slowly but surely, Michel begins to see the absurdity of life and his separation from it, and that allows him to engage in 'absurd reasoning' as a 'starting point' to contemplate the meaningless nature of the universe. He grasps its inhuman nature but attempts to persist and live without appeal and carries with him the trinity of the absurd man, passion, freedom and revolt and so experiences the 'pure flame of life'. For example, when he ponders on what he has done with the four decades of his existence compared to people who make things, he concludes that he has not produced very much working in the service sector (86). Referring to himself as a 'moderate parasite', he recognizes that it would be 'easy to get by without people like me' but justifies his right to be in the world by saying that his 'ineffectuality' was not that 'flamboyant' as he had never been a high-flyer in his job, and 'never felt the need to pretend to be'. He also perceives that 'his temperament . . . was less than warm' and that he 'had failed to make any real friends' (25–6). Part of him is already an outsider, an alien, a stranger, and this forces him to question why it is that he had never shown any passion in his work or life in general (26). While realizing that his 'dreams are run-of-the mill', he concludes that his real desire is to be a tourist, so he goes on his trip to Thailand (27). However, as we shall now see, while this strangeness is initially reinforced, aspects begin to unravel through his contact with Valérie.

As the holiday is an adventure one visiting various locations, he will be travelling in a group, so his outsider status will be challenged continually. When he is first alone with Valérie and senses that he likes her, he also becomes aware of his inability to interact with her socially, or be able to seduce her, due to his isolated existence (44, 62). Moreover, when he discovers that all the travellers are meant to eat together, he decides to go to his room instead because he thinks that 'relations with other people are unbearable' as 'it is in our relations with other people that we gain a sense of ourselves' (87). Consequently, he did not much like being in a group (95).

On the coach on one of the trips, he forgets to bring something to read to avoid talking to people and panics because his inner world is being encroached upon (102). When he reaches the hotel, he copes with the stress he has been under by getting drunk and falling asleep (103). Waking up at five in the morning with a hangover, he vomits into the toilet bowl. He then walks the streets of the resort, has a drink, and then returns to the hotel, satisfied with his free time, which he was determined to continue with (103–4). Repeating a phrase that he had read earlier in the day from the teachings of the Buddha, he states: '*I was attached to a delusive existence*', but is consoled by the thought that he still had the hostess bars to frequent later (104). So part of him knows that he is living this deluded life and is aware of the absurdity of his own existence. However, the catalyst that forces him to confront reality is the love engendered in him from Valérie as they form a relationship together when they return to Paris (135).

Early in their relationship, Michel asks Valérie what she sees in him because he sees himself as not particularly attractive or funny, a 'washed-up guy, not very sociable, more or less resigned to his boring life' (138). He sees her as amiable, caring and as someone who gives him so much pleasure, which leaves him perplexed at her interest in him. Valérie's reply is that she does not really know but she does like his insecurity. He lacks a sense of certainty when confronted with the absurdity that his life has no meaning. However, his passion for Valérie will offer him that meaning as he quickly perceives that happiness is a possibility for them, which gives him a feeling of elation and makes him want to cry (142). Strangely, Michel later muses that he has hardly any memories of being happy with Valérie and concludes that misery is our lot (161–2). Yet, on

the next page he contradicts himself because Valérie tells him that
to her he seems happy, and he agrees (163). He then switches back
into pessimistic mode by declaring that life has 'a whole series
of inevitable troubles, decline and death'. These contradictions,
these juxtapositions of happiness and unhappiness, are the workings of the absurd through Michel's consciousness. How can we
be happy faced with death and the day-to-day absurdities of our
own lives? We, along with Michel, confront it in all its absurdity and in doing so attempt to persist, knowing that life has little
consolation for us, but in recognizing that we still attempt to live.
Michel's self-interrogation is then contrasted with a brief moment
of deliberation from Valérie that she, too, is implicitly aware of
the absurd.

Contemplating on her own life, she tells Michel that she is not
ambitious in her job, is content to be happy and in love with him
and asks for nothing more (162–3). Nevertheless, she then adds
that she is forced to ask for more as she is 'trapped in a system'
from which there is no escape (163). She pleads for time to think
about life but concludes that she does not know how anyone can
find the time to do so. Valérie is aware of the absurd but does
not know how to confront it. Caught within the constraints of the
working day, which given her position is far more than eight hours,
there is no time to pursue those thoughts, even though she can
see the absurdity of her, and by implication, many other people's
existence. As Michel himself says, they 'were caught up in a social
system like insects in a block of amber', the amber of, we might
say, the absurd (165).

When Valérie suggests that she and Michel should move in
together, he sees this as a 'new' or rather 'first' beginning, and
opines that his previous independent life became a 'habit' and perhaps not always a good one (179–80). Prompted by the absurd,
he asks himself whether it was a conscious choice in his life to
live alone (180). He decides that it was just the habit of the everyday, but the everyday that he should have been questioning on the
meaning and nature of his own existence. He faces his possible
new situation by using 'lucid reasoning noticing its limits' from
Camus' perspective of the absurd. He accepts that at his time of
life, this was probably the right time to live with someone, but he
also notes the drawbacks, such as desire becoming 'dulled more
quickly when couples live together'. Even so, he concludes that it

'becomes dulled anyhow, that's one of the laws of life', although his own desire for Valérie was as strong as ever. Michel therefore does not turn away from the absurd but embraces it in all its anguish as he attempts to make sense of what seems his senseless life in a senseless world. He admits that on one level 'anything can happen in life, especially nothing', and so grasps its absurd aspect, but also recognizes that 'something had happened in his life', he had found a lover and she made him happy (207).

When he is about to leave his own apartment and move in with Valérie, the absurd is waiting to confront him yet again, as he suddenly felt no attachment whatsoever to anything there, or to any object during his life (181). He notes that he had only two suits, books, which he could just buy again. No photos or letters of any of the women he had been out with, nor any photos of himself, even when he was younger. He deduces that his 'identity could be contained in a couple of files which would easily fit into a standard-size cardboard folder'. The absurdity of his own existence then makes Michel generalize that humans are not in any way special and nor do they have an 'irreplaceable individuality'. He maintains that it is a pointless exercise to try to identify what determines our identity and fate, because we are not unique and the contention that we are is simply 'pompous absurdity'. He then recalls Schopenhauer's statement that we remember our own lives 'little better than a novel we once read', adding, 'that's about right: a little no more'. Such thoughts become particularly acute on the absurdity of the self if we now fast-forward and see how Michel reacts after the demise of Valérie.

After Valérie's murder by Muslim extremists, an absurd action in itself, Michel's hold on reality begins to slip. He is confronted again with the fundamental question of the meaning of life but is so psychologically disorientated that everything seems meaningless. He becomes mentally ill and is eventually admitted to a psychiatric unit when he returns to Paris (344–5). His general feeling is of being fatigued and a psychiatrist tells him he is suffering from 'extremely weakened reactivity' (345). When he is asked what his plans are he says he will stay for now and suggests that he will be happy again once all this sadness has gone. Michel says to himself that the psychiatrist did not seem convinced.

When Michel is transferred to a new psychiatric hospital, the same psychiatrist is there and advises him that he must free himself from attachments, meaning Valérie. Michel appears to be in denial because he has moments when he thinks she is not dead (345–6). He tells himself that if he can just stay tranquil and avoid excessive contemplation then he will return to normality (347). In his final conversation with the psychiatrist, the latter explains that denial is a 'problem of perception' rather than a 'disorder of mood'. He adds that the reason Michel has been detained in hospital for such a long time is that he was a suicide risk, which is often the case with sudden confrontations with a harsh reality, but he was now out of danger and so he could leave. The change in his mental state forces Michel to think again of the absurd. The inability to confront the death of Valérie means that he is engaging in an 'act of eluding' and returning to habitual existence of the everyday world. His eluding deepens further as he tries to resuscitate her memory by going back to Bangkok (348–9). He books into the same hotel that they stayed in last time, but he quickly understands that this is not a good idea and moves to a different one. Eventually, he decides to go back to Pattaya, the resort where the attack occurred (352).

However, his 'eluding' begins to lessen as he now becomes increasingly self-interrogatory. He considers that nothing in his story has been determined and that he could have spent the rest of his life with Valérie in Thailand, in Brittany or elsewhere, but this is now the end of his journey (352). He realizes that 'growing old is no joke; but growing old alone is worse than anything' and Pattaya was the place not to come to begin life, but to accept its eventual end (352, 354). He concludes that his own life is finished and the idea of embarking on a relationship with anybody is unthinkable (356). He then rents a room with basic amenities and buys an amount of A4 paper to write about his life. It is at this point that the absurd suddenly appears because he laments that it is strange how many people can spend their lives without saying anything or even uttering some form of protest. He adds the caveat that his own written comments may be meaningless and have no audience in mind, but that they must be stated nevertheless (357).

He spends the next six months writing these thoughts down and they constitute the novel we are reading. When his work is nearly completed he says that he misses Valérie (358). Wondering whether it was the case that writing all his recollections down would be some kind of cathartic experience to overcome her passing and make life less unbearable, he concedes that if so it has been a 'fail-ure' as her absence has 'never been more painful' to him. He then decides to go back to the massage parlours because they offered some kind of human interaction but soon stops due to the void that his life has now become, and passion anyway would only transform into pain (358–9).

His story is nearly at its end and he spends most of his days in his room. He resolves that when love has gone, life reverts back to the habit of the everyday that he can no longer engage with (359–60). As for Valérie, he sees her as a 'radiant exception' because she devoted her life to making someone else happy, the phenom-enon of which he thinks is a mystery (360). As for himself, he will 'remain a child of Europe, of worry and shame' with 'no message of hope to deliver' (360–1). He has only contempt for the West, because 'every single one of us reeks of selfishness, masochism and death' and 'we have created a system in which it has simply become impossible to live; and what's more we continue to export it' (361). All that is left for him after his long journey is that he knows what death is, but doubts that it will do him much harm. He has known 'hatred, contempt, decay' and 'brief moments of love', but overall he judges that he has been a 'mediocre individ-ual' in every way and does 'not deserve for anything' of him 'to survive'. A forlorn and broken man, he imagines that he will die in the night (361–2). However, what will survive is the work he has written and we can see from Camus' perspective that his life was a confrontation with the absurd. Michel showed immense cour-age at times in confronting the absurdity of the everyday existence that we all lead, and Valérie was an important part in making him do that, but in the end her loss meant that the absurd could be confronted no longer. Death was chosen over persistence and the confrontation with the harsh reality of life.

To support this reading of the novel, although without any spe-cific reference to the notion of the absurd, Jason Cowley rightly sees Houellebecq as a 'profoundly moral writer' who asks 'what does it mean to live in a world without belief or consolation?'[45] He deduces that the 'kind of answer' in *Platform* is that 'to live in this world is to suffer'. Cowley recognizes that, for Michel, 'no moral code of restraint determines his life' and so he descends into a debauched existence. For Cowley, reading the novel shows us 'what a flimsy construct the self is, and how provisional is the manner

in which we lead our lives'. He argues that 'Western individualism teaches us that we are free to remake ourselves in whichever
way we choose, that we are masters of our own destiny', and that
the 'modernist project taught us that individual consciousness is
supreme, that it is not what we do, but what we think that makes
us interesting'. Houellebecq, though, 'persuasively reminds us that
such notions are simply not true'. However, Cowley also notes
the optimism at the end of *Platform* because Michel never aban-
dons his love for Valérie even as he falls into his 'narcotised haze'.
Cowley concludes that there is no doubt that Houellebecq 'believes
in the possibility of love, if not redemption. Which means that
reading him is never deflating; it is, rather, a source of constant
inspiration and delight'. As we have seen, it is such a confrontation
with the absurd that gives even greater credence to such a perceptive interpretation of this novel and its power in making us think
about the meaning of our existence through its meaningless futility.

Islam

In the initial aftermath of the publication of the novel, a number
of reviewers highlighted the perceived Islamaphobia that was present in the work. Houellebecq was put on trial for incitement to
religious and racial hatred in September 2002, not for the views
expressed in *Platform*, but for 'provocatively worded opinions' he
gave to a literary magazine.[46] However, it does raise an important
issue around the way Islam is treated in the novel. The case against
Houellebecq was brought not by the French state, which called for
him to be acquitted, but by four Muslim organizations on 'behalf
of the six million Muslims in France' who wanted to see him 'punished for calling Islam "dangerous" and "the most stupid of all"
religions'. In court, Houellebecq replied to the charges by declaring
that he 'had never had a coherent idea in his life' but then went
on to express his opinion that 'all monotheistic religions promoted
hatred rather than love'. He added that the Bible was filled with
passages 'so boring they make you want to shit', although it did
contain some poetry, unlike the Koran. His gripe, he says, was not
with Muslims or Arabs: 'he just "hated" their "stupid" religion'.
   Salman Rushdie, in a spirited defence of Houellebecq, picked
up on this point and agreed that to 'attack people's ideologies or

belief-systems is not to attack the people themselves'.[47] For Rushdie, this is 'one of the foundation principles of an open society' because citizens should have the right to complain about discrimination against them, but that should not apply to dissent even where it is 'strongly worded' and 'impolite'. He states bluntly, and I would argue correctly, that 'there cannot be fences erected around ideas, philosophies, attitudes or beliefs'. Even the idea that Houellebecq's unfavourable comparison between the Koran and the Bible should be seen as stoking racial hatred is dismissed by Rushdie on the grounds that anyone should have the right to say that they prefer one book to another, especially in any society that purports to be free. Moreover, he continues, logic would dictate that if a Muslim said that the Koran was better than the Bible then they, too, would be guilty of stoking racial hatred and so 'absurdity would rule'.

Rushdie also notes that in court the anti-Islamic sections of *Platform* were mentioned as further evidence against Houellebecq, along with the fact that his mother, who abandoned him to be brought up by his grandmother, married a Muslim and converted to Islam. The inference is clear, Houellebecq the man had good cause to hate Islamic religion due to his personal experiences and not least because he also had a dislike for his own mother after what she had done to him. *Platform* was therefore evidence of his anti-Islamic stance and a further way to condemn him on that issue. However, Rushdie rejects the identification of the author with the characters in his text, which should preserve its 'autonomy' and 'its right to be considered on its own terms'. Elision of the author with the text is illegitimate and also strikes at the heart of the freedom of a writer to create characters of whatever sort, Nazis or bigots for example, without being accused of endorsing their views. For Rushdie, it is Houellebecq's Islamic adversaries that have miscalculated in bringing these 'ridiculously slight' accusations against him, because they 'have shown themselves, yet again, to be opponents of the rough-and-tumble-world of free speech'. Rushdie concludes that if the verdict were to go against Houellebecq then the 'law of blasphemy would have effectively been introduced' and he hoped that the judge would not take such a 'retrograde step'. As it transpired, the judge did not, and Houellebecq was acquitted. Free speech and the autonomy of the text had won the day.

How, though, were the Islamic sections of the book seen by some reviewers? Julian Barnes interprets the novel's discussions of Islam as an example of Houellebecq 'being a clever man who is less than a clever novelist'.[48] Barnes notes how there are three main outbursts against Islam in the novel, one from Aïcha, his father's cleaner, another from an Egyptian Michel meets in the Valley of the Kings, and finally a Jordanian banker he meets in Bangkok. Barnes finds it 'extraordinary' that these three casual meetings across three continents should produce 'three vociferous Arab Islam-despisers who disappear from the narrative immediately their work is done', and he asserts that this 'isn't so much an author with his thumb on the scales as one clambering into the weighing pan and doing a tap dance'. For Barnes, Houellebecq's offence is not necessarily his attack on Islam but his unconvincing 'fictional insolence' that instead of convincing the reader with the 'force of its rhetoric and the rigour of its despair' produces the reaction of implausibility. Barnes resolves that Houellebecq offers us only 'opinions and riffs and moments of provocation' rather than 'thorough narrative' as he allows questions such as: 'Are Muslims like this? Is humanity like this?' to enter the mind of the reader far too often. Concluding with a reference to Camus, Barnes contrasts the way the latter started by 'creating in Meursault one of the most disaffected characters in postwar fiction, and ended by writing "The First Man",[49] in which ordinary lives are depicted with the richest observation and sympathy'.[50] On that basis, he observes that the 'trajectory of Houellebecq's world-view will be worth following', no doubt to see if he can emulate the greatness and literary development of Camus. However, Barnes' criticisms become undermined once we pay due attention to the philosophy of the absurd in Camus. Barnes sees the attack on Islam as some kind of literary error, but in the world of the absurd it is a rupturing device to make the reader think about the issue of Islam and to ask the very questions that Barnes thinks it is a mistake for the reader to be asking. He is also identifying the author with the character, which again is an error, as Salman Rushdie pointed out earlier.

Such incoherence and illogical narrative has been identified by fellow novelist James Buchan too, who also notes the comparison to Camus, not simply in literary terms, but in the 'fame' that Houellebecq has achieved, which is described, or should it be decried, as 'quite unexpected'.[51] For Buchan, such fame is fortuitous because Houellebecq, 'a grown man . . . reads like an adolescent'. The story in *Platform* is 'preposterous . . . because we are not engaging with reality', although the Bali bombing that was to take place just over a month after Buchan wrote his review was to prove that life was to imitate Houellebecq's prophetic art.[52] Nevertheless, Buchan chides Houellebecq for being 'too inhibited to address the reader directly', although Buchan does not explain why a novelist should do this in the first place.[53] He derides Houellebecq's use of 'ready-made literary styles: television game-shows, holiday brochures', etc., along with 'page after page of ballast, including reviews to no purpose of novels by John Grisham, Frederick Forsyth and Agatha Christie'. However, it is not Houellebecq's use of these 'literary styles', but the preoccupations of his main character that is taking place here. It is Michel, not Houellebecq, who is astute enough to realize how mediocre the bestselling fiction of Grisham and Forsyth is, which is the reason why they are mentioned; but, Michel, to his credit, does admire Christie.

Buchan's quasi-rant continues with the love of Michel and Valérie described as 'bland, ill-informed and self-consciously tedious', and the novel itself as proceeding 'through assertion'. Michel, himself, 'is prone to flashes of pointless rage' with his 'main characteristic' being a 'fear of Muslims' who are the 'villains of the story' because they murdered his father and his mistress. For Buchan, Michel's expressed horror on the expanding immigration of Muslims across Europe 'sounds like Pim Fortuyn', the Dutch politician who was openly critical of Islam and as a result was assassinated in 2002. Buchan then states, 'remembering, no doubt, that he is offending against the rules of speech in polite society, Houellebecq brings on a pair of Muslim characters to criticise their religion and then depart'. The example Buchan alludes to is the Egyptian one, where the character states that 'there is no other God but God alone', and derides this as being 'nonsense' and a 'tautology'. Buchan counters by arguing that what the 'actual fatiha or creed of the Muslims' is in reality is 'there is no God but the God', which is 'not a tautology but a statement of radical monotheism'. Buchan deduces that 'here as elsewhere in the book, Houellebecq's characters simply do not know what they are talking about'. Buchan's final parting shot is to suggest that Michel's own view of the 'scary, over-feminised, lonely, demeaning, faithless' view of European culture 'is that of the worst sort of low-grade Muslim propaganda', which makes him, ironically, the 'Muslims' friend'. However, this seeming irony, this juxtaposition of conflicting viewpoints, that there can be a commonality between Michel's views and that of the Muslims he despises is lost on the one-dimensional reading of the book offered here. The edict is that everything must make sense and if it does not then the novel somehow fails. The problem, as Camus informs us, is that the world does not make sense and we have a terrible and absurd time trying to make it do so. Michel as the everyday man is immersed in this dilemma as he tries to grasp meaning in a world where those who give it meaning fail to see that their certainty undermines meaning itself.

As for the statement of 'there is no God but the God', not being a tautology but a statement of radical monotheism, Buchan seems unaware that this statement of radical monotheism can be tautological. It does not escape, even in this purportedly more precise form, its meaningless nature unless of course you believe in such a proposition, but belief is beyond the boundaries of logic, which is no doubt what the Egyptian was trying to say. Moreover, the language of the absurd is explicitly used by the Egyptian who declares: 'One God! What an absurdity! What an inhuman murderous absurdity' (252).

Jenny Turner, while being more sympathetic to and appreciative of Houellebecq the writer, expresses similar concerns to Buchan in relation to *Platform*.[54] Turner asks the question whether it is fair to demand of novels that they be 'articulate and reasonable' and 'attempt in some way to make the world a better place?' She responds by saying that if this is so, then *Platform* is a 'disaster' because, among other things, 'its politics are reactionary and xenophobic', and she also draws an analogy with the racism of Pim Fortuyn to make her case. However, Turner asks herself the question of articulacy and reasonableness a second time, with the addition of, 'or is it as important, sometimes, that what they are trying to say is real and new?' She concedes that at least *Platform* 'makes an imaginative purchase on the undeniably actual strand of thought in turn-of-the-century Europe, a continent that feels itself' to be, quoting from *Atomised*, '"sliding slowly, ineluctably, into the ranks of the less developed countries"'. Her last reflection is on Michel's comment that: 'In most circumstances in my life, I have had about as much freedom as a vacuum cleaner', which she adjudicates is 'not a noble thought, or one that lends much hope to the future. But it is apt and it is funny, and it is, unfortunately, likely to be true'.

The analogy, though, is important because Michel is just sucking up the commercial junk of capitalism that is presented before him. As the everyday man, he is as unfree as the vacuum cleaner is when switched on and directed to sucking up dust and dirt, just as he is sucking up the banalities of capitalist culture. Turner, therefore, comes close to realizing that *Platform* is absurd in the sense that it is making us, as readers, balk at its absurdity, in the hope that we question both what is being said in the book and what we ourselves think. Houellebecq is an agent provocateur,[55] forcing us to think the unthinkable and engage with the seemingly unimaginable, so it is no surprise that the book comes across as both these things. Logic is being looked for where it cannot be found. The logic must come out of our response to the outlandish opinions that are often espoused in the novel.

Andrew Hussey also noted how the 'attacks on Islam are bitter and, naturally, offensive to Muslims' and saw Houellebecq's own attempt to defend these sections of the book by saying it is only fiction, and that the vengeful response of Michel to Valérie's murder is demanded by the logic of the narrative, as 'weak'.[56] Instead, Hussey surmised that Houellebecq's 'real objection to Islam' is because it 'offers a total challenge to Western Enlightenment values'. Hussey makes this claim on the basis that Houellebecq 'began his career as a kind of Marxist', so the '"medieval nostalgia" of Islamic thought is bound to conflict with his way of thinking'. Hussey also thinks this is true of most on the French Marxist left to whom the 'term multiculturalism is still a mystery'. Additionally, he interprets the 'virulence of Houellebecq's dislike' emanating in a 'more complicated way, from his compassion', his 'horror of suffering and violence' and the 'touching pathos, even tenderness, with which the heterosexual orgies are described, in opposition to the murderous Puritanism of Islamic terror'. The pornography, if that is what it is, is of the 'highest poetic order', according to Hussey. He concludes by declaring that 'there are few writers in any language who understand the tensions of the present age as well as Houellebecq', who Hussey compares to Louis-Ferdinand Céline, the anti-Semitic novelist of the 1930s. Hussey argues that Houellebecq resembles Céline in terms of 'style and content', and while the latter's anti-Semitism was 'disgusting in the 1930s and is made more so by history', it 'did not make him a lesser novelist' and the 'same applies to Houellebecq'. Again, though, this attempt to elide the novelist with the novel must be resisted precisely on the grounds that Rushdie has outlined above. The autonomy of the text means that we should not be delving into the biography of the author to 'prove' his own views by showing them to be congruent with that of any of his or her characters. In this sense, Camus' philosophy forces us to confront the absurdity of established religion, and refuse its comforting solace. Such consolation is not open to the absurd man that is Michel, as he must go on persisting and suffering, that is, until the absurdity of what he takes Islam to be results in the destruction of Valérie and the disintegration of his own self.

Conclusion

Houellebecq's own judgement on *Platform* was that it was a failure, partly because the character of Michel was 'bland' in comparison to the character of Valérie who dominates the book too much.[57] However, what I hope to have shown here is that grasping Michel's existence through Camus' notion of the absurd should assuage the fears even of Houellebecq himself. Michel is bland in the sense that he is Camus' everyday man, but there is a richness to Michel's character as he probes and pushes the boundaries of his everyday existence and the conventional mores that govern our lives in his contact with the absurd. Certainly, Michel's feelings are more often than not mediated through Valérie, but that is after he is brought out of his outsider existence, and his love for her makes him confront the world to make it meaningful in its meaninglessness. Even when that love is gone, the force of its power can certainly not be denied in the story that Michel has told us. Moreover, the fact that Michel thinks he cannot love in that way again is a further testament to the power of that love in the first place: an affirmation in its negation in an absurd world.

Part IV:
J. M. Coetzee

7 • *Disgrace*: Thomas Aquinas and the Path to Prudence

Disgrace explores mainly white but also implicitly black South African identity through the characters of a father, David Lurie, a university teacher of Romantic poetry, and his daughter, Lucy, who lives an isolated life on a smallholding in 'old Kaffria', alongside Petrus, a black farm worker.[1] Lurie is the embodiment of the old apartheid South Africa as a white man with little or no concern for the consequences of his own actions on others, particularly black South Africans. Lucy is emblematic of the new South Africa with the white minority having to come to terms with a power shift towards black rule. Lurie is forced to resign his post due to an affair with a student, Melanie Isaacs, something he will not apologize for. Lurie visits Lucy on her farm and they suffer an horrific attack. Lucy is raped by three men who also beat Lurie and set part of his head on fire. The incident is pivotal in making Lurie question his own self-certainty, arrogance and general unconcern for other people: his disgrace. Despite his persistent attempts to resist self-analysis, he begins to alter his behaviour for the better. One important source for this change is the work he does in an animal welfare clinic with Lucy's friend Bev Shaw, which makes him rethink how he relates to the 'other'. What, though, is the basis of this self-interrogation and orientation to the good?

The aim of this chapter is to try to answer this question by showing that Lurie's actions can be accounted for by using Aquinas' moral theory and in particular through his notions of prudence and disgrace. Interestingly, Derek Attridge, one of the most perceptive commentators on Coetzee's work, makes the important point that Coetzee often turns to religious discourse to try to escape the terminology of the administered society, even where the characters may have no orthodox religious beliefs, because they need such a language to talk about their lives.[2] In relation to *Disgrace*, Attridge notes how Lurie, a confessed unbeliever, is an example of this, and Attridge then explores the various ways this occurs in relation to him throughout the novel. The implication is that the self-interrogation has a religious basis to it despite the fact that Lurie himself would not want to think or talk in that way about the moral dilemmas he will face.[3] For Attridge, Lurie implicitly engages with the religious notions of grace, disgrace and salvation through his actions, but the reasons why he does so 'seem as obscure to him, as they are to us'.[4] As Attridge explains further, 'something' leads Lurie while in his disgrace to 'undertake a life of toil in the service of others', but Attridge does not tell us what this 'something' is. Additionally, Attridge also contends that because of his actions, Lurie achieves 'something approaching a state of grace' at the end of the novel, which implies that 'his daily behaviour relates to some value beyond the formal structures – moral, religious, emotional, political, – of reward and punishment', that have brought about his disgrace.[5] For Attridge, Lurie is 'true to an excess, an overflow, an alterity that no calculation can contain, no rule account for'.

Attridge himself offers a nuanced analysis of the theological basis to the novel, so it is unclear why he suggests that neither Lurie, nor us as readers, cannot account for his actions. It is also unclear why, after identifying Lurie's need for religious discourse, he can claim that Lurie is beyond such a value system. Attridge's contention seems to be that this is because religion is rule-based, but Aquinas' moral theory opposes following rules and instead emphasizes a deed-based virtue ethics based on people acting as deliberating moral agents when faced with ethical dilemmas in their daily lives. Using this framework can give us an enhanced insight into Lurie's character and his movement from a state of disgrace to a position by the end of the novel where he is on the cusp of a more prudential life in Aquinas' sense of the term. For Aquinas, of course, the ethics point to God as a source that orientates us towards the good, but Lurie is not a theist, so that cannot be the end point for him. This is why he secularizes theological discourse in an attempt to make sense of his changing emotions and actions. So while a literal Thomist understanding of what is happening to him is possible, it must also be translated into a secular humanist interpretation to be true to Lurie himself, and to my own understanding of a non-theistic reading of Aquinas' virtue ethics. First, we need to outline the key concepts in Aquinas' theory.

Prudence

To understand Aquinas' notion of disgrace we need to begin with his understanding of prudence (*prudentia*), because it is through this notion that he sees humans as conducting themselves as moral agents, and from which we can fall into disgrace. Aquinas explains that 'prudence is a virtue most necessary for human life' because a good life consists in doing good deeds.[6] This means acting, not simply from impulse or passion, but from 'right choice' with due attention to the way we do a good deed, rather than just what the good deed is. When we deliberate in this way, we do so in relation to some end that will be achieved from our actions, and this involves the use of reason. Aquinas deduces that there needs to be an 'intellectual virtue' in our reasoning that both perfects and points us towards those things that will achieve the end. The ultimate end itself for which all human beings exist is to attain 'final and perfect happiness' in the 'vision of the Divine Essence' through 'knowing and loving God'.[7]

As Herbert McCabe elucidates, for Aquinas, prudence is the virtue of having practical wisdom or good sense, rather than just following rules or natural law, and it is indispensable if we are to lead a good life.[8] Prudence in Aquinas' sense differs markedly from the normal rendering of prudence in English to mean one who always counts the cost in the manner of a pragmatic businessman.[9] Aquinas' notion of prudence is opposed to the vice of *astutia*, which is a cunning, a kind of bogus prudence, involving the careful, rational pursuit of a bad end. Prudence, on Aquinas' understanding, involves being good at *consilium*, that is, deliberation on the means with respect to ends. So when we decide on a particular action, we need to question ourselves about the effect that it will have on another person. Prudence is not dry rationalism; rather, it embraces the emotional complexities of human decision and action. Out of this can come the opposite to prudence, which is self-deception, posturing, play-acting on your private or public stage, but when humans engage in the virtue of prudence they are guided to do what is right by God's grace.[10] God is the 'First Mover' in our deliberations and we are subject to the 'plan of his providence'.[11] God gives us an 'infused virtue' to allow us to engage in works of 'supernatural virtue' and 'do and wish supernatural good'.[12] We have a natural inclination to virtue, but we must also realize that this can be 'corrupted by vicious habits', just as our natural knowledge of what is good is 'darkened by passions and habits of sin'.[13] Yet, even when our nature has become corrupted by sin, this can never be total and it is through God's grace and his divine help that sinners can heal their intrinsically good nature so that they 'may entirely abstain from sin'.[14] As Aquinas states, 'grace does not destroy nature, but perfects it'.[15]

For Aquinas, the return of the human creature to God can be seen as the return of the sinner who has rejected God's grace, but by God's grace of forgiveness, returns to him because grace is the remedy for sin.[16] Human beings, having been separated from God, are in need of his grace and can do nothing of themselves to deserve it, which, as the word implies, is simply the free gift of God.

Aquinas' assertion that 'the whole community of the universe is governed by God's mind'[17] has led Eleonore Stump to consider whether determinism is present here.[18] She contends that we should resist this conclusion because during any interaction between the intellect and the will, the will could direct the intellect in a different way or even stop it thinking about the issue at hand. As Aquinas himself states, 'God who is more powerful than the human will, can move the will of man . . . But if this were by compulsion, it would no longer be by an act of the will'.[19] Consequently, human beings can determine themselves by their 'reason to will this or that, which is true or apparent good',[20] and they can direct themselves towards such an end 'through free will, because they can take counsel and they can choose'.[21] Prudence therefore informs our actions as moral agents so we now need to examine this specifically in relation to Aquinas' notion of disgrace.

Disgrace

Aquinas argues that there are two aspects to disgrace.[22] One type is inextricably linked to vice and involves the 'deformity of a voluntary act', but it does not have the 'character of an arduous evil'. This type of disgrace should not be feared as it can be overcome by human will. The other type of disgrace is 'penal' and involves reproach or disapproval in relation to a person, in contrast to a person being honoured, which is a part of glory. This type of reproach should be feared because it is an arduous evil and more difficult to overcome the blame received. This fear of disgrace, Aquinas informs us, is shamefacedness, which, as it involves reproach or ignominy, must also relate to the disgrace that is part of vice.

Aquinas proposes that shamefacedness regards fault in two ways. In one way, humans refrain from vicious acts through fear of reproach and this can involve them blushing. In another way, humans, while doing disgraceful deeds, avoid the public eye through fear of reproach, and here they are ashamed. Consequently, those who are ashamed act in secret, whereas those who blush fear to be disgraced. Additionally, Aquinas explains that when we notice something disgraceful in a person who we thought was good, then this makes the disgrace even worse, which brings him to the issue of shame.

Shame may be lacking in people for two reasons. The first is because the things that should make people ashamed are not seen by them as being disgraceful. These people are mired in sin without shame and instead of being critical of their sins they boast about them. The second is because they apprehend disgrace as impossible to themselves, or as easy to avoid, as is the case with the old and the virtuous. However, if there was anything disgraceful in their character then they would be ashamed of it, and so, following Aristotle, shame exists in the virtuous hypothetically.

If and when we fall into disgrace, how do we recover ourselves and put us on a path that might allow us to receive God's grace? Aquinas argues that atoning for our sins is part of the notion of penance and involves detesting our past sins, along with the purpose of changing our lives for the better, which itself is the 'goal of penance'.[23] Engaging in this process of penance involves a movement back towards God's grace, but the level of grace that can be achieved will depend on the level of intensity or remissness in the movement of free will. Sometimes it will be higher than before, sometimes lower, and sometimes the same.[24] Such gradations will also apply to the virtues that will be formed from God's grace. Additionally, Aquinas contends that although a person may have ceased sinning, there can be no immediate return to the state before the sins occurred; rather the person must engage in a motion of the will that goes against the previous motion of the will of sinning.[25] When we have committed a wrong, we have to counsel ourselves not just that we are sorry for what we have done, but will the opposite of what we sinfully willed at the time, and which now goes against our current will. With Aquinas' theory outlined, we now need to apply it to *Disgrace*, commencing with the character of David Lurie.

Lurie

From Aquinas' account, we can see that at the start of the novel Lurie is already steeped in disgrace and so far away from a prudential life that redemption appears to be impossible. The incident with Melanie is a culmination of his lack of concern for others and a total obsession with his own desires and needs. Self-centred, lacking in empathy and seemingly devoid of having a conscience, he epitomizes the white South African elite that subscribed to a brutal form of racist rule and oppression under apartheid. Lucy, far more attuned to these post-apartheid times, refers to him as a 'moral dinosaur' but Lurie does not feel the need to change (89).

When, after his resignation, Lucy tells him of the things that he can do to fill his time, such as volunteering to help Bev in the animal clinic, he makes the disparaging comment that 'it sounds suspiciously like community service. It sounds like someone trying to make reparation for past misdeeds' (77). Nevertheless, he agrees to do it but only with the proviso that he does not have to become a better person, because he is not prepared to be reformed and wants to go on being himself. Lucy responds by saying, 'so you are determined to go on being bad. Mad, bad and dangerous to know. I promise no one will ask you to change'.

Similarly, when he considers this type of philanthropic work further he makes the following proclamation:

> I just find it hard to whip up an interest in the subject. It's admirable, what you do, what she does, but to me animal-welfare people are a bit like Christians of a certain kind. Everyone is so cheerful and well-intentioned that after a while you itch to go off and do some raping and pillaging. Or to kick a cat. (73)

Lurie, though, is surprised by his outburst, especially as he is not in a bad temper. Lucy, however, is annoyed with him for his indifference to what she and Bev are doing and his seeming disdain for animal life (74). Unfortunately for Lurie, these words will come back to haunt him, because it is he, and even more tragically his daughter, that will suffer from those who also think like him. The intruders probably hate well-intentioned people too, especially if the latter are part of the white minority that has suppressed them, and 'raping and pillaging' is their own response, which Lurie, without any hint of irony, will be outraged by.

At this point, prior to the attack, Lurie is a sinner who has rejected God's grace, in Aquinas' literal understanding of the matter, and an egoist who is lacking a conscience in our secular understanding. He has fallen into a disgrace that seems to be the second type that Aquinas describes as 'penal' and an 'arduous evil', because it is difficult to overcome and so should be feared. Lurie's response to his disgrace should be to realize his shame, but he is incapable of doing this at the moment. Aquinas tells us that this can be due to a person not seeing their acts as being disgraceful, and instead of criticizing their sins they boast about them. This is Lurie exemplified. Nevertheless, as Aquinas also informs us, when people have fallen into disgrace, the path back to receiving God's grace must be through penance and atoning for our sins, which we should despise and make us change our lives for the better. It is also not simply a matter of saying sorry for what we have done, but actively opposing the sin itself on the path to redemption and a more prudential life. Lurie does not realize it yet but this call-ing back to God's grace, which secularly means living with a clear conscience and attaining self-respect, begins to happen to him after the attack, as he goes through certain fragmentations of his own identity and alterations in his attitude to the world.

When he reflects on the awfulness of the incident, for example, 'he has a sense that, inside him, a vital organ has been bruised, abused – perhaps even his heart' (107). He registers for the first time what it is like to be an old man 'without hopes, without desires, indifferent to the future'. He reflects that it will take a long time for him to recover and that he is 'bleeding' and will be 'bled dry', leaving him in a fragile state. He tries to convince himself that he only feels this way because of the offence and soon he will feel like his 'old self again', but he knows that the truth is different and he is sinking into a state of despair (107–8).[26] As we shall see, a Thomist understanding of the novel illuminates what is happening

to him and I want to focus on two main ways that this occurs. One
is in relation to his work with the dogs and his changing attitude to
animals in general, and the other is in the discussions and meetings
with Melanie's father Mr Isaacs.

Mr Isaacs

What I will be suggesting here is that Mr Isaacs plays a crucial
role in helping Lurie extract himself from the arduous evil of disgrace that he has fallen into, and so makes him begin to pursue
the path to prudence. For Aquinas, this is the receiving of God's
grace or, on a secular understanding, it is gaining self-respect by
acting with compassion and due moral deliberation. Indeed, the
contrast between the literal theistic understanding of Thomism
and a secular interpretation of it is counterpoised nicely between
Isaacs as a believer and Lurie as an unbeliever in their confrontations with each other. This is plotted early in the novel when
Isaacs telephones Lurie and asks him for help because Melanie has
said that she is leaving university and getting a job (36). He asks
Lurie to have a chat with her and persuade her to think again,
especially as she respects him so much (36–7). There is an indication that Lurie realizes that he is morally culpable here because he
remembers that Melanie no longer respects him, 'with good reason', and contemplates admitting this to Isaacs. He does no such
thing, of course, and instead says that he will see what he can do
(37). Nonetheless, that a moment of recognition of his wrongdoing
is present is important for noting his initial and contradictory path
to a more prudential life.

   After this brief conversation with Melanie's father, Lurie knows
that he will 'not get away with it' and that Isaacs will not forget this exchange with its 'lies and evasions'. Lurie then wonders
why he did not own up to the truth and surmises that he should
have said: '*I am the worm in the apple*' and '*the very source
of your woe*'. A few days later, Isaacs, guessing what Lurie has
done, accuses him of abusing his position. Isaacs exclaims that he
thought that he was sending his daughter to a university rather
than a 'nest of vipers' and continues to admonish him: 'you may be
high and mighty and have all kinds of degrees, but if I was you I'd
be very ashamed of myself, so help me God' (38). Lurie recognizes

that this is his chance to confess, but he decides to run off without answering because he is 'tongue-tied' with the 'blood thudding in his ears', while also accepting that he is undeniably a viper. Isaacs shouts after him that he cannot escape and nor has he heard the last of it, because he will be called back to atone for his sins or selfish ways, but Lurie does not comprehend that yet.

When the harassment charge is formally made against Lurie, he believes it is Isaacs, 'the little man in the ill-fitting suit', and Melanie's cousin Pauline, who are responsible, because Melanie is 'too innocent' and 'too ignorant of her power' to take such a step (39). He then imagines what the scene must have been like and in the process demonizes and mocks Isaacs for supposedly coercing Melanie into making the accusation. Lurie, though, is creating a false picture of his own making, which does not correspond with Melanie's boyfriend revealing to him that she would spit in his face, a revelation that causes a jolt to his imagined picture of her. Lurie is telling himself this to try to make him feel better and it is unlikely that Isaacs, given the nature of his character, would force his daughter into doing anything, unlike Lurie of course. The next time Isaacs appears in the novel is after the incident on Lucy's farm has taken place. By then, Lurie is already embarked on the path to prudence and the possibility of receiving God's grace, in Aquinas' sense of the term, as we shall now see.

A key moment that indicates this is at the end of the previous chapter before Lurie visits Isaacs' house. Lurie has a conversation with Bev and expresses his concern over Lucy. Bev reassures him that she and her husband will look after her. Bev then tells him it will be 'all right', and adds: 'You will see' (162). This comforting phrase can also be interpreted differently once we take into account what will happen in the next chapter when he meets Isaacs again. The contention here is that he certainly will 'see' because his eyes will be opened again given that he has previously been blind to the redemptive power of God's grace, or in a secular interpretation, human compassion. It is therefore no accident, and without any previous intimation, that he goes to Melanie's family house and then to the school to meet her father. The implication is that he is being driven there by God's guidance or his conscience, which is confirmed by what Melanie's father will say to him.

When Lurie arrives at Isaacs' house and meets Melanie's younger sister Desiree, his passions begin to be aroused again (163–4). The

sight of Desiree evokes the memory of Melanie, which 'comes over
him in a hot wave' (164). However, his first inclination is not,
as was previously the case, to embrace this desire, but instead to
think, '*God save me . . . what am I doing here?*' This is an important plea because later he is going to deny that he believes in God,
and it appears here that he is simply making a general exclama-
tion with no theological import. As the passion rises in him, he
determines that they tempted the gods by giving her a name,
Desiree, the desired one, like that. He reflects that both sisters are
'fruit from the same tree' and fantasizes being in bed with both
of them, which he describes as 'an experience fit for a king'. It
seems, then, that we have the same sinful or selfish Lurie who is
not penitent and has not tried to mend his evil ways. Nevertheless,
he then 'shivers slightly' and decides to go and meet Mr Isaacs at
his school, which again indicates the retreat from his disgraceful
state onto the path of prudence. As Aquinas indicates, even the
virtuous can fall into shame and disgrace, so while someone sinful can have these thoughts, it is how they are dealt with and the
course of action taken that is important, by willing a good rather
than a bad end. In this respect, Lurie has the good judgement and
practical wisdom to leave the house.

When Lurie arrives at the school and meets Isaacs, he explains
that he is visiting because he was at a loose end and was passing
through his city, George (165). Lurie wants to say what is on his
heart, but is unsure himself, although earlier he expressed surprise
that he had a heart in the first place. The disgrace he has descended
into, his arduous evil, is being challenged here and accounts for the
confusion that Lurie feels. As we have seen, this form of disgrace
is the most difficult to overcome so it is not surprising to see him
unsure of himself as his selfish identity begins to fragment.

He begins to inform Isaacs why he went after Melanie, call-
ing it an adventure and saying that she lit a fire in him (166). He
wonders whether Isaacs has adventures, deduces not, and then
thinks that 'he would not be surprised if Isaacs was something in
the church, a deacon or a server, whatever a server is'. This is not
confirmed in the novel but what is clearly evident is that Isaacs is
a religious man. It is also interesting to note the role of a deacon
within the church: in 1 Timothy 3: 8, St Paul tells Timothy that
'deacons must be chaste, not double tongued, not given to much
wine, not greedy of filthy lucre, holding the mystery of faith in a

pure conscience'.[27] He states that they must 'first be proved: and so let them minister, having no crime', and adds that they should be 'the husbands of one wife: who rule well their children and their own houses. For they that have ministered well shall purchase to themselves a good degree, and much confidence in the faith which is in Christ Jesus'. Deacons are the servants of God and Isaacs not only fits these characteristics but acts in this role in his exchanges with the atheist Lurie as now becomes clear.

Lurie expands on the fire theme and mentions how in the old days people worshipped fire and would think twice about letting a flame die, referring to this as a 'flame-god' (166). He explains how it was this kind of flame that Melanie 'kindled' in him, 'real fire', even though it was not hot enough to burn him up, but the narrator suggests otherwise because the next sentence states: 'Burned – burnt – burnt up'. He burned with his desire for Melanie, was literally burnt in the attack when he was set on fire and has been burnt by the identity crisis that has engulfed him.

Isaacs is astonished and asks Lurie 'what on earth' he is doing coming to his school and telling him stories. Lurie apologizes and admits that he is being outrageous, but maintains that he wanted to defend himself. After asking how Melanie is, Isaacs informs Lurie that she is now back at university and doing well, but enquires how he is. Lurie says that he will be spending time helping his daughter on her farm, and completing a book. Isaacs regards Lurie with what the latter perceives as 'piercing attention' and Isaacs responds by saying: 'So', and the 'word leaves his lips like a sigh: how are the mighty fallen!' (167).

Lurie considers that while it is probably correct to say that he has fallen, he does not know why he should be described as mighty because he 'thinks of himself as obscure and growing obscurer. A figure from the margins of history'. But, of course, he did not think like that before the fall. He was assured and arrogant in his disgrace, which he is now beginning to question. Lurie then concedes that it probably does us good to have a fall now and then as long as we do not break. However, that we do not break means that we have a possibility of atoning for our sins or selfish ways and he has fallen from God's grace, or secularly, acting with due conscience, which Lurie still does not fully realize yet. Isaacs still fixes an intent look on him and declares: 'good, good, good', as he is beginning to see the change in his identity. Isaacs is acting the role of deacon or server because he is the servant of God but, of course, the path to prudence must come from within Lurie himself, albeit with Isaacs' probing.

Isaacs then asks Lurie if there is something more he wants to tell him given that he mentioned that there was something on his heart. Lurie seems surprised and answers in the negative, stipulating that he only came round to see how Melanie was. Isaacs perceives that this is not the real reason at all, and although Lurie denies that he had something on his heart now, he did not earlier. So God's call to his grace is working its way through him from a literal Thomist perspective, or he is beginning to develop a conscience on a secular interpretation, and Isaacs as the server and deacon is helping to bring this out.

Lurie departs but when he has nearly left the outer office, Isaacs calls him back and asks him what plans he has for the evening. Lurie replies that he has not got any and Isaacs invites him to his house for dinner. Lurie remarks that Isaacs' wife might not like that, but Isaacs comments that it does not matter and tells him to come anyway and 'break bread with us'. The breaking of bread service takes us back to our salvation from sin through Christ, which was made possible on the cross and a further indication of Isaacs acting as mediator and servant of God.[28]

When Isaacs goes to write down his address, Lurie tells him not to bother because he has been to his home already and met his younger daughter who has 'directed' him there. Isaacs says 'good' and 'does not bat an eyelid' (167–8). Again, the reason why is because Isaacs, from a literal Thomist perspective, sees Lurie as being called by God's grace and knows that he is on the path of penance and atoning for his sins, whereas Lurie is still only coming to terms with the journey he is taking. On the secular interpretation, Lurie is being guided by his conscience to rectify his wrongdoings on the path to prudence.

When Lurie arrives at the house, Isaacs introduces Desiree to him, and when she tosses her hair back to expose her face, Lurie thinks, 'My God, my God!' (169). He now surmises what is going through her mind and he senses that she is shocked that her sister could get naked and sleep with such an old man. So, from a literal Thomist perspective, the appeal to God could be asking him to save Lurie from his passion and a realization of how disgraceful he has been. On the secular interpretation, it is a call to one's conscience for help in not giving in to selfish acts and instead pursuing a more virtuous life.

Lurie concludes that he is just causing upset in the home and suggests that it is better if he leaves, but Isaacs gives a gay smile and tells him that they will be 'all right', they 'will do it' and encourages him to be strong, which chimes with Bev's comment that Lurie will see that things will be 'all right'. Isaacs, from his theistic perspective, is aware that Lurie needs his strength to come back to God and not to give into his weaknesses and sin again. Once the dinner is finished and Desiree and Mrs Isaacs have left the table, Lurie motions to leave but Isaacs again asks him to stay. Lurie continues with his reminiscences about Melanie, conjecturing that things might have turned out differently between them if he had been more lyrical, but his problem is that he manages love too well and when he burns he does not sing.

Lurie eventually apologizes and asks for Isaacs' pardon. He declares that Isaacs' family is wonderful, but on second thoughts thinks exemplary would describe them better. Isaacs wondered how long it would take until Lurie apologized and adds that we are all sorry when we are found out, but that is not the question, the important question is 'what lesson have we learned' and 'what are we going to do now that we are sorry?' (171–2). Lurie is about to reply, but Isaacs asks if he can pronounce the word of God in his hearing and whether he gets upset when hearing God's name (172). He then questions Lurie about what he thinks God wants from him besides being very sorry. The narrator tells us that Lurie 'tries to pick his words carefully' even though he has been distracted by Isaacs' questioning. He tells Isaacs that normally he would accept that lessons cannot be learned once a person gets to a certain age, and all one can expect is to be punished. However, in his new state of heightened awareness, he ponders that it might not now always be true and he will wait and see what happens. Lurie then states that in relation to God, he is not a believer so he translates what Isaacs calls God and God's wishes into his own terms, and the contrast between a literal Thomist approach and a secular interpretation of it begins to come to the fore as follows:

> I am being punished for what happened between myself and your daughter. I am sunk into a disgrace from which it will not be easy to lift myself. It is not punishment I have refused. I do not murmur against

it. On the contrary, I am living it out from day to day, trying to accept
disgrace as my state of being. Is it enough for God, do you think, that I
live in disgrace without term? (172)

This is an important admission from Lurie. From our Thomist
perspective we can see that he now realizes that he has fallen into a
disgrace which will be difficult to extract himself from: an arduous
evil. Difficult, yes, but not impossible in Aquinas' understanding
of the word. The fact that Lurie accepts his punishment is also
to his credit, although he still cannot see that instead of accepting disgrace as his state of being, he needs to act and atone for
his wrongdoings. As Isaacs has intimated to him, this is what God
requires rather than simply saying sorry, and on the secular interpretation it is what a decent society would require within which a
more prudential and virtuous life could flourish.

So what lesson has Lurie learned? Isaacs advises that normally he
would tell him to ask God but he cannot do that as Lurie does not
pray. From the literal Thomist perspective, it is as though Isaacs
can see that Lurie is moving away from disgrace to the possibility of God's grace, so he then enquires as to why he thinks he has
come to the house. Lurie makes no response so Isaacs tells him his
own theory, namely that although Lurie did not plan on it, he was
passing through George, remembered his student's family was from
there and thought why not visit? He makes the point that Lurie
did not plan it, but now finds himself there and Isaacs wonders if
that surprises him (172–3). Lurie says not quite, as he did come to
speak to Isaacs and had been thinking of doing so for some time
(173). Isaacs will not be shaken off so quickly and explains that
he is easy to speak to; even his schoolchildren know that with him
they get off lightly. So he repeats his request to Lurie again, who
did he really come to speak to? This unnerves Lurie and he begins
to dislike this man with his tricks. The interface between Isaacs'
theism and the atheism of Lurie is reaching a crucial point here.
Isaacs wants Lurie to see that he is being called to God's grace, but
Lurie, as an unbeliever, cannot think in that way, even though he
realizes that something is making him think differently.

In his own way of trying to understand this in secular terms,
Lurie's conscience has been pricked and this forces him to go and
seek out Desiree and her mother. When he finds them, 'with careful ceremony' he goes on his knees and touches his forehead to the

floor. He wonders to himself if that is enough, and as they both stare at him in silence, he meets first the mother's eyes, and then Desiree's and the 'current leaps, the current of desire'. He thanks them for their kindness and for the meal and then leaves. So, again, the sinful and disgraceful side of Lurie has not completely gone yet as his desire is still flowing through him. However, that he is on a journey to a more prudent life is evident when later that night Isaacs rings him at his hotel and wishes him strength for the future. This links back to Isaacs encouraging him to be strong, not to give into temptation and to repent for his sins. After a pause, Isaacs is suspicious that Lurie, whose cause is not redeemed yet, might be expecting him to intervene on his behalf to get reinstated at the university. Lurie seems genuinely surprised and contends that the thought had never crossed his mind (173–4). Isaacs informs him that such interference is impossible because 'the path you are on is the one that God has ordained for you. It is not for us to inter-fere' (174). Lurie replies: 'understood'. On the level of the literal Thomist understanding, this 'understood' becomes clear, because he is being called towards God's grace. But Lurie is an unbeliever so it needs to be understood secularly, just as Lurie secularly inter-preted what was happening to him in terms of falling into a state of disgrace. The path he is on is the path to prudence and a more virtuous life. He understands from Isaacs' theistic perspective that the end point and guide in this journey is God, but he will need to find his own non-theistic source, which will be his conscience and the urge to do good in exercising his practical wisdom, which he is still learning to do. Isaacs is therefore crucial in making Lurie confront his disgrace and attempt to atone for it.

In his discussion of this pivotal scene, Attridge explains that the verbal doublet of disgrace/grace does not occur in the novel, and ventures further that grace is in fact not the opposite of disgrace, whereas something like honour is.[29] He argues that the *OED* def-inition of disgrace links it frequently with dishonour and concludes that disgrace can only be redeemed by honour, so public shame can only be redeemed by public esteem, but this is a path he thinks Lurie refuses to go down. Attridge sees Lurie's visit to the Isaacs family as 'his most significant effort in this direction' of 'public confession', but he concludes that because of Lurie's uncontrollable desires, and the fact that he imagines Melanie and her schoolgirl sister in bed with him, any appeal for forgiveness is undermined.

Even so, Attridge recognizes that Lurie does not simply shrug off what he has done and in fact does admit to his disgrace, as in his declaration to Isaacs quoted above. Attridge concludes that the disgrace Lurie finds himself in cannot be equated with the public disgrace his actions and words have produced. He suggests that Lurie never wholeheartedly regrets his seduction of Melanie as her memory constantly flickers his desire, and he has no regrets at all about his behaviour before the committee. Attridge claims that what Lurie experiences is a deeper sense of being unfit for the times in which he lives.

From our Thomist perspective, this see-saw moral response by Lurie that Attridge finds difficult to account for – the attempt to come out of his disgrace and yet at times still clinging to it – is perfectly understandable once we see that Lurie is struggling along the path to prudence and the possibility of receiving God's grace or self-respect and redemption on the secular interpretation. It is not that Lurie is unfit for the time he is living in, but that he is trying to come to terms with those times, where his previously unfeeling selfish persona must change and orient itself to a good rather than a bad end. He has still got a bit of this journey to travel, and that leads us nicely to how he begins to emerge out of his disgrace through his work with animals.

The lives of animals

The way humans treat animals is a persistent concern for Coetzee the writer and he expresses this decisively in *Disgrace*. It also raises an issue in relation to a Thomist reading of the novel because Coetzee has written of his hostility to Aquinas' understanding of the relation of humans to animals in the Tanner Lectures given at Princeton University in 1997–8.[30] On Coetzee's interpretation, Aquinas contends that because humans alone are made in the image of God, how humans treat animals is irrelevant, except that being cruel to animals might make people cruel to each other. Coetzee then contemplates asking Aquinas what is the being of God and knows that Aquinas would respond that it is reason.[31] Coetzee, though, rejects reason as a basis for distinguishing between humans and animals. He suggests that reason is neither the being of the universe nor the being of God but simply a tendency in human thought and should not be bowed down to.[32] However, Coetzee has not fully grasped either Aquinas' understanding of humans' relation with animals, or his notion of reason. As regards the first point, as Stump indicates, while 'Aquinas subordinates all other species of animals to the human species, this feature of his theory cannot be interpreted as sanctioning wanton cruelty towards non-human animals or their gratuitous destruction', because any destruction of being is always on the face of it bad.[33] It is just that in certain circumstances the least worst act of destruction might have to be rationally chosen over another, but that act should bring about a greater good and an enhancement of being, and not be destruction for destruction's sake. In relation to the second point, as we have seen, Aquinas' emphasis on reason is intrinsically linked to his notion of prudence with the deliberating moral agent willing a good end. Taking these two aspects together, there is no reason why a moral agent cannot deliberate on how being is better enhanced when considering our relation to animals. I now want to explore this in relation to Lurie.

The animals that dominate the book are dogs, but there is a crucial incident involving two tethered sheep that will be slaughtered for Petrus' party (123). Petrus leaves them on bare ground where they have been bleating for most of the day in protest. Lurie cannot bear their bleating any longer and asks Petrus to tie them where they can graze. Petrus tells him it is not worth it as they are being killed soon anyway, but Lurie persists and maintains that they still should be allowed to graze. Petrus is unmoved but once he is out of the way Lurie unties them and takes them to the damside where they can drink and feed. Lurie then ruminates on the sheep and discerns that they are black-faced Persians, twins perhaps, and destined to be butchered from birth. At first he thinks that this is perfectly reasonable as they are bred to be used and sheep neither own themselves or their lives, but he then tells Lucy that he is perturbed by how Petrus can bring the sheep to see the people who will eat them (124). She responds by asking him if he would rather that they were killed in an abattoir so he would not be aware of it, to which he assents. She snaps back at him to be realistic and remember that this is the way country life is.

The next day the sheep are back tethered on the bare patch. Lurie surmises that this is an awful way 'to spend the last two days of one's life' (125). If this is the way things work in the country, then he concludes that the country is a world of 'indifference' and 'hardheartedness'. What, though, can he do? He considers buying the sheep but realizes that this is pointless as Petrus will just buy another two, and the idea that he can either set them free or look after them himself seems ridiculous (126).

He suddenly understands that a bond has developed between himself and the sheep but he cannot work out how. On reflection, he thinks it is not a bond of affection and it cannot be with these two sheep in particular, because he would not be able to pick them out from a herd of similar sheep. Even so, 'suddenly and without reason' their concerns have become his. He then stands before them as the sun beats down 'waiting for the buzz in his mind to settle, waiting for a sign'. We might ask a 'sign' from where? On a literal Thomist reading the sign will be from God as he suffuses Lurie's being with the capacity for prudence as a moral agent who should use his practical wisdom and deliberation to will a good end. The narrator says 'without reason', but 'reason' in Aquinas' understanding of the term is not dry rationalism because it covers the emotional complexities of human action and decision, and is what will be used by Lurie to do what is right. This also questions further Coetzee's own reading of Aquinas and its apparent inapplicability to animals. Additionally, the adjectives of 'indifference' and 'hardheartedness' that Lurie uses to describe and deride country ways could easily be applied to Lurie's previous and current aspects of his behaviour, not simply in relation to animals but in his treatment of his fellow human beings. Nonetheless, this new awareness of suffering and consideration of the 'other' is a further indication that he is on the prudential path to the possibility of a more virtuous life.

As he contemplates the sheep, he decides to step forward towards them but they retreat, and he reflects on how well Bev relates to animals compared to him. He refers to this in theological language as her 'communion with animals' as she enters into their lives, a 'trick' he thinks he does not possess. A link back to Isaacs should be noted here, as Lurie also said of the former that he was using his tricks against him when he was urging Lurie to realize that he was being called to God's grace. He then wonders if he is too complicated a person to develop this communion, to be a certain type of person like Bev, and asks himself, as the 'sun beats on his face with all its springtime radiance', whether he needs to change. The imagery of the sun's radiance implying an illumination of his path to a more prudential life is pertinent as he morally deliberates on the course of action he should take both immediately in relation to the two sheep and, as we shall see shortly, in relation to animals in general.

He has already decided that it is impractical for him to buy the sheep, so he determines that the most appropriate course of action is not to go to the party. He asks Lucy if that is possible without causing Petrus any offence. When Lucy asks if this has anything to do with the 'slaughter-sheep', he says yes straight away and then immediately corrects himself and replies no, adding, in a very defensive manner, that he has not changed his ideas, and still does not believe animals can have proper individual lives. He also concludes that it is not worth agonizing over which animal gets to live or die, but then utters the word 'nevertheless', indicating he is 'disturbed' although he does not know why (127). Lucy tells him that Petrus and his guests are certainly not going to give up their mutton chops because of him and his sensibilities, but he already knows that and decides he would prefer not to go to the party. He is again disturbed about the way he is behaving and never thought that he would end up talking in this way. She replies: 'God moves in mysterious ways, David', or as we have seen Aquinas say, 'the whole community of the universe is governed by God's mind'.[34] To which Lurie retorts: 'Don't mock me'. So the literal Thomist understanding of his predicament seems fairly evident here. Lucy may be teasing him but we know from Aquinas that we need the practical wisdom of prudence to help us decide on the right action to will a good end, as a secular interpretation of his ethics would understand it.

On the day of the party, he smells the stench of boiling offal and realizes that the 'deed has been done, the double deed, that it is all over'. He can no longer, it seems, use the word slaughter, which implies a heightened sensitivity to their fate. He wonders to himself if he should mourn their passing but questions if it is correct to mourn the 'death of beings' that do not themselves practice mourning. He looks into his heart, and can only find there a 'vague sadness'. He tries to cope with his feelings by tiring himself out by going for a long walk. Later, he changes his mind, goes to the party and is given two mutton chops from the dead sheep (131). He says to himself that he will eat them and 'ask forgiveness

afterwards'. Again, we can ask here forgiveness from whom? On
a literal Thomist reading, it will be forgiveness from God, because
Lurie has had to make the difficult decision of being part of, albeit
indirectly, the destruction of beings that has improved a greater
good and enhancement of being in the form of Petrus and his
guests. Lurie realized earlier that he cannot impose his own view
on them, but he has deliberated that his best considered course of
action was to go to the party and be civil, at the expense of how
he really felt towards the destruction of the sheep. On the secular interpretation, Lurie will be asking forgiveness from his newly
found conscience and his developing compassion to consider the
'other'. Indeed, this heightened sense of awareness of the lives of
animals and his movement along the path to prudence is to take an
even more intense turn with his relationship with the dogs.

As discussed earlier, Lurie works at the animal welfare clinic to
pass the time while he is at Lucy's farm. He thinks it is curious
that someone as selfish as he should give himself to the service of
dead dogs (146). He both helps Bev put the animals to sleep and
then takes their corpses to the incinerator (144). He could leave
the corpses there overnight for the incinerator crew to dispose of
them in the morning, but as they would be left with the other rubbish he decides that he cannot treat them with such 'dishonour'.
He instead takes them home and brings them back in the morning, but when he sees how the crew beat their stiffened corpses to
make them fit on the trolley that goes into the furnace, he decides
to do the job himself. He thinks that over time he will get used to
doing this but the more he assists in the killings the 'more jittery he
gets', making him stop at the roadside when driving home to find
his hands shaking and tears streaming down his face (142–3). He
confesses to himself that he does not understand what is happening to him, as he had, until recently, been indifferent to animals,
although in an abstract manner he has always been opposed to
cruelty (143). As with the sheep incident, he is confronted with the
destruction of beings that is having a profound and complex emotional effect on him, pulling him towards a more prudential life.

His previous identity fragments further when he ponders on
why he has taken the job and he deduces that it is not to lessen
the burden for Bev, because if it were he would just drop off
the bags at the dump and drive away (145–6). It also cannot be
for the dogs because they are dead and what do dogs know of

honour and dishonour anyway (146). He concludes that he does
it for himself and for 'his idea of the world, a world in which men
do not use shovels to beat corpses into a more convenient shape
for processing'. His bewilderment is then further encapsulated in
his assessment that there is no one else stupid enough to save the
honour of corpses and that is 'what he is becoming: stupid, daft,
wrongheaded'. Of course, he is not any of these things. On the
literal Thomist reading, he is trying to come to terms with the pull
he is being made to feel towards the possibility of God's grace,
and the dogs are a mediation of this. Part of him, the sinful part,
is attempting to resist this call, which is why he feels so confused
about the way he feels and why he still engages in sinful thoughts
and acts. On the secular interpretation, we can see that the pull is
away from his egoistic self and towards a more prudential life of
being a caring being who is attentive to the suffering of others.

By the end of the novel, Lurie is on the cusp of prudence. To
his disbelief, Lucy discovers that she is pregnant as a result of the
rape, and decides to keep the baby. When he questions her about
it she says she will grow to love the baby due to Mother Nature,
and she is determined to be a good mother and a good person. She
advises him that he 'should try to be a good person too' (216). His
response is to say that it is too late for him: 'I am just an old lag
serving out my sentence'. However, he thinks to himself that trying to be a good person is not a bad resolution to make in dark
times and it appears that he is moving away from his sinful or selfish past.

Because of his disagreement with Lucy over the baby, he stays
away from her farm, but once a week he drives to the hillside above
it and surveys the landscape. As he does so, he notices the beauty
of the countryside and sees Lucy working among the flowers
(216–17). He makes his way down the hill and, in a very moving
paragraph, he describes in detail the way she looks, and realizes
that she is at peace with both herself and her surroundings, even
after what has happened to her (217). As for him, he reflects that
he is 'a grandfather. A Joseph. Who would have thought it!' and
his sinful or egoistic self rears its head because he will no longer be
able to woo a pretty girl into bed given his aged state.

He then imagines that he will be a poor grandfather because he
'lacks the virtues of the old: equanimity, kindliness, patience. But
perhaps those virtues will come as other virtues go: the virtue of

passion for instance' (217–18). So the call to a more virtuous life
is being made to him, even as he is resisting aspects of it with his
regrets. He is awoken from this reverie by again seeing Lucy and
the beauty of both her and her rural surroundings, which takes his
breath away, even though he has 'never had much of an eye for
rural life, despite all his reading in Wordsworth. Not much of an
eye for anything except pretty girls; and where has that got him?
Is it too late to educate the eye?' (218). It is not too late because
the power of the scene he has just witnessed, the epiphanic nature
of the moment, suggests that redemption can be at hand for Lurie,
should he wish it. This is affirmed when Lucy eventually sees him
there and asks him to come in and have some tea. The narrator
then tells us that 'she makes the offer as if he were a visitor. Good.
Visitorship, visitation: a new footing, a new start'. Visitation is
what Lurie did when he went to see Isaacs and the link back with
that is the word 'good', which Isaacs says three times as Lurie
stumbles towards his apology and confession of his disgrace. Even
more importantly is the narrator's stipulation that this is a 'new
start'. One would think, or perhaps hope, that a possible reconciliation between himself and his daughter will enable him to begin to
re-educate his eye.

Attridge deduces that this is one of the few positive mentions of
the new in the novel, but he contends that this new intimation cannot be called the achievement of grace, because grace is by definition
something given, not something earned in the way that Lurie has
earned it in his relationship with Lucy.[35] For Attridge, although one
may seek grace 'it comes, if it comes at all, unsought'.[36] To support
this interpretation, Attridge refers to the 'paradox of the theological
concept of grace' as a 'spur'. He argues that the notion of grace here
raises on a secular level the ancient quarrel between Augustine and
Pelagius, which has been prevalent in many a later controversy, as
to whether a prior gracious gift from God is necessary to make the
individual fit to seek and receive grace, or whether the human freedom to accept or reject the offer of grace is primary. Attridge argues
that if Lurie achieves something that can be called grace then it is
possible to say that he both finds it and is found by it, rather than
one or the other. This certainly ties in with Aquinas' understanding
of the notion of grace, but what is missing is the role of prudence
because that will make Lurie lead a more virtuous life in his moral
deliberations and in doing good deeds.

Attridge also mentions here Rita Barnard's more positive rendition of the use of visitation, which he interprets more ironically and ambiguously.[37] However, unlike Attridge, Barnard rightly recognizes the religious overtones of visitation because it 'expresses the hope of some new annunciation and the arrival, perhaps, of an unexpected grace'.[38] To this extent, Barnard correctly posits a more forward-looking and slightly transformed Lurie, as I have tried to depict him here. This is certainly the case once we look at what a religious understanding of visitation is meant to consist of.

Visitation is described as the act of an ecclesiastical superior who in the discharge of his office visits persons or places with a view of maintaining faith and discipline, and of correcting abuses by the application of proper remedies.[39] Such visitation is incumbent on the shepherd who would properly feed and guard his flock. The main aspect of a visitation is to lead people to sound and orthodox doctrine by banishing heresies, maintain good morals, and to correct any evil acts. The shepherd is meant to also animate the people to religion, peace and innocence, and to put in vogue whatever else may be dictated by the prudence of the visitors for the benefit of the faithful, as time, place and opportunity shall permit. Understood secularly, Lurie as a visitor can be seen as guarding the flock that is Lucy and his future grandchild, which may also change his own identity towards willing a good end.

One might think that this positive moment would be the end of the novel but it is the dogs that have the last word. There is one dog Lurie has befriended and has a particular fondness for, a young male that has a left hindquarter that it drags behind it; Bev calls the dog *Driepoot* ('three legs') (214–15).[40] No visitor has wanted to adopt it so 'its period of grace is almost over; soon it will have to submit to the needle' (215). The dog adores Lurie and would die for him, and it is with this dog that the novel ends in a poignant last few pages.

Lurie and Bev have been carrying out the terminations and through all of them they do not speak because he has learned from her to concentrate all his attention on the animal they are killing, giving to it what 'he no longer has difficulty in calling by its proper name: love' (219). The young dog with the three legs that likes him is the last one. Lurie describes what is about to happen to the dog as having the 'smell of the released soul'. He thinks that the dog can never work out that you enter this room and never come out again.

The soul is yanked out of the body, briefly hangs in the air twisting and contorting and then it is sucked away and gone.

Lurie realizes that he could save the dog for one more week but knows it will only be a matter of time (219–20). He imagines himself caressing and supporting the dog as the needle finds the vein and his legs buckle beneath him, his soul escapes, and then he is put into the black bag, to be inserted in the incinerator the next day where he will be 'burnt, burnt up'. Again, the link back with Lurie's meeting with Isaacs should be noticed here, because Lurie said exactly the same about himself as he was coming to terms with the alteration of his identity on the path to prudence.

Lurie then changes his mind and decides to get the dog now. He takes it from its cage and bears it in his arms like a lamb as it licks his face (220). Bev says what he already knew, that she thought he would save him for another week. She then asks Lurie if he is giving him up, to which he replies: 'Yes, I am giving him up', which is also the last line of the novel. Interestingly, but in my view incorrectly, Laura Wright wants to reject any anthropomorphic interpretation that sees the dogs as being somehow symbolic of any of the characters in the book.[41] Consequently, she argues that the sacrifice of the dog here is to show that Lurie has learnt to give without expecting anything in return.[42] He has accepted responsibility for the dog as a 'being inherently entitled to love'.[43] Wright sees this reciprocity in its 'potential for ethical productivity' as being 'utterly promising'. But the 'him' here, given the signposts that we have seen at the end of the book, should allow us to see that the dog *is* symbolic of himself. The self he is giving up is his former arrogant, uncaring self. This new one will be different and offer a new start, a willing of a good end, as Lurie stands on the cusp of prudence and the possibility of a more virtuous life.

Conclusion

A Thomist reading of the novel, and in particular the character of Lurie, highlights the reasons behind the confused and often contradictory thoughts and actions that he has. On the literal Thomist interpretation, his resistance to God is juxtaposed with his attempt to make sense of his changing identity, and in doing so sets him on the path to God's grace. After all Lurie has gone through, it seems highly unlikely that he would slip into his sinful self as much as he has previously. As Aquinas reminds us, even the virtuous can fall into sin and disgrace, but it is what we do to atone for those actions that is important. The signs at the end of the novel seem to point to a much changed Lurie who we can imagine being far more sensitive to the plight of others in the altered world of post-apartheid South Africa. Should he stumble, should he have a fall, a literal Thomist understanding would indicate to us that he now has the power to pull himself up again and receive God's grace or, on the secular interpretation, he will find himself groping towards a more prudential wisdom on the path to a more virtuous life.

This brings us finally to the political dimension of Lurie's journey in the context of his membership of the white minority that ruled without conscience or compassion over the non-white majority in the previous apartheid state. Early in the novel when Lurie is before the university committee for what he has done to Melanie, he pleads guilty as charged, but refuses to show any contrition (51–2). The parallel between this committee and the Truth and Reconciliation Committee (TRC), chaired by Archbishop Desmond Tutu, has been aptly noted here by Andrew van der Vlies, because part of its remit in the post-apartheid era during the middle and late 1990s was to expose human rights abuses under the apartheid regime and to consider applications for amnesty by the perpetrators.[44] The latter were expected but not required to show contrition because amnesty was interpreted as essential for reconciliation and Lurie does not fulfil that expectation in any way. Similarly, van der Vlies also notes how, in a very subtle manner that is cleverly concealed but ultimately intimated by Coetzee, that Melanie is in fact 'coloured',[45] making Lurie guilty of not only professional misconduct but also engaging in and perpetuating 'white-on-black exploitation'.[46] However, this is at an early stage in his moral development and as we have seen in relation to the Isaacs family, he eventually does apologize and shows real remorse for his behaviour, albeit as he continues to fight his egoistic self along the path to prudence. To some extent, then, Lurie can be seen as epitomizing the white minority's need to confront their brutal and racist past and rediscover their conscience, self-respect and concern for others in order for reconciliation to succeed.

8 • *Diary of a Bad Year*: Theodor Adorno on Commitment

Diary of a Bad Year centres on JC, an ageing writer, Anya, a jobless, beautiful young woman, and her boyfriend Alan, an investment consultant, who all live in the same apartment block in Sydney, Australia.[1] JC meets Anya in the laundry room and is attracted to her. He then persuades her to be his secretary and type his piece for a book that he has been asked to contribute to, entitled *Strong Opinions*. *Diary* is divided into two parts: the aforementioned 'Strong opinions' and 'Second diary', which contains the more personal and 'soft opinions' of JC. Each page is split with JC offering his strong opinions on matters of art and politics such as the role of the state, the invasion of Iraq, torture, Harold Pinter, Bach and so on at the top, while beneath are his thoughts and conversations with Anya. Underneath that are then the words and thoughts of Anya who is often making comments on judgements, mostly negative, about what has been written by JC. As the book progresses Alan also gets his own part as well.

Anya develops a Platonic relationship with JC and eventually leaves Alan, seeing him for the shallow moneymaker he is. She sends letters to JC telling him what she is doing in her new life as he edges ever closer to death. His last words are to praise Russian writing in general and Tolstoy and Dostoevsky in particular because they set the standard to which all novelists must toil, even though they have little chance of emulating them. JC asserts that 'by their example one becomes a better artist; and by better' is meant not in terms of skill, but in terms of being 'ethically better' (227). As such, 'they annihilate one's impurer pretensions; they clear one's eyesight; they fortify one's arm'. The final words are left to Anya as she writes to him promising that she will 'hold his hand tight and give him a kiss on the brow, a proper kiss, just to remind him of what he is leaving behind' when he dies. She 'will whisper in his ear: sweet dreams, and flights of angels, and all the rest'.

Diary is an innovative novel in terms of its structure and by also having a main character who shares certain similarities with Coetzee himself. They both share the same initials, JC. They are both novelists. JC is Australian and Coetzee took Australian citizenship. JC has been awarded the Nobel Prize for Literature as has Coetzee. JC has also written two books that have the same titles as two of Coetzee's. So it is as though Coetzee is tempting us to make this identification, especially as JC is engaging in the 'strong opinions', many of which we can imagine Coetzee holding. But this raises the issue of what I want to focus on in this chapter through the work of Adorno, which is the place of commitment in art and the role of the artist. To do so, I begin by outlining Adorno's theory on this issue, and then explore Coetzee's own pronunciations on this matter. In general, Adorno insists that committed art must not be didactic in any way otherwise it will descend into bad art. It will be shown that Coetzee is very close to Adorno in this respect, which will then be highlighted by considering the use of politics in the novel in the 'strong opinions' of JC and through the opinions of Anya, who I interpret through JC as being a representative of the conventional wisdom of the masses. What I will argue is that although Coetzee appears to want us to draw inferences between the opinions of JC and himself, this has to be resisted because of Coetzee's own understanding of what art is meant to do, along Adornoan lines. What Coetzee is offering us through the creation of JC is a way to play with ideas and confront and problematize them in the aesthetic form of the novel, which ultimately subverts the possibility of didactic authorial intervention. *Diary* will be shown to be a piece of committed art in the true Adorno sense of the term. We first need to begin with Adorno's discussion on the role of committed art.

Adorno on commitment in art

Adorno's concern is to re-examine the issue of 'committed and autonomous literature' since Sartre.[2] Adorno contends that committed art exposes the falsity and fetish character of, supposedly, apolitical artworks that simply want to exist as an 'idle pastime', and ignore or detract us from the clash of real interests in society. However, the problem with committed art is that it can also descend into preaching and sermonizing when it puts itself at the service of a cause, and so end up where it was originally created, that is, in the academic seminar.[3] Adorno stipulates that in terms of theory, commitment should be distinguished from tendentiousness or advocating a cause or particular position.[4] Committed art should work towards an attitude, rather than lead to specific measures or laws. Adorno is therefore opposed to Sartre on this issue because his emphasis on partiality ignores what is crucial for committed art, namely, that the content the author is committed to should be ambiguous. Moreover, Sartre's emphasis on choice and decision making in his works are merely empty assertions because the possibility of choice itself depends on what is to be chosen in a pre-determined world. Adorno also cites Herbert Marcuse's criticism of Sartre's contention that the idea that one is free to accept or reject torture inwardly, for example, is 'nonsense'. Sartre's dramatic situations contain within themselves the whole administered world that his existentialism actually ignores: the world of unfreedom.[5]

For Adorno, art is not, as Sartre thinks, a matter of putting up alternatives, but rather of resisting, solely through artistic form, the course of the world, which 'continues to hold a pistol to the heads of human beings'. Sartre's overemphasis on subjective decisions to be made as the criteria for his art means that the choices themselves become interchangeable, and this eventually led Sartre to admit that he does not expect any real change in the world to be achieved through literature.

For Adorno, even Sartre's contention that the reason we write is from a deep conviction about some issue is mistaken because the writer's intention is only one moment in the process, which also involves objective requirements in the construction of the artwork. Adorno asserts that the writer's intention is also irrelevant to the written work because it takes on a life and meaning of its own when it is produced. Moreover, artworks themselves, as Sartre comes close to admitting himself, following Hegel, increase in stature the more they untangle themselves from the real person that produced them. For Adorno, the writer should also not be obliged to engage in choice, as Sartre emphasizes, but should engage with substance. In contrast, Sartre's plays are mere vehicles for what the author wants to say, using traditional plots and faith in meanings that are meant to be transferred from art to reality.[6] They fail to keep pace with the evolution of aesthetic forms and this has made

Sartre, against his intentions, acceptable to the culture industry of capitalism. Adorno concludes that Sartre's emphasis on the personal, on choice, on subjective responsibility, means that he does not recognize the very hell that he is rebelling against. He fails to realize that it is an 'anonymous machinery', and not the people in charge, that make decisions in society. So the weaknesses in Sartre's notion of commitment strike at the very cause to which Sartre is committed, according to Adorno.

Adorno then considers Brecht who uses his dramas to educate the audience away from the illusion of empathy and identification, to a detached, thoughtful and experimental attitude.[7] Adorno suggests that Brecht's drama surpasses Sartre, especially in its abstractness, which is raised to a formal principle of a didactic *poésie* (poetry) that excludes the traditional concept of the dramatic character. Adorno commends Brecht for realizing that the psychological action of individuals is played out in the sphere of consumption and exchange where the real essence of society is concealed and made abstract. Unlike Sartre, Brecht does not prioritize the sovereignty of the subject but sees the subject as being an agent and a function of a gruesome social process: capitalism. In this way, Brecht also provoked thought through the use of theatre.[8] However, despite seeing Brecht as a greater artist than Sartre, Adorno also notes some problems with his work because he wrongly used his drama to glorify the Communist Party.[9]

In his approach to exposing the evils of capitalism, such as showing cattle dealers slitting each other's throats when squabbling over money, Brecht dislocates them from the economic logic of the system, and makes their squabble seem almost childish.[10] For Adorno, Brecht is politically naive because his opponents simply grin at how silly his characters are as they present no real threat to the system.[11] For example, Brecht's play *The Resistible Rise of Arturo Ui* is meant to be an attack on fascism with Ui, a Chicago gangster, representing Hitler. Brecht depicts him as being ridiculous and in doing so detracts from the true horrors of fascism as a concentration of social power into a mere accident, a misfortune or a petty crime.[12] Brecht is therefore guilty of 'preaching to the saved' and sacrificing political reality to political commitment.

Having exposed the weaknesses in Sartre's and Brecht's understanding of the aim of art, Adorno points out that the best way to express the impulse that should animate committed art is to put it negatively with the edict that it is 'barbaric to continue to write poetry after Auschwitz'.[13] He recommends that literature must recognize, but also resist this claim, and so not descend into cynicism.[14] The sheer amount of suffering in the world means that art should contain an awareness of affliction, as Hegel calls it, and it is through art that suffering finds its own voice.[15] Adorno maintains that the most radical artists have followed this edict, such as the composer Arnold Schoenberg[16] and the writers Samuel Beckett and Franz Kafka.[17]

Adorno eulogizes Schoenberg's music because it was deliberately atonal and through this technique he was able to offer a frightening power in his work through harshness and discordance.[18] In particular, he mentions Schoenberg's piece, *A Survivor from Warsaw*, a tribute to the Jewish victims of Nazism, as an example of how autonomous art can evoke the sheer hell of the suffering endured, and as an affront to the consciences of the German people. Nonetheless, even Schoenberg is not immune from allowing his art to turn these victims into works of art themselves, because the musical rendering of the physical pain suffered by the Jews offers the possibility that some pleasure can be gained from it.

Adorno then considers Picasso's painting *Guernica*, which depicts the bombing of the town in 1937 during the Spanish Civil War by twenty-eight German planes. Adorno retells the story of how an occupying German officer visited Picasso in his studio and, pointing at the picture asked, 'Did you make that?' to which Picasso responded, 'No, you did'.[19] For Adorno, *Guernica* is an autonomous work of art because it offers a determinate negation of empirical reality that destroys what destroys, and shows the guilt of what happened forever. Adorno also praises Sartre in this respect for recognizing that the autonomy of the work of art is connected to a will that is not inserted into the work, but rather connected to the work's own gesture towards reality. So the work of art does not have an end because it is an end, and each painting, statue and book issues forth an appeal to the viewer or reader.

Adorno then argues that the autonomy of artworks that do not allow themselves to be adapted to the market involuntarily become an attack against the status quo. Such an attack is not abstract from empirical reality because it is mediated through that reality within which the artist is also embedded. Adorno identifies this in the eccentric works of Beckett because they force people to recoil in horror, which they should do because he is discussing some of the darkest parts of the human condition that everyone knows, but dare not talk about, which is the dismantling of the subject.[20] Beckett's plays and his 'colossal novel *The Unnamable*', along with Kafka's prose, arouse the anxiety that existentialism only talks about, and so make works of committed art look like children's games. Any minimal promise of happiness in their works cannot be traded for consolation of any sort. Happiness can only be attained through thorough articulation to the point of wordlessness. All commitment to the world has to be cancelled if the idea of committed art is to be fulfilled.

Adorno concludes by praising the artist Paul Klee as an important figure in the production of committed and autonomous art because his work had literary roots.[21] Adorno mentions Klee's famous painting the *Angelus Novus*, in which the machine-like image of the angel forces the viewer to ask whether it is a portent of disaster or salvation. Adorno suggests that the image surpasses any overt marks of caricature and commitment and instead, in the words of Walter Benjamin who owned the painting, is an angel that takes rather than gives.

For Adorno, then, an autonomous work of art should help human beings but in a way that it seems it is not doing so and contain a hidden edict of 'it shall be different'. Its autonomy should mediate its intention through the form of the artwork, which crystallizes into a likeness of an 'other' that ought to exist and instruct us on how our lives ought to be, but again not overtly. The autonomous artwork should also present itself as politically dead even though it is inherently political.[22] Adorno specifically mentions Kafka's parable of the children's guns here because the issue of non-violence that is discussed is combined with the realization of a developing 'political paralysis'.[23] What we now need to consider is whether *Diary* can fulfil these criteria and be seen as a potent form of committed art. To help us do that, I first want to consider Coetzee's own understanding of the art of the novel.

Coetzee

In an interview with David Attwell, Coetzee considers the difference between writing fiction and writing literary criticism.[24] He admits that he finds the former allows him the 'greater freedom' to follow where his thinking takes him. One reason for this, he explains further, is that he is not a trained philosopher and 'much of contemporary criticism has become very much a variety of philosophizing'. Additionally, he also thinks in a 'slow . . . painstaking and myopic manner' and he does not 'think or act in sweeps'. It would, therefore, be pointless for him to rethink Dostoevsky in Derridean terms or, what interests him more, rethink Derrida in Dostoevskian terms, because he does not have the mind or philosophical equipment to do so.

Another reason Coetzee gives for preferring to write fiction rather than literary and philosophical criticism is the difference between these two discursive modes. Writing stories is a process of freedom and irresponsibility, or rather a responsibility to something that is yet to emerge, a 'that which is not'. Writing criticism, in contrast, imposes a responsibility to a goal that has already been set by the argument, the whole philosophical tradition, and the narrow discourse of criticism itself. Coetzee indicates that if he was a truly creative critic then he would make that discourse less monological and so try to liberate it. However, he acknowledges that he does not have enough of an investment in criticism to try, because his liberating and playing with possibilities is in his fiction. Or, putting it another way, he wants to write the type of novel and work in the novel form so as not to be as contained as the philosopher when he or she plays or works with ideas. Coetzee is therefore a committed artist in the Adornoan sense because he is avoiding tendentiousness and so exploring the dilemmas and ambiguities of the issues he is concerned with.

Another way that Coetzee can be seen as a committed artist is evinced in a review he wrote of Phillip Roth's *The Plot Against America*.[25] Coetzee notes how Roth made a public declaration that tried to dispel a particular interpretation of the novel. Coetzee rejects such an attempt and states that 'a novelist as seasoned as Roth' should know that the stories they set out to write 'sometimes begin to write themselves' and that 'their truth and falsehood' is no longer within their jurisdiction, so 'declarations of authorial intent carry no weight'. Additionally, Coetzee makes the pertinent point that once the book is published it 'becomes the property of its readers, who, given half a chance, will twist its meaning in accord with their own preconceptions and desires'. Coetzee notes that Roth is aware of this because he reminds us that even though Kafka did not write his novels as political allegories, East European Communists interpreted them in that way to use for their own political ends.

In Coetzee's own case the picture that has been painted of him is that he is an apolitical figure. This began with his fellow South African writer Nadine Gordimer's book review of his first Booker prize winner, *The Life and Times of Michael K*.[26] Coetzee makes an interesting response to this charge as he explains why, from the novel, he could be construed in this way.[27] He relates the scene where Michael K hides away while a group of guerrillas are close by. K thinks about joining them but ultimately decides not to and Coetzee admits that this is the 'most politically naked moment in the novel'. On a simple reading it seems that K is a 'model either of modest prudence or of cowardice masquerading as commitment to a humbler function', which in his case is to grow pumpkins for those fighting on the front line. Moreover, it also implies that being 'humble' is being 'noble' and that growing pumpkins is more important than shooting people, which leads to the questions levelled at him by Gordimer: why does K not go off and fight and why is it that Coetzee could not offer us a different book with a more courageous hero? What type of moral behaviour was K meant to show us? As Coetzee explains, to a reader taking this interpretation, K is simply evading the 'overriding political question: how shall the tyranny of apartheid be ended?' From this viewpoint, Coetzee continues, the text seems to turn upon itself by reflecting upon its own textuality and becomes simply 'evasion'.

Coetzee's response is to state that 'one writes the books one wants to write. One doesn't write the books one doesn't want to write'. The emphasis here, he specifies, is on the 'want' and not the 'one'. The 'want' has a resistance to being known but the different book where K is a hero and joins the guerrillas is not a book that he wanted to write in the sense that he felt he could do so successfully, to be 'able to bring it off', however much he may have wanted to.[28] In contrast, Coetzee considers that what he wants to write is a 'question to prospect, to open up, perhaps, in the present dialogue, but not to mine, to exploit: too much of the fictional enterprise depends on it'.[29] He then contends further that it is as unproductive to find the answer to why one desires because in doing so the answer can mean the end of desire and its production.

It is clear from these comments, then, that Coetzee could not use his own art in the way Sartre and Brecht have, as a form of didactic preaching, which Adorno is so critical of. Coetzee's emphasis on, in Adorno's language, the autonomy of the artwork, its capacity to go beyond authorial intention and take on a life of its own, shows that as a novelist he is being true to committed art in the Adornoan sense. If he had conceded to Gordimer's charge to make Michael K a more overtly political character it would have descended into the bad art of sermonizing as in the case of Sartre and Brecht. Coetzee as a committed artist cannot reduce himself to that because he wants to probe and open up discussion and problematize it rather than close it down. Asking Coetzee to be overtly political is as crude and meaningless as asking Kafka to be, even though his own works, as we saw above, can be interpreted in this manner. As Adorno states, committed art gets its commitment politically by not being political and that is why Kafka, Beckett and so on are the great writers of the twentieth century – a judgement that Coetzee would also agree with.

This raises the issue that we mentioned at the outset: if Coetzee is an adherent of committed art in the Adornoan sense, as we have tried to show here, then how do we understand what appears to be an overtly political novel with *Diary*, especially as its main character JC seems to represent the author? The answer must be that if Coetzee were to engage in such preaching then he would be failing what he thinks great art should be doing. To see whether he accomplishes this means first examining some examples of politics in the novel through the strong opinions of JC.

JC and politics

There is much discussion on what political thought JC subscribes to. Anya and Alan think at first that he is a socialist but Anya notes that his hostility to the state puts him in the anarchist camp. JC himself in the chapter entitled 'On having thoughts' ponders on this issue (203). He pronounces that if he were to give his brand of political thought a label, he would call it 'pessimistic anarchistic quietism, or anarchist quietistic pessimism, or pessimistic quietistic anarchism'. Anarchism, because what is wrong with politics is power itself. Quietism, as he has his own doubts about the will to change the world because the will contains the drive to power, and pessimism because he is sceptical that things can be changed. He also links pessimism to the notion of original sin and the fact that humankind is imperfectable. As he reflects on these thoughts, he then questions whether he qualifies as a thinker at all – a thinker in the sense that they have thoughts about politics or anything else. He then confesses that this is because he has never been easy with abstractions or good at abstract thought (203).

Politically this view is similar to Adorno's own pessimistic hopefulness or hope without hope.[30] Adorno was sceptical of social movements because he saw them as ideological and lusting after power. In opposition to this, he had his own negative pessimism or negative utopianism which we discover in art rather than through political activity and engagement. JC seems to be saying something similar in terms of political action and that, for him, as a novelist, the artwork is enough. It is then up to philosophers and critics to analyse the artwork.

This tension between the aesthetic and the political is also evident when Anya asks JC to write another novel rather than give his strong opinions, and he replies that he does not have the endurance any more (54). She thinks that given we have all got opinions about politics, it is better to tell a story as people will sit up and listen to you (55). She asserts that she enjoys a good story with human interest that she can relate to, and there is nothing wrong with that (77). JC responds by asserting that 'stories tell themselves, they don't get told' and you should 'never try to impose yourself', but 'wait for the story to speak for itself' and 'hope that it isn't born deaf and dumb and blind'. In this way, *Diary* can be seen as a form of committed art in the positive Adornoan sense of the term because it is refusing didacticism in the very process of seemingly enunciating it, and the author is not pursuing a particular angle on an issue but waiting for the inspiration to emerge. Anya wants immediacy and a direct relation with the storyteller, which is bad art on an Adornoan reading and also in the opinion of JC.

Such tension and ambiguity is also present in a discussion of terrorism. JC notes the increased level of surveillance by governments throughout the world, and bemoans how their one-dimensional understanding assumes that anything worth knowing can be uncovered without much effort (22). A world of surveillance and curbs on freedom of speech means a world without secrets and the loss of a world when secrets exerted their power over people's lives, as in the novels of Dickens and Henry James. JC disparages these 'masters of information' because they have 'forgotten about poetry, where words may have a meaning quite different from what the lexicon says, where the metaphoric spark is always one jump ahead of the decoding function, where another, unforeseen reading is always possible' (23). The juxtaposition that JC seems to be making is between the political elites that see the world in stark terms, as in the case of George W. Bush's refrain that you are either with us or against us on the war on terror, and the means used to prosecute that war (20). JC is telling us what makes great art and why those in power, the 'masters of surveillance', are incapable of appreciating it. They miss the subliminal message, the saying without saying, which is the basis of committed art, and a less one-dimensional understanding of society.

This again raises the issue of the role of the artist in relation to politics, and JC makes some pertinent points in this regard when he comments on Harold Pinter's speech at the award ceremony for his Nobel Prize for Literature (127). Pinter made a sustained and savage attack on Tony Blair for his part in the war in Iraq, and called for him to be put on trial as a war criminal. JC then states:

> When one speaks in one's own person – that is, not through one's art
> – to denounce some politician or other, using the rhetoric of the agora,
> one embarks on a contest which one is likely to lose because it takes
> place on ground where one's opponent is far more practised and adept.

Consequently, JC concludes that anyone doing so will be quickly disparaged and ridiculed. In actuality, Pinter's speech was largely, and perhaps deliberately, ignored in the media. JC sees what Pinter has done as being foolhardy but certainly not cowardly, and suggests that there is a time when the shame is so great that you must put prudence to one side and 'act, that is to say, speak'. And of course the irony is that Coetzee appears to be doing this in *Diary*, given the main narrator is very close to the identity of the author. On one level Adorno would find this to be a form of preaching and by definition bad art. However, that Anya is allowed to undermine such preaching with her common sense view of the world problematizes it in a way that suggests an irony and ambiguity that results in committed art in the good sense of the term. Coetzee's novel is, therefore, following Adorno, mediating its intention through the form of the artwork, which crystallizes into a likeness of an 'other' that ought to exist. The 'other' is the possibility of a change in the consciousness of Anya and her siding with JC over her boyfriend Alan, as we shall now see.

Anya

Anya's place in the novel is pivotal because she is seemingly representative of the masses. She is portrayed, initially at least, as having limited political and cultural knowledge and she stands midway between the strong opinions against the status quo by JC and Alan's support of neoliberalism. She refers to both of them at one point in the middle of the novel as the old bull and the young bull fighting it out, while she is the young cow they are trying to impress who is getting bored with their antics (109). This mirrors her attitude at the start of the novel when she bemoans how bored she is because all JC writes about is politics, which is pointless because people have had enough of it (26). But of course the type of politics that JC is writing about and criticizing is the politics of neoliberalism, which her boyfriend Alan, obsessed by greed and money, epitomizes. JC offers a more nuanced politics that is against the status quo, but Anya cannot see that yet. Her awareness increases developmentally throughout the novel as she mediates between the views of JC and Alan and I will now highlight some of the ways in which this is done.

Anya notes how JC has tried to compare the Australian prime minister of that time, John Howard, and the Liberals in general, as being Kurosawa's *The Seven Samurai* all over again, which leads her to exclaim: 'Who is going to believe that?' (33). She has seen the film herself in Japanese with Chinese subtitles and most of the time it was incomprehensible to her. She instead focused on the naked thighs of the crazy man with the topknot. The implication is that Anya, as a representative of the general masses, will not understand JC's hidden message, and neither will anyone else. JC is using cinematic art to try to rupture the status quo subliminally, but Anya's contention is that it will only be appreciated among the elite. What this incident highlights for us is that through JC the consequences of endorsing high art in this way are being problematized or, in Coetzee's terms, opened up and contended. From our Adornoan perspective, JC is being true to committed art because he is using the analogy to fuse aesthetics and politics, not in a crude manner, but in terms of a juxtaposition that through the effort of interpretation can be grasped for those prepared to make the effort to discern it. If JC is overtly tendentious then the aesthetic moment of his analogy will descend into bad art, but Anya's challenge is a pertinent one. How are people going to believe that when most people have not seen the film or might not, as in Anya's case, understand it?

This is evinced a little later when she again tells him that he should write about anything except politics because his kind of writing does not work with it (35). Politics, she continues, is people shouting each other down, getting their own way and it has nothing to do with logic. She then compares politics to air or pollution and reasons that we cannot fight pollution, but we should either ignore it or adapt to it. So in one sense, Anya is expressing an oft-heard refrain that turns many people off from, in this description, bourgeois politics centred on political elites that seem estranged from the mass of people that they are meant to represent. Nevertheless, we then discover that for her this political apathy is not total because she does vote. Alan, unsurprisingly, votes for Howard and she informs JC that she was not going to but in the end she also did, justifying her decision with 'better the devil you know than the devil you don't' (41). Nevertheless, there is a hint here that she was coerced to do so by Alan as he said to her: 'shall we?' She reflects that she could have said no to him, but she decided not to and now finds herself living with him as 'Ms Needle' to his 'Mr Haystack, tight as twins'. The saying implies a near impossible search for something, and it raises the question of what the search is meant to be symbolic of. Could it be Anya's own identity and emerging awareness of both the inner world she inhabits between the competing perspectives of JC and Alan? That is what I will be arguing as we see the further development of her identity throughout the novel.

The suspicion that Alan coerced her into voting for Howard is raised further because their initial conversation extends into the evening when they go to a restaurant and he reiterates his question to her: 'Shall we or shan't we?' (42). The fact that he is posing the question collectively is even more evident that he is pressurizing her, because, given his own views, it would be unthinkable that he would not vote for a neoliberal such as Howard. This forces her to say to herself: 'Shall I or shan't?', a thought she cannot say to him as he expects her to go along with his decision. She finally makes her choice unreflectively by saying the nursery rhyme 'eeny-meeny-miny-mo' and reveals 'that is how Howard got elected. The nigger you catch by the toe. The nigger you know. Oops. Negro'. This comment is taken from the crudest use of the rhyme and is not expanded on further but it seems an implicit criticism of the racism of Howard and his administration, perhaps reflecting the impact it had on people such as Anya, even though she is from the Philippines herself.

Indeed, the racism issue is discussed explicitly by JC in the chapter 'On asylum in Australia', where he considers the way refugees are handled in that country (111). What baffles him is not necessarily the harsh laws that are used, but the way they are implemented. He finds it hard to make sense of how a 'decent, generous, easygoing people' can 'close their eyes' and treat such vulnerable people with 'such heartlessness, such grim callousness'. His answer is that to save their own sense of being generous and caring, they close their eyes to it. The implication appears to be that Anya is, at this point, representative of such a view. She realizes that what she has said is wrong – 'Oops' – but quickly covers over it and moves on, no doubt as the vast majority of the general Australian public also do, from JC's perspective that is.

The other example of the inherent racism in Australian society is of course the treatment of the Aboriginal Australians. JC examines whether white Australians should issue an apology to them, and if such an apology has any meaning without some form of restitution (107). He compares this situation to that in South Africa where the handing back of land from white to black is a 'practical possibility', whereas in Australia 'nothing so dramatic can be projected' because the 'pressure from below is, by comparison, slight and intermittent'. So Anya, as part of the general populace, seems to have absorbed these views but the hope is, both for JC and for us, that she will become more enlightened as she engages with his own opinions.

We get the sense that Anya is beginning to change about a third of the way into the novel when she starts to feel sorry for JC, as he is on his own and sits in his flat all day or goes to the park to talk to the birds (78). Alan bluntly tells her not to feel too sorry for him because he is lucky to be turning his idle opinions into cash (79). Alan sees it as 'ingenious' that JC can be working in the two dimensions, the individual and the economic, at the same time. For Alan, the individual dimension is nobody's business but your own, and the economic dimension is the bigger picture. Anya admits that she probably agrees and can see that it makes sense but she argues about it anyway and ponders on whether 'that is all there is'. A critical spark has been lit that is starting to make Anya think differently about the world, especially as it is seen through the neoliberal eyes of Alan. He detects this and it makes him realize that she has some 'spunk' and a 'mind of her own', and is not some dummy with a nice body that he dumped his wife for. However, as Anya indicates, she has not got as much spunk as her 'lord and master', which is how she normally refers to him, although she does then tell us that she learned a long time ago that it was not worth getting into an argument with him and winning (83). Even so, she reveals that they still argue a lot (84), so there is a more determined side to Anya's character but she chooses to hide that for an easy life with someone, secure in the knowledge that a neoliberal world is the only possible one. Unfortunately, for Alan that world will soon come crashing down as she begins to see the type of warped human values that such an ideology gives expression to.

The key event is when Anya discovers that Alan has inserted a spying device on JC's computer, and he sees that he has got $3 million or more in saving accounts that are earning hardly any interest (121–4). She is angry when Alan suggests that both of them could make better use of the money and remonstrates with him on what it has got to do with them (126). Alan suggests that they take the money, invest it, and then give JC a share back, unbeknown to him (127). Anya thinks that Alan is crazy and could jeopardize his career but he tells her if anything went wrong it would be traceable only to a clinic for Parkinson's disease in Switzerland and then a holding company in the Cayman Islands (131). Alan is starting to be exposed for the fraudster he is, especially when Anya asks how he got the spyware onto JC's computer (133). He readily admits that he put it on one of the disks she gave him, and she responds: 'So you used me'. Unperturbed, Alan informs her that even if he had not used her he would have found some way of doing it (134). His justification for doing so is that a serious amount of money is being wasted and what he is doing is 'not a game'. She suddenly becomes aware of the immorality of Alan's way of life, because she thinks to herself that it certainly is not a game, but not in the way that he thinks (135). For her, it is 'the real thing' and while she knows that he has never hidden from her that he works in the 'shades of grey that are neither dark nor light', she concludes that in the case of JC, Alan is 'crossing the line from grey into black, into the out-and-out blackest'.

In her new heightened state of ethical awareness, Anya now tells Alan that she is not sure she is with him on his plan (136). Alan advises her to just forget that they ever had this conversation, and he can do it all on his own while she continues being nice to JC (137). She then ponders that Alan does this with people's money in the stock market every day so in one sense it is harmless, but then she asks herself whether she is living with a professional swindler (139). Anya then states quite clearly that she is suddenly seeing Alan in a different way and she tells him that if he goes ahead with his scheme then things will never be the same between them (143). She asks him if this is the type of person he actually is and intimates that, if so, things will change (149). He agrees to drop the idea, but she only half believes him (150–1). Eventually, they do separate over the issue, and she tells JC that she is going to see her mother (171). She treats it is a trial separation but there will be no going back for Anya now. It is therefore fitting that Alan tells JC that Anya saved him from being robbed: 'She pleaded on your behalf. He is a good man, she said, his heart is in the right place, with the downtrodden and oppressed, with the voiceless ones, with the humble beasts' (172). So her turnaround from a seemingly unthinking apolitical figure is clear, but this does not stop Alan from undermining her by also telling JC that Anya has told him in confidence that she is disappointed in the way his book on strong opinions has turned out (190). He ironically says to JC that he hopes that has not hurt him and suggests that Anya is not a political animal anyway, so his adumbrations on politics had no effect on her, as she wanted something more 'toothsome' and 'personal' (191). However, she has had something personal and political, because her relationship with JC has made her see that Alan's way of living is not for her and it has also exposed Alan for what he is: a crook.

With Alan out of her life, she sends a letter to JC and discloses to him that she blushes when thinking about the comments she made about his opinions, especially as he is a world-famous author (196). But then she thinks to herself that *'maybe he appreciated having a perspective from below, so to speak, an opinion of his opinions'* given that he was a bit out of touch with the modern world. In the letter, she also maintains that she does not think JC influenced her, but she was lucky to meet him when she did (203). She concedes that she would still probably be with Alan if it was not for JC, but maintains that he did not influence her as she was herself before she met him and has not changed. Even so, she then concedes that JC did open her eyes and showed her that there was a different way of living, of having ideas and expressing them, although she thinks that she does not have the talent to do that, unlike him (204). So there was a potential for a raising of her consciousness there in the first place, it just needed someone – JC – and something – the behaviour of Alan – to bring it out. Indeed, her changed consciousness also breeds a new-found confidence as she tells him that:

> If I have to be honest, the strong opinions on politics and so forth were not your best, maybe because there is no story in politics, maybe because you are a bit out of touch, maybe because the style does not suit you. But I really do hope you will publish your soft opinions one day. If you do, remember to send a copy to the little typist who showed you the way. (222)

It is as though Coetzee is mocking himself here, in that the style does not suit him because it is not the role of the author to put these strong opinions forward in this way. JC should remain within his role as a novelist and avoid the temptation to engage in overt politics, just as Coetzee seems to do. Consequently, it is not just the way Anya's consciousness changes through her contact with JC, but also the way in which JC's consciousness develops through his involvement with Anya. By staying within his art and making it committed in the Adornoan sense, the didacticism of JC's strong opinions will be subverted as the artwork takes on an autonomous life of its own.

9 • Conclusion: The Aesthetic Moment

We have been in the company of a cast of characters conjured up by four great novelists that have allowed us to explore various facets of human identity through the medium of contemporary fiction and via the lens of social and political philosophy. The emphasis on exploring identity through the characters is an important one and it is of note that Michel Houellebecq made a telling comment on how his own work is viewed in this respect. An interviewer reminded him that he had rebuked book reviewers for not focusing enough on the characters in his novels. Houellebecq's reflection on this issue was as follows:

> One precious thing about ordinary readers is that sometimes they develop feelings for the characters. This is something critics never discuss. Which is a shame. The Anglo-Saxon critics do good plot summaries but they don't talk about the characters either. Readers, however, do it uninhibitedly.[1]

Whether Houellebecq was being fair with his reviewers is another matter, but it is clear that the approach taken in this book falls into the category of 'ordinary reader'. The focus is on the characters and my 'feelings' towards them. From the outset, the aim has been to examine the operations of the aesthetic self in aesthetic moments that challenge the status quo and make us think differently about the conventional wisdom that governs our respective worlds in all their complexity. The theorists I have called upon here to illuminate the dilemmas that these characters face have hopefully brought forth different ways to contemplate, not only their condition, but the universal moment of the human condition, as they and we forge our identities and, hopefully, from my perspective, our aesthetic selves. To those of us who are Houellebecq's 'ordinary readers', the feelings that we have towards these characters should therefore make us engage in a reflexive process as we see how they begin, through often unexpected happenings and circumstances, to question their own identity. By being drawn into their worlds and the dilemmas that they face, we can engage in a self-interrogation of our own selves aided by the different theoretical frameworks that have been discussed throughout this book. If we do, then, what questions might we ask from the selected novels that have just been examined?

Did you feel crushed under the weight of the despotism suffered by the four main characters in *Unbearable Lightness* and identify with their own responses to such a terrible predicament? Did it make you consider those who are under tyrannical rule today and empathize with their plight? Did it make you want to become a free spirit? Or did you come to the conclusion that the flight into lightness might not be the answer, and instead you need to embrace the dialectical interplay of both weight and lightness in life?

Did Chantal and Jean-Marc make you question the identity of both yourself and a significant 'other'? Are you now on a quest to achieve moments of mutual recognition, both interpersonally and collectively, to avoid the damaging inequalities that can arise from the life and death struggle of the master/slave dialectic?

Did you deem that Robbie's downfall under the weight of class prejudice means little today in a society where class has apparently disappeared? Or can you see how Robbie's plight is manifest in the lives of many different people who either embark on the path of cultural dislocation, with all the pressures of conformity and a rejection of one's class background that might impose, or never even make it to that stage in life? Did you see Cecilia's rejection of her comfortable upper-middle-class existence to engage in a form of class solidarity with those supposedly beneath her as a form of folly, or were you heartened by the courage and affirmation that encapsulated her new identity?

If Lurie and Perowne should somehow meet and share their own experiences, would they both realize how their identities have changed for the better, that their previous, insulated selves, demarcating the 'other' as something to be avoided or abused, was something to be ashamed of? Is it necessary that they have to be confronted with such a mistaken view of the world by their own world being invaded in such a horrific manner? Did you identify with them? Perhaps you identified with Baxter, the outcast, made even worse by the degenerative disease that was engulfing him. Or perhaps, like Perowne, you eventually empathized with him, even though he had violently threatened both you and your own family, but all the same, whose actions you came to understand, although not completely forgive. Or perhaps you thought it was all Baxter's own fault and just down to bad luck; so you turned your back on him.

Were you fired by Michel's love for Annabelle and did you weep over her life cut short and endured under a logic of instrumentalism that emanates from a system that knows nothing of compassion? Did the depiction of the atomized world we inhabit make you consider whether you, too, might be alienated, and being conscious of this affirm moments of disalienation, while also being aware of its contingency and the possibility of falling into further alienations? Or perhaps you might be in the even worse state of not being conscious of your own alienation?

Did the absurdity of Michel's existence and his brash challenge to conventional mores shock you, or could you appreciate that a junk culture can produce junk people who rage at the world but can only find tragic solace in individualism and hedonism? Have you confronted the absurd's terrifying question of what the meaning of life is, as he did or, like Valérie, have you not even got the time for contemplation due to the monotony of the eight-hour day and the excessive pressures that it produces and makes it into a twelve-hour day or even more? Perhaps you are not even allowed into this daily grind and exist as best as you can in exclusion zones on the outskirts of Paris where the middle classes dare not go for fear of attack. Or perhaps you were shocked to find that such places actually existed, or rather that you knew that they did but would prefer not to let it penetrate your consciousness, until *Platform* forced you to, that is.

Did you identify with the neoliberal Alan of *Diary of a Bad Year*? Was that the path we should go down in these catastrophic times where a flawed model of economic and social organization still exerts its hegemonic power, as it impoverishes and destroys the lives of the majority of people while lining the pockets of a minority? Where making money and the pursuit of narrow self-interest with little concern for anyone else is lauded as the best foundation on which to construct a society, albeit if that society is not even meant to exist in the first place? Do you identify with that?

My own answers to these questions are here in what has gone before through the utilization of social and political philosophy to illuminate our understanding of these great novels, and the human predicaments that are explored within. By making us think differently about the world, by inspiring us to question what is, and imagine what might be, we can perhaps begin to realize our aesthetic selves on the path to a transcendence of identity, as we explore the varied experiences that constitute the aesthetic moment.

Notes

Introduction

1 Herbert Marcuse, *The Aesthetic Dimension* (London: Macmillan, 1979), p. 1.
2 Ian Fraser, *Dialectics of the Self: Transcending Charles Taylor* (Exeter: Imprint Academic, 2007), ch. 7.
3 Martha Nussbaum, *Love's Knowledge. Essays on Philosophy and Literature* (Oxford and New York: Oxford University Press, 1990), p. 50.
4 Pauline Johnson, *Marxist Aesthetics. The Foundations within Everyday Life for an Emancipated Consciousness* (London: Routledge and Kegan Paul, 1984), p. 1.
5 Nussbaum, *Love's Knowledge.* See also her *Upheavals of Thought. The Intelligence of the Emotions* (Cambridge: Cambridge University Press, 2007).
6 Richard Rorty, *Contingency, Irony and Solidarity* (Cambridge: Cambridge University Press, 1989).
7 Judith Butler, 'Judith Butler: reanimating the soul', in Mike Gane (ed.), *The Future of Social Theory* (London and New York: Continuum, 2004), pp. 47–76. Cf. Judith Butler et al., *What's Left of Theory?* (London: Routledge, 2000).
8 John J. Joughin and Simon Malpas (eds), *The New Aestheticism* (Manchester and New York: Manchester University Press, 2003).
9 Terry Eagleton, *The Ideology of the Aesthetic* (Oxford: Blackwell, 1990).

Chapter 1

1 Milan Kundera, *The Unbearable Lightness of Being* (London: Faber and Faber, 1995). Page references to this text will appear in parentheses throughout.
2 For a useful and succinct overview of these events, see Lawrence Wilde, *Modern European Socialism* (Aldershot: Dartmouth, 1994),

pp. 147–52. For a personal account, see Alexander Dubček's autobiography, *Hope Dies Last* (London: Harper Collins, 1993).

3   Friedrich Nietzsche, *The Birth of Tragedy* (Cambridge: Cambridge University Press, 2008), 1. Numbers refer to sections for this text.

4   Ibid., 1, 2, 9, 16. Cf. Julian Young, *Nietzsche's Philosophy of Art* (Cambridge: Cambridge University Press, 1999), 32–3.

5   Daniel Came, 'The aesthetic justification of experience', in Keith Ansell Pearson (ed.), *A Companion to Nietzsche* (Oxford: Wiley-Blackwell, 2009), p. 51.

6   Nietzsche, *The Birth of Tragedy*, 1.

7   Young, *Nietzsche's Philosophy of Art*, p. 35

8   Nietzsche, *The Birth of Tragedy*, 1.

9   Ibid., 16.

10 Martha Nussbaum, 'The transfiguration of intoxication: Nietzsche, Schopenhauer and Dionysus', in Salim Kemal, Ivan Gaskell and Daniel W. Conway (eds), *Nietzsche, Philosophy and the Arts* (Cambridge: Cambridge University Press, 2002), p. 56.

11 Richard Schacht, 'Introduction' to Friedrich Nietzsche, *Human, All Too Human* (Cambridge: Cambridge University Press, 2007), p. ix.

12 Milan Kundera, *Testaments Betrayed* (London: Faber and Faber, 1996), p. 168.

13 Alexander Nehamas, *Nietzsche: Life as Literature* (Cambridge, Mass.: Harvard University Press, 1985), p. 3.

14 Friedrich Nietzsche, *Human, All Too Human* (Cambridge: Cambridge University Press, 2007). HH, I, Preface, P6. Abbreviated to HH, followed by volume number, I or II, P for paragraph and then the number of the paragraph.

15 HH, I, Preface, P6.

16 HH, I, Preface, P2.

17 HH, I, Preface, P7.

18 HH, Preface, P5.

19 Nehamas, *Nietzsche*, p. 72.

20 Schacht, 'Introduction', pp. xv–vi.

21 Nehamas, *Nietzsche*, p. 3.

22 Ibid., pp. 3–4.

23 Ibid.

24 HH, II, P174.

25 HH, I, Preface, P1.

26 Friedrich Nietzsche, *The Gay Science* (Cambridge: Cambridge University Press, 2008), P341. P refers to paragraph.

27 Bernd Magnus and Kathleen M. Higgins, 'Nietzsche's works and their themes', in Bernd Magnus and Kathleen M. Higgins (eds), *The Cambridge Companion to Nietzsche* (Cambridge: Cambridge University

Press, 2007), p. 37. Aaron Ridley links the demand explicitly but only briefly to Kundera's *Unbearable Lightness* in his *Nietzsche on Art* (London: Routledge, 2007), pp. 106, 107 n.20.

28 Magnus and Higgins, 'Nietzsche's works', pp. 39, 62 n.38.
29 Nehamas, *Nietzsche*, pp. 150, 169.
30 Ibid., p. 151.
31 Ibid., pp. 164, i. He cites Nietzsche, HH, I, P208 for support.
32 Nehamas, *Nietzsche*, p. 165.
33 Ibid., p. 168.
34 See Milan Kundera, *The Art of the Novel* (London: Faber and Faber, 2005), p. 29.
35 Ibid., pp. 29–30.
36 Ibid., p. 31.
37 Ibid., p. 44.
38 Milan Kundera, *The Curtain* (London: Faber and Faber, 2007), p. 64.
39 Kundera, *The Art of the Novel*, pp. 27, 34.
40 Ibid., p. 35.
41 Kundera, *Testaments*, p. 172.
42 Ibid., pp. 172, 148.
43 Ibid., 172.
44 Ibid., pp. 172–3
45 Ibid., p. 173.
46 Ibid., p. 174.
47 It is translated as 'return' in the novel but I will follow the translations of Nietzsche that consistently refer to it as 'recurrence'.
48 Friedrich Nietzsche, *Twilight of the Idols*, in Friedrich Nietzsche, *The Anti-Christ, Ecce Homo, Twilight of the Idols and Other Writings* (Cambridge: Cambridge University Press, 2005), P2, P1. P refers to paragraph.
49 Tomas has a similar thought when he refuses to sign a petition asking for the release of political prisoners (pp. 214–18).
50 Sabina also realizes that when she receives the letter informing her of their deaths (p. 121).
51 This, therefore, challenges the claim by Marijeta Bozovic that none of the characters can reconcile the 'key dichotomy' of lightness and weight. See her 'Sparknote on *The Unbearable Lightness of Being*'. Available at *http://www.sparknotes.com/lit/unbearablelightness*, accessed 9 February 2009.
52 Kundera, *The Art of the Novel*, pp. 17–18.
53 Nietzsche, *The Birth of Tragedy*, 19.
54 Kundera, *The Art of the Novel*, p. 18.
55 John Banville, 'Light but sound', *The Guardian*, 1 May (2004). Available at *http://www.guardian.co.uk/books/2004/may/01/fiction.johnbanville*, accessed 9 February 2009.

56 E. L. Doctorow, 'Four characters under two tyrannies'. Available at *http://www.kundera.de/english/Bibliography/The_Unbearable_Lightness_of_Be/the_unbearable_lightness_of_be.html*, accessed 20 April 2011.

Chapter 2

1 Milan Kundera, *Identity* (London: Faber and Faber, 1998). Page references to this text will appear in parentheses throughout.
2 G. W. F. Hegel, *Phenomenology of Spirit* (Oxford: Oxford University Press, 1997). Referenced by paragraph number.
3 Ibid., para. 178.
4 Ibid., para. 179.
5 Ibid., para. 184.
6 Ibid., para. 186.
7 Ibid.
8 Ibid., para. 187.
9 Ibid., para. 188.
10 Ibid., para. 189.
11 Ibid., para. 190.
12 Ibid., paras 191, 192.
13 Ibid., para. 192.
14 Ibid., para. 195.
15 Ibid.
16 Ibid., para. 196.
17 Alexandre Kojève, *Introduction to the Reading of Hegel: Lectures on the Phenomenology of Spirit* (London: Basic Books, 1969), p. 29.
18 Allen W. Wood, *Hegel's Ethical Thought* (Cambridge: Cambridge University Press, 1990), p. 89.
19 Kojève, *Introduction to the Reading of Hegel*, p. 58.
20 George Armstrong Kelly, 'Notes on Hegel's "Lordship and Bondage"', in Alasdair McIntyre (ed.), *Hegel. A Collection of Critical Essays* (Notre Dame: University of Notre Dame Press, 1972), p. 195.
21 Ibid., pp. 191–2, 195.
22 Ibid., p. 195.
23 Ibid., pp. 195–6.
24 G. W. F. Hegel, *Elements of the Philosophy of Right* (Cambridge: Cambridge University Press, 1991), para. 158A. Para. refers to paragraph and A to addition.
25 Armstrong Kelly, 'Notes on Hegel's "Lordship and Bondage"', pp. 195–6.
26 Hegel, *Elements of the Philosophy of Right*, Part 3.
27 For the argument that once Hegel's notion of love enters into the

family it is denied to women, see Patricia J. Mills, 'Hegel and the "woman question": recognition and intersubjectivity', in L. M. G. Clarke and L. Lange (eds), *The Sexism of Social and Political Theory* (Canada: University of Toronto Press, 1979), p. 89. For the rejection of the master/slave relation and the recognition on which it is based, see Genevieve Lloyd, *The Man of Reason* (London: Methuen, 1984), p. 92.

28 See, for example, the dismissive review by George Steiner, 'She's scared to blink in case her man turns into somebody else', *The Observer*, 19 April (1990). Available at *http://books.guardian.co.uk/print/0,,3924440-99930,00.html*, accessed 23 June 2008. For a more positive reading see, for example, Christopher Lehmann-Haupt, 'Nothing is as it seems but who can be sure?', *New York Review of Books*, 7 May (1998). Available at *http://www.nytimes.com/books/98/05/03/daily/kundera-book-review.html*, accessed 23 June 2008.

29 François Ricard, *Agnès's Final Afternoon. An Essay on the Work of Milan Kundera* (London: Faber and Faber, 2003), p. 107.

30 Ibid., p. 108.

31 Ibid., p. 112.

32 Ibid. Cf. Milan Kundera, *The Art of the Novel* (London: Faber and Faber, 2005), p. 16.

33 Ricard, *Agnès's Final Afternoon*, p. 113.

Chapter 3

1 Ian McEwan, *Atonement* (London: Jonathan Cape, 2001). Page references to this text will appear in parentheses throughout.

2 Ian McEwan, 'The master', *The Guardian*, 7 April (2005).

3 Robert McCrum, 'The story of his life', *The Observer*, 23 January (2005).

4 E. P. Thompson, *The Making of the English Working Class* (Harmondsworth: Penguin, 1970) and 'Class and class struggle', in Peter Joyce (ed.), *Class* (Oxford and New York: Oxford University Press, 1995).

5 The few exceptions are Anne Rooney, *Atonement* (London: York Press, 2006), pp. 138–41, and even more briefly in Patrick Parrinder, *Nation and Novel. The English Novel from its Origins to the Present Day* (Oxford: Oxford University Press, 2006), p. 406.

6 As James Wood points out, even this might not be 'true' as Briony appears to 'float a hypothesis' that Cecilia and Robbie might have died, rather than actually confirm it. James Wood, 'Ian McEwan, *Atonement*', in Liam McIlvanney and Ray Ryan (eds), *The Good of the Novel* (London: Faber and Faber, 2011), p. 18.

7   Thompson, *The Making*, p. 9
8   Ibid., pp. 9–10.
9   Ibid., p. 11.
10 Ibid., p. 12.
11 Ibid., p. 13.
12 Ibid., p. 10.
13 Ibid., p. 11.
14 Ibid., p. 10.
15 Thompson, 'Class and class struggle', p. 134.
16 Ibid., pp. 134–5.
17 Ibid., p. 136.
18 Karl Marx, *Capital*, vol. 1 (Harmondsworth: Penguin, 1988), p. 165.
19 Georg Lukács, *History and Class Consciousness* (London: Merlin, 1990), p. 90; Cf. Matt Perry, *Marxism and History* (Basingstoke: Palgrave, 2002), p. 100.
20 Thompson, 'Class and class struggle', p. 137.
21 Ibid., p. 138.
22 Ibid., p. 139.
23 Ibid., p. 141.
24 Ibid., pp. 141–2.
25 Ibid., p. 142.
26 The controversy arose due to the division that was created between his approach based on class experience through which subjects actively constitute themselves, and the Althusserian structuralism that appeared to see subjects determined by the capitalist system.
27 Beverley Skeggs, *Class, Self, Culture* (London: Routledge, 2004); Diane Reay, 'Beyond consciousness? The psychic landscape of social class', *Sociology*, 39/5 (2005), 911–28; Valerie Walkerdine, Helen Lucey and June Melody, *Growing Up Girl: Psychosocial Explorations of Gender and Class* (Basingstoke: Palgrave, 2001).
28 Andrew Sayer, *The Moral Significance of Class* (Cambridge: Cambridge University Press, 2005), p. 17.
29 Ibid., pp. 53, 97–8.
30 Stephanie Lawler, 'Introduction: class, culture and identity', *Sociology*, 39/5 (2005), 797.
31 Skeggs, *Class, Self, Culture*, pp. 41–2.
32 Ibid., p. 42.
33 Ibid., pp. 175, 194 n.1.
34 Ibid., p. 173. For the two other feminists mentioned, first Diane Reay offers what she terms a 'psychic landscape of social class', which involves a 'generative dynamic' of 'thinking, feeling and practices' in relation to class ('Beyond consciousness', 912). She therefore suggests that there is a powerful dynamic between the emotions, and psychic

responses to class and class inequalities that contribute powerfully to
the making of class, and which is why she is also concerned to re-
emphasize the importance of class consciousness and class awareness.
The resonance with Thompson should be clear here, even though Reay
does not explicitly refer to him. The very use of such an important
word as 'making' in relation to class and one of the key categories
of class consciousness reveals the continued importance of Thompson's framework even where it is unacknowledged. This also seems
remiss given that Reay adopts the theories of Bourdieu for her inves-
tigations (ibid., 913) as it was Bourdieu himself, as Skeggs points out,
that praised Thompson for his emphasis on the 'making' aspect for his
understanding of class (Skeggs, *Class, Self, Culture*, p. 18). Secondly,
Walkerdine et al. also make no reference to Thompson's work, but in a
brief and appreciative discussion of Marx, who, of course, Thompson
is drawing on, they state that Marx argued that the working class was
'made' through class struggle (*Growing Up Girl*, p. 13). Consequently,
the working class did not exist automatically, nor was it simply produced by its relation to the means of production. Rather the 'working
class is a group of people who exist historically and their designation is
heavily contested'. The link with Thompson could not be clearer here
in understanding class as a process. Moreover, the emphasis on understanding class as culture, as Thompson does, is also what Walkerdine
et al. claim is a defining characteristic of their work (ibid., p. 45).

35 Karl Marx and Frederick Engels, *The German Ideology*, in Karl Marx
and Frederick Engels, *Collected Works Vol. 5* (London: Lawrence and
Wishart, 1976), p. 47.
36 Penny Gay, 'Introduction' to William Shakespeare, *Twelfth Night*
(Cambridge: Cambridge University Press, 2003), p. 11.
37 Jonathan Noakes, 'Interview with Ian McEwan', in Margaret Reynolds and Jonathan Noakes (eds), *Ian McEwan. The Essential Guide to
Contemporary Literature* (London: Vintage, 2002), pp. 19–20.
38 Ian McEwan, 'Only love and then oblivion. Love was all they had
to set against their murderers', *The Guardian*, 15 September (2001);
Cf. Peter Childs (ed.), *The Fiction of Ian McEwan* (Houndmills: Palgrave Macmillan, 2006), p. 5.
39 Rooney, *Atonement*, p. 44.
40 Ibid., p. 77.

Chapter 4

1 Ian McEwan, *Saturday* (London: Vintage, 2006). Page references to
this text will appear in parentheses throughout.

2 Julia Kristeva, *Powers of Horror: An Essay on Abjection* (New York: Columbia University Press, 1982).
3 Julia Kristeva, *Revolution in Poetic Language* (New York: Columbia University Press, 1984), p. 21.
4 Ibid., p. 27.
5 Ibid. Cf. Nöelle McAfee, *Julia Kristeva* (New York and London: Routledge, 2004), p. 17.
6 Ibid.
7 Ibid.
8 Kristeva, *Revolution in Poetic Language*, p. 22.
9 McAfee, *Julia Kristeva*, p. 2.
10 Ibid.
11 Kelly Oliver, *Reading Kristeva. Unravelling the Double-bind* (Bloomington and Indianapolis: Indiana University Press, 1993), p. 13.
12 Kristeva, *Powers of Horror*, p. 1.
13 Ibid., p. 2.
14 Ibid., pp. 1–2.
15 Ibid., p. 4.
16 Ibid.
17 Ibid., p. 5.
18 Oliver, *Reading Kristeva*, p. 56.
19 Kristeva, *Powers of Horror*, p. 2.
20 Ibid., pp. 2–3.
21 Ibid., p. 3.
22 Ibid., p. 8.
23 Ibid., p. 5.
24 Ibid.
25 Ibid., p. 207.
26 Ibid., p. 208.
27 Anna Smith, *Julia Kristeva. Readings of Exile and Estrangement* (Houndmills: Macmillan, 1996), p. 13.
28 McAfee, *Julia Kristeva*, p. 50.
29 Lynn Wells, *Ian McEwan* (Houndmills: Palgrave, 2010), p. 117.
30 Ibid., p. 117.
31 Ibid., p. 131.
32 Ibid., p. 118.
33 Ibid.
34 Ibid., p. 129.
35 Ibid.
36 Ibid., p. 131.
37 Ibid.
38 Ibid., pp. 131–2.

39 Elizabeth Kowaleski Wallace, 'Postcolonial melancholia in Ian McEwan's *Saturday*', *Studies in the Novel*, 39/4 (winter 2007), 476. Cf. Wells, *Ian McEwan*, pp. 112–13.

40 David Lynn, 'A conversation with Ian McEwan', in Ryan Roberts (ed.), *Conversations with Ian McEwan* (Jackson: University of Mississippi Press, 2010), p. 144.

41 Ian McEwan, 'The child in time', *The Guardian Review*, 12 July (2008). Quoted in Sebastian Groes, 'Introduction. A cartography of the contemporary: mapping newness in the work of Ian McEwan', in Sebastian Groes (ed.), *Ian McEwan* (London: Continuum, 2009), p. 11.

42 Wells, *Ian McEwan*, p. 123.

43 John Banville, 'A day in the life', *New York Review of Books*, 52/9, 26 May (2005).

44 Dominic Head, *Ian McEwan* (Manchester and New York: Manchester University Press, 2007), p. 196.

45 I would like to thank Lawrence Wilde for drawing this parallel to my attention.

46 Peter Childs (ed.), *The Fiction of Ian McEwan* (Houndmills: Palgrave Macmillan, 2006), p. 147.

47 Ibid.

48 Thanks again to Lawrence Wilde for pointing this out to me.

49 Ryan Roberts, '"A thing one does": a conversation with Ian McEwan', in Ryan Roberts (ed.), *Conversations with Ian McEwan* (Jackson: University of Mississippi Press, 2010), p. 194.

Chapter 5

1 Michel Houellebecq, *Atomised* (London: Vintage, 2001). Page references to this text will appear in parentheses throughout.

2 Nancy Huston, 'Michel Houellebecq: the ecstasy of disgust', *Salmagundi*, 152 (2006), 20–37; Katherine Gantz, 'Strolling with Houellebecq: the textual terrain of postmodern flanerie', *Journal of Modern Literature*, 28/3 (spring 2005), 149–61; Jerry Andrew Varsava, 'Utopian yearnings, dystopian thoughts: Houellebecq's *The Elementary Particles* and the problem of scientific communitarianism', *College Literature*, 32/4 (2005), 145–67; Jack I. Abecassis, 'The eclipse of desire: l'affaire Houellebecq', *MLN*, 115/4 (2000), 801–26; Michael Karwowski, 'Michel Houellebecq: French novelist for our times', *Contemporary Review*, July (2003), 40–6.

3 Henri Lefebvre, *Critique of Everyday Life. Vol. I* (London and New York: Verso, 1992), pp. 169–70.

4   Henri Lefebvre, *Critique of Everyday Life. Vol. II* (London and New York: Verso, 2002), pp. 206–7.
5   Ibid., p. 207.
6   Ibid., pp. 207–8.
7   Ibid., p. 208.
8   Ibid., p. 209.
9   Ibid., pp. 209–10.
10 Ibid., pp. 213–14.
11 Ibid., p. 214.
12 Ibid., p. 215.
13 Ibid., pp. 215–16.
14 Ibid., p. 216.
15 Ibid., p. 341.
16 Ibid., pp. 341–2.
17 Ibid., p. 342.
18 Ibid., p. 211.
19 Ibid., p. 212.
20 Ibid., pp. 212–13.
21 Ibid., p. 213.
22 Huston, 'Michel Houellebecq', 23; Cf. Gantz, 'Strolling with Houellebecq', 149.
23 Huston, 'Michel Houellebecq', 31.
24 Ibid., 34.
25 Ibid., 31.
26 Abecassis, 'The eclipse of desire'.
27 Ibid., 813.
28 Ibid., 804.
29 Ibid., 804, 824.
30 Ibid., 804.
31 Ibid., 809.
32 Varsava, 'Utopian yearnings', 164 n.4.
33 Ibid., 156. Varsava refers to this second-hand from Hayden White, *Metahistory: The Historical Imagination in Nineteenth-century Europe* (Baltimore: John Hopkins University Press, 1973), p. 284. For the actual text, see Karl Marx, 'Preface' to *A Contribution to the Critique of Political Economy* (Moscow: Progress Publishers, 1977).
34 Varsava, 'Utopian yearnings', 155.
35 Again, Varsava refers to this second-hand from White, *Metahistory*, p. 284. For the actual text, see Karl Marx, *Theses on Feuerbach*, in Karl Marx and Frederick Engels, *Collected Works*, vol. 5 (London: Lawrence and Wishart, 1976).
36 Varsava, 'Utopian yearnings', 156.
37 Ibid.

38 Ibid.
39 Ibid., 162.
40 Karwowski, 'Michel Houellebecq', 42.
41 Ibid., 44.
42 Ibid., 46.
43 Ibid., 45–6.
44 Ibid., 46.
45 Ibid.

Chapter 6

1   Michel Houellebecq, *Platform* (London: William Heinemann, 2002).
    Page references to this text will appear in parentheses throughout.
2   Albert Camus, *The Myth of Sisyphus* (London: Penguin, 2005).
3   Albert Camus, *The Outsider*, in *The Collected Fiction of Albert Camus*
    (London: Hamish Hamilton, 1970).
4   This has been noted by, among others, Julian Barnes in his review
    essay 'Hate and hedonism: the insolent art of Michel Houellebecq',
    New Yorker, 7 July (2003).
5   John Foley, *Albert Camus. From the Absurd to Revolt* (Stocksfield:
    Acumen, 2008), p. 14.
6   Camus, *Myth of Sisyphus*, p. 1.
7   Ibid., pp. 1–2.
8   Ibid., p. 2.
9   Ibid., p. 3.
10 Ibid., pp. 3–4.
11 Ibid., pp. 4–5.
12 Ibid., p. 5.
13 Ibid., pp. 5–6.
14 Ibid., pp. 6–7.
15 Ibid., p. 8.
16 Ibid., p. 9.
17 Ibid., pp. 9–10.
18 Ibid., p. 10.
19 Ibid., p. 11.
20 Ibid., pp. 11–12.
21 Ibid., pp. 12–13.
22 Ibid., p. 14.
23 Ibid., pp. 18–19.
24 Ibid., pp. 19–20.
25 Ibid., p. 20.
26 Ibid., p. 26.

27 Ibid., p. 29.
28 Ibid., pp. 27–8.
29 Ibid., pp. 28–9.
30 Ibid., p. 29.
31 Ibid., pp. 29–30.
32 Ibid., pp. 37, 39.
33 Ibid., pp. 40, 47.
34 Ibid., pp. 47–48.
35 Ibid., p. 51.
36 Ibid., pp. 51–2.
37 Ibid., pp. 53, 58.
38 Ibid., p. 58.
39 Ibid., pp. 59–60.
40 Ibid., p. 59.
41 Ibid., pp. 59–60.
42 Ibid., p. 60.
43 Ibid., p. 61.
44 Ibid., p. 62.
45 Jason Cowley, 'French kisses. . .and the rest', *The Observer*, 11 August (2002).
46 John Lichfield, 'Drunken racist or one of the great writers? The jury is out', *The Independent*, 21 September (2002).
47 Salman Rushdie, 'A platform for closed minds', *The Guardian*, 28 September (2002).
48 Barnes, 'Hate and hedonism'.
49 See Albert Camus, *The First Man* (London: Penguin, 2001).
50 Barnes, 'Hate and hedonism'.
51 James Buchan, 'The sum of private parts', *The Guardian*, 7 September (2002).
52 Jason Cowley, 'The prophetic novelist', *New Statesman*, 21 October (2002).
53 Buchan, 'Sum of private parts'.
54 Jenny Turner, 'Club bed', *The New York Times*, 20 July (2003).
55 Andrew Hussey, 'Agent provocateur', *The Observer*, 6 November (2005).
56 Andrew Hussey, 'The pornographer's manifesto', *New Statesman*, 19 August (2002). Available at *http://www.newstatesman.com/node/143634*, accessed 15 January 2012.
57 Expressed in an interview with Susannah Hunnewell, 'Michel Houellebecq, the art of fiction', *The Paris Review*, 206 (2012). Available at *http://www.theparisreview.org/interviews/6040/the-art-of-fiction-no-206-michel-houellebecq*, accessed 20 February 2012.

Chapter 7

1 J. M. Coetzee, *Disgrace* (London: Vintage, 2000). Page references to this text will appear in parentheses throughout.
2 Derek Attridge, *J. M. Coetzee and the Ethics of Reading* (Chicago and London: University of Chicago Press, 2004), p. 180.
3 Ibid., p. 181.
4 Ibid.
5 Ibid., p. 182.
6 Thomas Aquinas, *Summa Theologica* (New York: Christian Classics, 2000), IaIIae.57.5. Hereafter referred to as *ST* and following the standard referencing to this work. This reference, therefore, refers to the fifth article, of the fifty-seventh question, of the second part of the first part.
7 *ST* 1aIIae.3.8.; *ST* 1aIIae.1.8
8 Herbert McCabe, *On Aquinas* (London: Continuum, 2008), pp. 103–4. Cf. Eleonore Stump, *Aquinas* (London and New York: Routledge, 2003), pp. 76–7, and Fergus Kerr, *Thomas Aquinas* (Oxford: Oxford University Press, 2002), p. 80.
9 McCabe, *On Aquinas*, p. 104.
10 *ST* 1aIIae.109.
11 *ST* 1aIIae.109.1.
12 *ST* 1aIIae.109.2.
13 *ST* 1a.IIae.93.6.
14 *ST* 1aIIae.109.8.
15 *ST* 1a.1.8.
16 McCabe, *On Aquinas*, p. 106.
17 *ST* 1a.IIae. 94. Cf. Kerr, *Thomas Aquinas*, p. 76.
18 Stump, *Aquinas*, p. 23.
19 *ST* 1a.IIae.6.4.
20 *ST* 1a.IIae.9.6.
21 *ST* 1aIIae.94. Cf. Kerr, *Thomas Aquinas*, p. 76.
22 *ST* IIa.IIae.144.2.
23 *ST* III.90.2; Cf. Stump, *Aquinas*, p. 434.
24 *ST* III.90.2.
25 *ST* 1aIIae.86.2; Cf. Stump, *Aquinas*, p. 434.
26 Despite what the narrator states here, Attridge argues that one symptom of Lurie's state is that irrespective of the 'trials he faces, he does not fall into despair – in its theological sense a loss of faith in the capacity of God's grace to exceed human deserving – but exhibits an obscure tenacity of will, not even strong or clear enough to be called faith or optimism'. Attridge, *J. M. Coetzee*, pp. 182–3. I will show that

the path to prudence can account for this tenacity through a Thomist reading of Lurie's actions and behaviour.

27 *New Advent*, 'Deacons'. Available at *http://www.newadvent.org/ cathen/04647c.htm*, accessed 20 September 2011.

28 *Biblebasicsonline*, 'The breaking of bread'. Available at *http://www. biblebasicsonline.com/english/Study11LifeinChrist/110305TheBreakn gOfBread.html*, accessed 10 September 2011.

29 Attridge, *J. M. Coetzee*, p. 178.

30 J. M. Coetzee, *The Lives of Animals* (Princeton: Princeton University Press, 1999), p. 22. Coetzee writes this through the character Elizabeth Costello, but I will refer to his name to avoid confusion. Coetzee is referring to *ST* 3.2.112, which he has referenced second-hand from Tom Regan and Peter Singer, *Animal Rights and Human Obligations* (Englewood Cliffs, N.J: Prentice-Hall, 1976), pp. 56–9. The reference to *ST* used here does not correspond to the normal referencing system so it is not possible to check this interpretation of what Aquinas has said precisely.

31 Coetzee, *Lives*, pp. 22–3.

32 Ibid., p. 23.

33 Stump, *Aquinas*, p. 76.

34 *ST* 1a.IIae. 94. Cf. Kerr, *Thomas Aquinas*, p. 76.

35 Attridge, *J. M. Coetzee*, p. 179.

36 Ibid., p. 180.

37 Ibid., p. 179 n.21.

38 Rita Barnard, 'Coetzee's country ways', in Derek Attridge and Peter D. McDonald (eds), 'J. M. Coetzee's *Disgrace*', Special Issue, *Interventions: International Journal of Postcolonial Studies*, 4/3 (2002), 390.

39 *New Advent*, 'Canonical visitation'. Available at *http://www. newadvent.org/cathen/15479a.htm*, accessed 13 May 2010.

40 Andrew van der Vlies, *J. M. Coetzee's Disgrace* (London: Continuum, 2010), p. 98.

41 Laura Wright, *Writing 'Out of all the Camps'. J. M. Coetzee's Narratives of Development* (London and New York: Routledge, 2006), p. 109.

42 Ibid., p. 107.

43 Ibid., p. 108.

44 Van der Vlies, *J. M. Coetzee's Disgrace*, p. 66.

45 See ibid., pp. 25, 45. Van der Vlies cites the following pages in the novel that he suggests support his assertions about Melanie's race. See Coetzee, *Disgrace*, pp. 18, 43, 48, 50, 53, 78.

46 Van der Vlies, *J. M. Coetzee's Disgrace*, p. 25.

Chapter 8

1 J. M. Coetzee, *Diary of a Bad Year* (London: Vintage, 2008). Page references to this text will appear in parentheses throughout
2 Theodor Adorno, 'Commitment', in Theodor Adorno, *Notes to Literature* Vol. 2 (New York: Columbia University Press, 1992), p. 76.
3 Ibid., p. 77.
4 Ibid., p. 79.
5 Ibid., p. 80.
6 Ibid., p. 81.
7 Ibid., p. 82.
8 Ibid., p. 85.
9 Ibid., p. 82.
10 Ibid., pp. 82–3.
11 Ibid., p. 83.
12 Ibid., p. 84. Adorno sees Charlie Chaplin's *The Great Dictator* as committing a similar error in parodying Hitler in particular and Nazism in general.
13 Ibid., p. 87.
14 Ibid., pp. 87–8.
15 Ibid., p. 88.
16 Ibid.
17 Ibid., p. 90.
18 Ibid., p. 88.
19 Ibid., p. 89.
20 Ibid., p. 90.
21 Ibid., p. 95.
22 Ibid., p. 93.
23 Ibid., p. 94.
24 J. M. Coetzee, *Doubling the Point. Essays and Interviews* (Cambridge, Mass. and London: Harvard University Press, 1992), p. 246.
25 Phillip Roth, *The Plot Against America* (London: Jonathan Cape, 2004); J. M. Coetzee, *Inner Workings. Literary Essays 2000–2005* (London: Vintage, 2008), p. 229.
26 J. M. Coetzee, *The Life and Times of Michael K* (London: Vintage, 1983); Nadine Gordimer, 'The idea of gardening', *New York Review of Books*, 2 February (1984). Cf. Peter D. McDonald, 'Stony ground', *London Review of Books*, 20 October (2005).
27 Coetzee, *Doubling the Point*, p. 207.
28 Ibid., pp. 207–8.
29 Ibid., p. 208.

30 For a more detailed discussion of this aspect of Adorno's thought and its relation to art, see my *Dialectics of the Self: Transcending Charles Taylor* (Exeter: Imprint Academic, 2007), Ch. 5.

Conclusion

1 Susannah Hunnewell, 'Michel Houellebecq, the art of fiction', *The Paris Review*, 206 (2012). Available at *http://www.theparisreview. org/interviews/6040/the-art-of-fiction-no-206-michel-houellebecq*, accessed 20 February 2012.

Bibliography

Abecassis, Jack I., 'The eclipse of desire: l'affaire Houellebecq', *MLN*, 115/4 (2000).

Adorno, Theodor, 'Commitment', in Theodor Adorno, *Notes to Literature*, vol. 2 (New York: Columbia University Press, 1992).

Aquinas, Thomas, *Summa Theologica* (New York: Christian Classics, 2000).

Armstrong Kelly, George, 'Notes on Hegel's "Lordship and Bondage"', in Alasdair McIntyre (ed.), *Hegel. A Collection of Critical Essays* (Notre Dame: University of Notre Dame Press, 1972).

Attridge, Derek, *J. M. Coetzee and the Ethics of Reading* (Chicago and London: University of Chicago Press, 2004).

Banville, John, 'Light but sound', *The Guardian*, 1 May (2004). Available at *http://www.guardian.co.uk/books/2004/may/01fiction.johnbanville/print*, accessed 9 February 2009.

____, 'A day in the life', *New York Review of Books*, 52/9, 26 May (2005).

Barnard, Rita, 'Coetzee's country ways', in Derek Attridge and Peter D. McDonald (eds), 'J. M. Coetzee's *Disgrace*', Special Issue, *Interventions: International Journal of Postcolonial Studies*, 4/3 (2002).

Barnes, Julian, 'Hate and hedonism: the insolent art of Michel Houellebecq', *New Yorker*, 7 July (2003).

Biblebasicsonline, 'The breaking of bread'. Available at *http://www.biblebasicsonline.com/english/Study11LifeinChrist/110305TheBreaknOfBread.html*, accessed 10 September 2011.

Bozovic, Marijeta, 'Sparknote on *The Unbearable Lightness of Being*'. Available at *http://www.sparknotes.com/lit/umbearablelightness*, accessed 9 February 2009.

Buchan, James, 'The sum of private parts', *The Guardian*, 7 September (2002).

Butler, Judith et al., *What's Left of Theory?* (London: Routledge, 2000).

____, 'Judith Butler: reanimating the soul', in Mike Gane (ed.), *The Future of Social Theory* (London and New York: Continuum, 2004).

Came, Daniel, 'The aesthetic justification of experience', in Keith Ansell Pearson (ed.), *A Companion to Nietzsche* (Oxford: Wiley-Blackwell, 2009).

Camus, Albert, *The Outsider*, in *The Collected Fiction of Albert Camus* (London: Hamish Hamilton, 1970).

_____, *The First Man* (London: Penguin, 2001).

_____, *The Myth of Sisyphus* (London: Penguin, 2005).

Childs, Peter (ed.), *The Fiction of Ian McEwan* (Houndmills: Palgrave Macmillan, 2006).

Coetzee, J. M., *The Life and Times of Michael K* (London: Vintage, 1983).

_____, *Doubling the Point. Essays and Interviews* (Cambridge, Mass. and London: Harvard University Press, 1992).

_____, *The Lives of Animals* (Princeton: Princeton University Press, 1999).

_____, *Disgrace* (London: Vintage, 2000).

_____, *Diary of a Bad Year* (London: Vintage, 2008).

_____, *Inner Workings. Literary Essays 2000–2005* (London: Vintage, 2008).

Cowley, Jason, 'French kisses . . . and the rest', *The Observer*, 11 August (2002).

_____, 'The prophetic novelist', *New Statesman*, 21 October (2002).

Doctorow, E. L., 'Four characters under two tyrannies'. Available at *http://www.kundera.de/english/Bibliography/The_Unbearable_Lightness_of_Be/the_unbearable_lightness_of_be.html*, accessed 20 April 2011.

Dubček, Alexander, *Hope Dies Last* (London: Harper Collins, 1993).

Eagleton, Terry, *The Ideology of the Aesthetic* (Oxford: Blackwell, 1990).

Fraser, Ian, *Dialectics of the Self: Transcending Charles Taylor* (Exeter: Imprint Academic, 2007).

Foley, John, *Albert Camus. From the Absurd to Revolt* (Stocksfield: Acumen, 2008).

Gantz, Katherine, 'Strolling with Houellebecq: the textual terrain of postmodern flanerie', *Journal of Modern Literature*, 28/3 (spring 2005).

Gay, Penny, 'Introduction' to William Shakespeare, *Twelfth Night* (Cambridge: Cambridge University Press, 2003).

Gordimer, Nadine, 'The idea of gardening', *New York Review of Books*, 2 February (1984).

Groes, Sebastian, 'Introduction. A cartography of the contemporary: mapping newness in the work of Ian McEwan', in Sebastian Groes (ed.), *Ian McEwan* (London: Continuum, 2009).

Head, Dominic, *Ian McEwan* (Manchester and New York: Manchester University Press, 2007).

Hegel, G. W. F., *Elements of the Philosophy of Right* (Cambridge: Cambridge University Press, 1991).

_____, *Phenomenology of Spirit* (Oxford: Oxford University Press, 1997).

Houellebecq, Michel, *Atomised* (London: Vintage, 2001).

_____, *Platform* (London: William Heinemann, 2002).

Hunnewell, Susannah, 'Michel Houellebecq, the art of fiction', *The Paris Review*, 206 (2012). Available at *http://www.theparisreview.org/interviews/6040/the-art-of-fiction-no-206-michel-houellebecq*, accessed 20 February 2012.

Hussey, Andrew, 'The pornographer's manifesto', *New Statesman*, 19 August (2002). Available at *http://www.newstatesmen.com/ 200208190026*, accessed 15 January 2012.

___, 'Agent provocateur', *The Observer*, 6 November (2005).

Huston, Nancy, 'Michel Houellebecq: the ecstasy of disgust', *Salmagundi*, 152 (2006).

Johnson, Pauline, *Marxist Aesthetics. The Foundations within Everyday Life for an Emancipated Consciousness* (London: Routledge and Kegan Paul, 1984).

Joughin, John J. and Simon Malpas (eds), *The New Aestheticism* (Manchester and New York: Manchester University Press, 2003).

Karwowski, Michael, 'Michel Houellebecq: French novelist for our times', *Contemporary Review*, July (2003).

Kerr, Fergus, *Thomas Aquinas* (Oxford: Oxford University Press, 2002).

Kojève, Alexandre, *Introduction to the Reading of Hegel: Lectures on the Phenomenology of Spirit* (London: Basic Books, 1969).

Kristeva, Julia, *Powers of Horror: An Essay on Abjection* (New York: Columbia University Press, 1982).

___, *Revolution in Poetic Language* (New York: Columbia University Press, 1984).

Kundera, Milan, *The Unbearable Lightness of Being* (London: Faber and Faber, 1995).

___, *Testaments Betrayed* (London: Faber and Faber, 1996).

___, *Identity* (London: Faber and Faber, 1998).

___, *The Art of the Novel* (London: Faber and Faber, 2005).

___, *The Curtain* (London: Faber and Faber, 2007).

Lawler, Stephanie, 'Introduction: class, culture and identity', *Sociology*, 39/5 (2005).

Lefebvre, Henri, *Critique of Everyday Life. Vol. I* (London and New York: Verso, 1992).

___, *Critique of Everyday Life. Vol. II* (London and New York: Verso, 2002).

Lehmann-Haupt, Christopher, 'Nothing is as it seems but who can be sure?', *New York Review of Books*, May 7, 1998. Available at *http:// query.nytimes.com/gst/fullpage.html?res=9C0DEFD91431F934A357 56C0A96*, accessed 23 June 2008.

Lichfield, John, 'Drunken racist or one of the great writers? The jury is out', *The Independent*, 21 September (2002).

Lloyd, Genevieve, *The Man of Reason* (London: Methuen, 1984).

Lukács, Georg, *History and Class Consciousness* (London: Merlin, 1990).

Lynn, David, 'A conversation with Ian McEwan', in Ryan Roberts (ed.), *Conversations with Ian McEwan* (Jackson: University of Mississippi Press, 2010).

Magnus, Bernd and Kathleen M. Higgins, 'Nietzsche's works and their themes', in Bernd Magnus and Kathleen M. Higgins (eds), *The Cambridge Companion to Nietzsche* (Cambridge: Cambridge University Press, 2007).

Marcuse, Herbert, *The Aesthetic Dimension* (London: Macmillan, 1979).

Marx, Karl, *Theses on Feuerbach*, in Karl Marx and Frederick Engels, *Collected Works*, vol. 5 (London: Lawrence and Wishart, 1976).

——, 'Preface' to *A Contribution to the Critique of Political Economy* (Moscow: Progress Publishers, 1977).

——, *Capital*, vol. 1 (Harmondsworth: Penguin, 1988).

—— and Frederick Engels, *The German Ideology*, in Karl Marx and Frederick Engels, *Collected Works Vol. 5* (London: Lawrence and Wishart 1976).

McAfee, Nöelle, *Julia Kristeva* (New York and London: Routledge, 2004).

McCabe, Herbert, *On Aquinas* (London: Continuum, 2008).

McCrum, Robert, 'The story of his life', *The Observer*, 23 January (2005).

McDonald, Peter D., 'Stony ground', *London Review of Books*, 20 October (2005).

McEwan, Ian, *Atonement* (London: Jonathan Cape, 2001).

——, 'Only love and then oblivion. Love was all they had to set against their murderers', *The Guardian*, 15 September (2001).

——, 'The master', *The Guardian*, 7 April (2005).

——, *Saturday* (London: Vintage, 2006).

——, 'The child in time', *The Guardian Review*, 12 July (2008).

Mills, Patricia J., 'Hegel and the "woman question": recognition and intersubjectivity', in L. M. G. Clarke and L. Lange (eds), *The Sexism of Social and Political Theory* (Canada: University of Toronto Press, 1979).

Nehamas, Alexander, *Nietzsche: Life as Literature* (Cambridge, Mass.: Harvard University Press, 1985).

New Advent, 'Canonical visitation'. Available at *http://www.newadvent.org/cathen/15479a.htm*, accessed 13 May 2010.

——, 'Deacons'. Available at *http://www.newadvent.org/cathen/04647c.htm*, accessed 20 September 2011.

Nietzsche, Friedrich, *Twilight of the Idols*, in Friedrich Nietzsche, *The Anti-Christ, Ecce Homo, Twilight of the Idols and Other Writings* (Cambridge: Cambridge University Press, 2005).

——, *Human, All Too Human* (Cambridge: Cambridge University Press, 2007).

——, *The Birth of Tragedy* (Cambridge: Cambridge University Press, 2008).

——, *The Gay Science* (Cambridge: Cambridge University Press, 2008).

Noakes, Jonathan, 'Interview with Ian McEwan', in Margaret Reynolds and Jonathan Noakes (eds), *Ian McEwan. The Essential Guide to Contemporary Literature* (London: Vintage, 2002).

Nussbaum, Martha, *Love's Knowledge. Essays on Philosophy and Literature* (Oxford and New York: Oxford University Press, 1990).

____, 'The transfiguration of intoxication: Nietzsche, Schopenhauer and Dionysus', in Salim Kemal, Ivan Gaskell and Daniel W. Conway (eds), *Nietzsche, Philosophy and the Arts* (Cambridge: Cambridge University Press, 2002).

____, *Upheavals of Thought. The Intelligence of the Emotions* (Cambridge: Cambridge University Press, 2007).

Oliver, Kelly, *Reading Kristeva. Unravelling the Double-bind* (Bloomington and Indianapolis: Indiana University Press, 1993).

Parrinder, Patrick, *Nation and Novel. The English Novel from its Origins to the Present Day* (Oxford: Oxford University Press, 2006).

Perry, Matt, *Marxism and History* (Basingstoke: Palgrave, 2002).

Regan Tom and Peter Singer, *Animal Rights and Human Obligations* (Englewood Cliffs, N.J: Prentice-Hall, 1976).

Reay, Diane, 'Beyond consciousness? The psychic landscape of social class', *Sociology*, 39/5 (2005).

Ricard, François, *Agnès's Final Afternoon. An Essay on the Work of Milan Kundera* (London: Faber and Faber, 2003).

Ridley, Aaron, *Nietzsche on Art* (London: Routledge, 2007).

Roberts, Ryan, '"A thing one does": a conversation with Ian McEwan', in Ryan Roberts (ed.), *Conversations with Ian McEwan* (Jackson: University of Mississippi Press, 2010).

Rooney, Anne, *Atonement* (London: York Press, 2006).

Rorty, Richard, *Contingency, Irony and Solidarity* (Cambridge: Cambridge University Press, 1989).

Roth, Phillip, *The Plot Against America* (London: Jonathan Cape, 2004).

Rushdie, Salman, 'A platform for closed minds', *The Guardian*, 28 September (2002).

Sayer, Andrew, *The Moral Significance of Class* (Cambridge: Cambridge University Press, 2005).

Schacht, Richard, 'Introduction' to Friedrich Nietzsche, *Human, All Too Human* (Cambridge: Cambridge University Press, 2007).

Skeggs, Beverley, *Class, Self, Culture* (London: Routledge, 2004).

Smith, Anna, *Julia Kristeva. Readings of Exile and Estrangement* (Houndmills: Macmillan, 1996).

Steiner, George, 'She's scared to blink in case her man turns into somebody else', *The Observer*, 19 April (1990). Available at *http://books.guardian.co.uk/print/0,,3924440-99930,00.html*, accessed 23 June 2008.

Stump, Eleonore, *Aquinas* (London and New York: Routledge, 2003).

Thompson, E. P., *The Making of the English Working Class* (Harmonds-worth: Penguin, 1970).

____, 'Class and class struggle', in Peter Joyce (ed.), *Class* (Oxford and New York: Oxford University Press, 1995).

Turner, Jenny, 'Club bed', *The New York Times*, 20 July (2003).

Varsava, Jerry Andrew, 'Utopian yearnings, dystopian thoughts: Houellebecq's *The Elementary Particles* and the problem of scientific communitarianism', *College Literature*, 32/4 (2005).

Vlies, Andrew van der, *J. M. Coetzee's Disgrace* (London: Continuum, 2010).

Walkerdine, Valerie, Helen Lucey and June Melody, *Growing Up Girl: Psychosocial Explorations of Gender and Class* (Basingstoke: Palgrave, 2001).

Wallace, Elizabeth Kowaleski, 'Postcolonial melancholia in Ian McEwan's *Saturday*', *Studies in the Novel*, 39/4 (winter 2007).

Wells, Lynn, *Ian McEwan* (Houndmills: Palgrave, 2010).

White, Hayden *Metahistory: The Historical Imagination in Nineteenth-century Europe* (Baltimore: John Hopkins University Press, 1973).

Wilde, Lawrence, *Modern European Socialism* (Aldershot: Dartmouth, 1994).

Wood, Allen W., *Hegel's Ethical Thought* (Cambridge: Cambridge University Press, 1990).

Wood, James, 'Ian McEwan, *Atonement*', in Liam McIlvanney and Ray Ryan (eds), *The Good of the Novel* (London: Faber and Faber, 2011).

Wright, Laura, *Writing 'Out of all the Camps'. J. M. Coetzee's Narratives of Development* (London and New York: Routledge, 2006).

Young, Julian, *Nietzsche's Philosophy of Art* (Cambridge: Cambridge University Press, 1999).

Index